D0163251

LIBRARY
MURRAY STATE UNIVERSITY

THE POLITICS OF LOYALTY

CONTRIBUTIONS IN
AMERICAN HISTORY

SERIES EDITOR

STANLEY I. KUTLER
Department of History
University of Wisconsin

THE POLITICS
OF LOYALTY

*The White House and the
Communist Issue,
1946–1952*

Alan D. Harper

*CONTRIBUTIONS IN
AMERICAN HISTORY*
Number Two

Greenwood Publishing Corporation
WESTPORT, CONNECTICUT

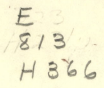

Copyright © 1969 by Alan D. Harper

All rights reserved. No portion of this book may be repro-
duced, by any process or technique, without the express written consent of the author and publisher.

Library of Congress Catalog Card Number: 73–95509
SBN: 8371–2343–7

Greenwood Publishing Corporation
51 Riverside Avenue, Westport, Conn. 06880
Greenwood Publishers Ltd.
42 Hanway Street, London, W. 1., England

Printed in the United States of America

Designed by Mina Greenstein

FOR MY WIFE ELIZABETH

200887

LIBRARY
MURRAY STATE UNIVERSITY

Contents

Preface

MUCH has been written about the so-called McCarthy period of our recent history—a good deal of it in refutation, and rather less in defense, of the exuberant Senator from Wisconsin. We possess a smaller body of literature on the anti-Communist activities of other elements in Congress and on the operation of the federal loyalty and security programs. Nothing yet, however, has been written from what we might call the center of the stage, from the angle of vision of the man vested with ultimate executive authority.

The loyalty question, as seen from the White House, constituted more than one problem. Harry S. Truman had to deal not only with the potential threat of Communist subversion within the government, but also with the politically exploitable fears that this unprecedented danger stimulated among members of Congress and their constituents in the country. As he saw it, he was frequently diverted from the hunt for red sharks by intrusive schools of red herrings. Yet the President had also to balance the essential claims of liberty with the legitimate requirements of security. The quarrels he faced had largely to do with determining the bounds of legitimacy relevant to those requirements.

The President was to find that he had to keep at least half an eye on the loyalty boards of his own creation, to ensure that the basic rights of government employees were respected. He was forced into an unsuccessful fight for internal security legislation consonant with constitutional freedoms. And he was compelled to try to forward a rational foreign policy in the face of Senator McCarthy's charges that the State Department was an asylum for Communist sympathizers—charges masking a thorough effort by the opposition to restrict the administration's policy options. In the course of these contests, Mr. Truman and the White House staff that gave him eyes and ears and hands (but not commonly, as has been true of more recent Chief Executives, a stick) had to cope with a variety of human obstacles: officials of the permanent bureaucracy for whom the administration of the moment is always a transitory nuisance; officers of the executive departments either anxious for the President's success, and valuing their own estimates of the situation above his, or tenderly solicitous of their own ambitions; a Republican congressional leadership committed to the idea that an opposition's duty is to oppose; and a Democratic leadership in the Senate hobbled by party factionalism, constituent pressure, and want of political stature.

Against such barriers the President and his aides often pushed in vain. No notion of government could be more wildly inaccurate than the easy assumption that what is ordered done gets done. We shall therefore be concerned in these pages not only with actions and counteractions in a dramatic, if somewhat contrived, atmosphere of crisis, but also with continuing problems of the business of governing.

In setting forth, and attempting to account for, the story that follows, I have incurred numerous debts of gratitude. No historian really works alone, although his task is in an important sense a lonely one, since he, and no one else, must be responsible for his conclusions.

I am grateful to those friends who have read this manuscript in whole or in part: Professor Stanley I. Kutler of the University of Wisconsin, Professor Martin Ridge of Indiana University, editor of the *Journal of American History,* and Professor M. S. Venkataramani of the Indian School of International Studies, New Delhi. Their suggestions have sharpened my focus on the issues at hand, and they have done much to improve this study, while remaining innocent of its failings.

The numerous colleagues with whom I have talked over various aspects of the work have made a major contribution to the result. I appreciate both their wisdom and their friendship.

I am greatly indebted to those former members of Mr. Truman's White House staff who have freely given me the benefit of their reflections, insights, and experience—particularly George M. Elsey, Donald A. Hansen, and Stephen J. Spingarn. Mr. Spingarn's special kindness is more readily acknowledged than repaid.

Two grants-in-aid from the Harry S. Truman Library Institute have been of decisive importance in completing this book. And without the resources and personnel of the Harry S. Truman Library itself, it could not have been written. Dr. Philip C. Brooks, Director of the Library, has been of unfailing assistance and encouragement to me, as he has been to all who have attempted research in the Truman period. James

R. Fuchs, who has served from time to time as Acting Director of the Library, has more than once lent a helping hand when one was badly needed. Philip D. Lagerquist, the Research Archivist, has not merely provided invaluable general guidance but has been available to answer a great variety of questions—some of them apparently impossible. The archivists who have assisted with day-to-day problems of research deserve special thanks. Jerry N. Hess, who was my first guide to the Library's holdings, helped open unseen doors on unexpected possibilities. After Mr. Hess's assignment to the Library's Oral History project, my work went forward under the thoughtful and perceptive care of Harry Clark, Jr., John T. Curry, and Willie L. Harriford, Jr. Cecil H. Schrepfer, whose inimitable management of the Library's photographic reproduction service has been well remarked, has permitted me to do hours of research at times when I could not possibly have been in Independence. Anna M. Parman, who has maintained calm in the Research Room for many years, has uncomplainingly offered reasonable satisfaction for unreasonable demands. Helen C. Luckey, who masquerades as an administrative assistant, makes everything possible.

No one who has ever gone to Independence to work in the Truman Library will ever forget Mrs. L. Howard Carvin, who, with the late Mr. Carvin, has provided scholars a place to live as well as a place to stay; 400 North Delaware will always be a kind of "home" address.

It is customary, at this point, for an author to thank his family for the patience and forbearance that have enabled him to complete his work. Since candor occasionally possesses more merit than convention, I prefer to thank my family for a happy mixture of impatience and curiosity that has helped bring this book to a conclusion.

A. D. H.

Sea Cliff, New York
May 8, 1969

And the Lord said unto Satan, From whence
comes thou? And Satan answered the Lord,
and said, From going to and fro in the earth,
and from walking up and down in it.

—Job 2 : 2

1

An Introduction to
the Problem

THE internal security of the United States became a public question—and a political issue—in the years after World War II. The beginning of the so-called cold war pressed upon government officials the recognition that the nation faced a potential enemy who had a remarkable reputation for conquest through subversion of its foes' key institutions. By playing upon the appeal of Communism for men of good will and ailing conscience who saw no hope in the status quo, the Soviet Union appeared able to command the obedience of many in the service of foreign governments, including some in positions of trust. A revival of the climate of the religious wars, in which countless men assumed that loyalty to an ideology took precedence over loyalty to their state, was a reasonable possibility. The threat was in truth real enough, although the power of the Soviet Union to conquer by subversion alone was acutely overrated in the United States. Quite naturally, under the circumstances, the Truman administration took

1

steps to protect the federal establishment against disloyal or suborned employees. Executive action sought to establish political stability while meeting the requirements of security; it failed to achieve the first goal at all and only tentatively reached the second. Contradictions in a hastily contrived plan, the inability of the American people to adjust readily to the unwonted atmosphere of tension, and the accumulation of easily manipulated political grievances soon served to cast doubt on the efficacy of the government employee loyalty program. Unhappily, the subsequent process of inquiry took on a vengeful aspect. The hazards of living in the same world with the International Communist Conspiracy, as agitated first by the House Committee on Un-American Activities, then later (and even more sensationally) by the dramatic, and dramatized, Senator Joseph R. McCarthy, acted to blur the definition of loyalty and confuse the determination of subversive potential. The search for an impossible absolute security against internal dangers seemed to challenge the civil liberties indispensable to a free society. After the spring of 1950, the fight over loyalty and security lent a new poignancy to Lincoln's famous question, "Must a government, of necessity, be too strong for the liberties of its own people, or too weak to maintain its own existence?"

The administration was very much on the defensive in facing the dilemma. Espionage cases in the United States, Canada, and Great Britain exposed the delivery of American atomic secrets into Soviet hands. Sensational charges by ex-Communists like Louis Budenz, Elizabeth Bentley, and Whittaker Chambers permitted President Truman's more ruthless opponents to draw a picture of a government honeycombed with subversive elements. This picture was brought into sharp focus by the investigation and subsequent trial for perjury of Alger Hiss, which raised to the surface many emotions irrelevant to the issue of his guilt or innocence.[1] The triumph of Communist forces in China—as a result of the administration's "selling Chiang Kai-shek down the river," according to the opposition[2]—appeared to some to reflect a sinister failure not only of Mr. Truman's policies but of his predecessor's, as well.[3] A few extreme critics were convinced that the President was a dupe of international Communism.[4]

McCarthy's attacks on the State Department, beginning in February, 1950, proved so serious—in terms of apparent popular response—that they put the administration squarely on the spot. "I have in my hand . . .," roared the Wisconsin Senator, and good citizens fell to calculating the number of Communists probably directing the key desks at State. The McCarthy onslaught, indeed, threatened to undermine the effective management of our foreign relations. President Truman clearly had to guard against such an eventuality. Recognizing the necessity for action, however, was one thing; deciding what to do was quite another.

Why, precisely, was the Truman administration brought to so sorry a plight? To what degree, if any, was it responsible itself for the atmosphere in which it was compelled to operate? How was McCarthy able to recruit a noisy, ardent, crude, and—for a few years—large following on the basis of a single issue? How did the unprecedented situation confronting the United States after World War II (and more particularly after the full-blown development of the "cold war" in 1947 and 1948) affect the course of American politics?

NOTES

1. James Reston pointed out, in an unusually perceptive column, that many could not consider Hiss guilty because his guilt would discredit the Roosevelt Administration, while at least as many others could not believe him innocent because his guilt would be proof of their conviction that "communism is only the New Deal in a hurry." *New York Times,* June 9, 1949.

2. Senator Taft's words. Cited in Norman A. Graebner, *The New Isolationism: A Study in Politics and Foreign Policy Since 1950* (New York: The Ronald Press Company, 1956) , p. 4.

3. Ibid., p. 45.

4. Samuel Lubell, *Revolt of the Moderates* (New York: Harper & Bros., 1956) , pp. 73–74. Senator McCarthy made the charge indirectly in a letter to the President concerning a "cover-up" by the State Department and the Tydings subcommittee investigating his charges against State. July 12, 1950, Papers of Harry S. Truman, Official File 20, Harry S. Truman Library (hereafter cited as Papers of HST) . (All manuscript collections cited are located in the Harry S. Truman Library, unless otherwise noted) .

2

Anti-Communism in the United States, 1917–1945

AMERICAN anti-Communism, as we now know it, was born with the Bolshevik Revolution of November, 1917, and manifested itself in especially virulent form over the succeeding five or six years. Behind this reaction lay a long-standing suspicion of radicalism. Educated Americans had recoiled in horror from the Paris Commune of 1871, and a widespread response of the same order greeted the Haymarket riots and the Pullman strike. The popular view was quite simple and unsophisticated, attributing such disturbances to foreign-born "anarchists" and "socialists." "Bolshies" were easily assimilated to the earlier categories, all being casually lumped together as "Reds." The ordinary citizen's antiradical feelings, in any case, probably owed more to nativism and nationalism than to political conservatism; the cartoon figure of the bearded foreigner clutching a bomb did not grossly distort the native American's picture of the "Red."

The American people, nevertheless, distinguished between

"good" and "bad" revolutions. The independence of the United States, after all, was the prime consequence of a successful revolution. President Wilson, in his war message of April 6, 1917, explicitly observed that the overthrow of the tsardom had made Russia a fit ally for the democratic powers of the West. It might be said that a revolution aiming at an approximation of the current condition of the United States was good; one that rejected the values and denied the achievements of American society was bad.

The Bolshevik coup d'état gave Russia a regime that not only scoffed at American values but publicly declared its enmity to the United States and the rest of what it called the capitalist world. American response to this declaration of hostility fed upon a xenophobia exacerbated by wartime emotions. Antiforeign feeling at first concentrated on persons and things German in a very simple way. Later it became more complicated, if no more worldly-wise. Because many Germans and Jews with German-sounding names held high rank in the Socialist party, and because a number of American Socialists, pacifists like most of their European brethren, had opposed the President's program of "preparedness" before the war, socialism was quickly equated with unpatriotism. The Bolshevik Revolution strengthened the political bias while it encouraged expansion of the permissible "hate list" to include Slavs, East European Jews, and foreign-born radicals generally. The antiwar and anticapitalist activities of the International Workers of the World (IWW), popularly known as Wobblies, gave a touch of plausibility to public alarm. And because many prominent Wobblies were foreign-born, the association of alien birth with unpatriotic sentiment was confirmed as truth for citizens throughout the country.[1]

The entry of the United States into the first World War caused the Wilson administration to seek means of shoring up the internal security system. The Alien Enemies Act of 1798, last survivor of the notorious Alien and Sedition laws of that year, was immediately invoked by the President. His powers to arrest, control, and deport enemy aliens by executive order were exercised, however, with great restraint. In June, 1917, the Congress responded to a request from Wilson by passing the Espionage Act. This new measure imposed penalties upon persons making false statements injurious to the war effort or tending to offer aid and comfort to the enemy. It also closed the mails to disloyal literature. Presumably the law penalized only such statements as might lead to a dangerous act, but its language was not clear enough to guarantee that it might not be applied more generally. It was certainly used in 1918 and 1919 to justify the roundup of Wobblies under conditions possibly outside the supposed intent of the act. Judges construed the terms of the law to punish a wide spectrum of antiwar sentiment.[2]

President Wilson also instructed the Civil Service Commission to

> remove any employee when . . . the retention of such employee would be inimical to the public welfare by reasons of his conduct, sympathies, or utterances, or because of other reasons growing out of the war. Such removal may be made without other formality than that the reasons shall be made a matter of confidential record, subject, however, to inspection by the Civil Service Commission.[3]

Wilson did not anticipate a systematic infiltration of the federal service by pro-German elements; rather, he sought to guard against the possibility of espionage by "hyphenated" Americans (notably German-Americans and anglophobe Irish-Americans) already in the government's employ. The Civil Service Commission, to be sure, took upon itself the job of screening applicants for employment to prevent hiring potentially disloyal persons, but the number of people involved was small and the threat was not taken too seriously. For the first time, nevertheless, an organized effort was made to ensure the loyalty of civil servants.

The search for saboteurs and spies was principally conducted outside the government, with the steel, munitions, and shipping industries receiving particular scrutiny. Universities and newspapers were also watched with some care. Attorney General Gregory asked for citizen participation in the fight against espionage and sabotage, and the Justice Department accepted the services of a private patriotic organization, the American Protective League, formed specifically to help out in the spy hunt. The APL gave its attention to the activities of Wobblies, Socialists, labor unions, and—in the South—Negroes in seeking out the sources of subversion.[4] The Bolshevik Revolution and the consequent Russian withdrawal from the war helped tie radicalism to the cause of the Central Powers, since the Soviet capitulation at Brest-Litovsk was frequently taken as proof of the common belief in the West that Lenin and his associates were German agents. So great was the excitement aroused by Bolshevik treachery that Congress responded to the Attorney General's plea for some stronger legislation than the Espionage Act by passing the Sedition Act in May, 1918. This law, providing severe penalties for the expression of disloyal opinions, insults to the flag, and slighting references to the Constitution and the government obviously opened the door to the prosecution of a variety of dissidents. It was, at least, designated as a wartime measure, to expire with the conclusion of hostilities.

A. Mitchell Palmer, who became Attorney General in March, 1919, made the best of such emergency statutes in crushing what he believed was the Bolshevik threat. Since the state of war would not be legally terminated until the United States signed peace treaties with the defeated Central Powers, he had some time to play with even though the shooting had stopped on November 11, 1918. Palmer also importuned congressional leaders to pass a peacetime sedition act, and he operated partly on the assumption that a new law would be enacted.

Palmer, however, did not initiate the anti-Bolshevik drive, although he was to bring it to its maximal intensity. A month before he assumed office, the Immigration Bureau tried precipitately to deport thirty-nine alien Wobblies already in its custody. The nation's press applauded the stroke, *The New York Times* inveighing heartily against the "bewhiskered ranting, howling, mentally warped, law-defying aliens."[5]

Throughout the summer of 1919, the Bureau of Investigation (immediate ancestor of the present FBI) accumulated data on suspected dangerous radicals and intervened in Labor Department proceedings to "assist" the Immigration Bureau to speed up deportations. The Attorney General struck, in the first of the famous "Palmer raids," on November 7, the second anniversary of the Bolshevik Revolution. Meetings of the Union of Russian Workers, a radical immigrant fraternity, were raided and members were rounded up. The next month, 249 alien Unionists were bound for Finland, en route to Russia, aboard a ship popularly christened the "Soviet Ark." On

January 2, a yet broader series of raids netted thousands of suspected Communists. Nearly 3,000 aliens were marked for deportation by the Department of Justice. The arrests and detention of the suspects, however, had been characterized by so flagrant a disregard of due process of law that Acting Secretary of Labor Louis Post insisted that each deportation case be subjected to prolonged and careful examination. While most of the proposed deportations were thus held up, public opinion cooled on the radical issue. The labor unrest of 1919, which had been highlighted by some violent strikes, died down, and the greatest of the strikes—that in the steel industry —was broken early in 1920. The Attorney General's ready predictions of enormities to be perpetrated by the radicals went unfulfilled, and his increasingly shrill insistence on the danger was met by skepticism at first, then by rough humor. Palmer hoped to parlay his defense of Americanism into the Democratic presidential nomination in 1920, but his one issue lost momentum before the delegates met.

The external policy of the United States, at the same time, rested upon a more rational fear of Russian intentions and motives. The Soviet leaders, Secretary of State Bainbridge Colby wrote in August, 1920,

> have declared that it is their understanding that the very existence of Bolshevism in Russia, the maintenance of their own rule, depends, and must continue to depend, upon the occurrence of revolutions in all other great civilized nations, including the United States, which will overthrow and destroy their governments and set up Bolshevist rule in their stead. . . .
>
> We cannot recognize, hold official relations with, or give friendly reception to the agents of a government which is determined and bound to conspire against our institutions.[6]

However much the policy of nonrecognition may be debated, and however much the wisdom of American intervention in Siberia may be questioned, the Wilson administration realized that the Russian Communist regime was a new force in the history of the world and set itself to meet the threat. The Republican administrations of the 1920s continued the policy of nonrecognition, partly to punish the Soviets for their attitude on the debt question, partly out of distaste for radicalism in general; fear of the Soviet state, however, abated. American businessmen were glad enough to enter into trade with the pariah nation, even if such trade helped stabilize the Soviet economy—a clear contravention of their government's aims.[7] Lenin's confidence that capitalist greed could be enlisted in the cause of communism was not wholly unjustified.

By 1933 President Franklin D. Roosevelt, who was uninterested in the questions of debts and claims that formed the legal basis of past policy, was able to extend full recognition to the Soviet Union. There was vocal opposition to the move, but it proved to have more voice than votes. Nonrecognition had long since lost whatever utility it might once have had, and various advantages to acknowledging the existence of the USSR were widely perceived. Manufacturers and shippers hoped that something might be done with the opportunities for fuller trade opened by recognition. Defenders of the "Open Door" in China saw the new policy as a gesture against Japan, newly embarked on a career of expansion in Manchuria and North China. Still other persons applauded recognition out of admiration for what they saw as the Soviet achievement.

The "depression decade" of the 1930s produced a stronger body of pro-Soviet opinion than had yet existed in this country. Numerous disenchanted and fearful intellectuals, labor organizers, professional people, and "plain citizens" came to agree with Lincoln Steffens that the future had arrived in good working order in Russia. Accordingly, they associated themselves with movements favorable to the Soviet cause and, to many people of this stripe, the Communists' "Popular Front" tactics of the mid-thirties seemed the fulfillment of a dream. Within the government itself men thought that to advance communism was to serve mankind—even if it required, at the least, a very great solicitousness for the interests of the Soviet Union. An established Communist party "cell" in the Department of Agriculture flourished mightily, and a new one was created within the staff of the National Labor Relations Board.[8]

Between 1930 and 1940, however, the Soviet Union lost its appeal for countless American liberals and native radicals. The political and military purges of 1936–1938 seemed symptomatic of a mindless barbarism, at best the paranoiac defense of a personal dictatorship. And the Molotov-Ribbentrop Pact of August, 1939, however realistic a response to Russian weakness, was an extreme act of political cynicism that left Soviet sympathizers around the world with an overriding sense of betrayal. The Russian invasion of Finland in November, 1939, aroused millions of Americans to hostility against the Soviet regime.

On the other side of the fence, a strong current of anti-Bolshevik feeling had run continuously from the time of the November Revolution. In some circles, the novelty, both real and apparent, of New Deal measures to fight the depression was taken as evidence of the "socialistic" tendencies of the Roosevelt administration. Policies regarded as indicative of this trend came to be considered as characteristic of the New Deal; and Socialists, for any number of Americans, were indistinguishable from Communists—despite the fate of European Social Democracy, which was then suffering as much from Communist as from Fascist enmity.[9] For believers in the equation, liberalism = socialism = communism, the acts of Stalin that had served to disillusion so many reformers simply confirmed what they had believed all along. And more sophisticated critics of the Soviet system reacted to the purges and the rapprochement with Nazism with sorrow rather than surprise.

Anti-Communists in Congress were increasingly active during the 1930s. Allying themselves with legislators fearful of the activities of Nazi sympathizers and native fascist groups, they sought an investigation of un-American propaganda. A motion to create an investigating committee was put forward by Representative Samuel Dickstein of New York, the House's most urgent anti-Nazi, in April, 1937, but it was conclusively defeated. The German occupation of Austria and the acceleration of the Soviet purges altered opinion, however, and thirteen months after Dickstein's failure, a similar resolution offered by Representative Martin Dies of Texas was carried. The Dies resolution called for a special committee of seven to investigate

(1) the extent, character, and objects of un-American propaganda activities in the United States, (2) the diffusion within the United States of subversive and un-American propaganda that is instigated from foreign countries or of a domestic origin and attacks the principle of the form of government as guaranteed by our Constitution, and (3) all other questions in relation thereto that would aid Congress in any necessary remedial legislation.[10]

Although most supporters of the resolution were probably motivated by fear of the Third Reich, Dies himself was more concerned with the Communist party. While his committee looked into the German-American Bund and other Nazi-supported activities and investigated anti-Semitism in America, it gave greater attention to Communist influence in the CIO, the Farmer-Labor party in Minnesota, and Brooklyn College, sit-down strikes, the Federal Theatre and the Federal Writers' Project (both believed to be havens for radicals), and the American Civil Liberties Union.[11]

Legislation to curb subversive activity passed Congress toward the end of the decade. It was probably aimed more at Communists than Nazis because of the well-founded belief that the former were more expert at political sabotage. The Nazi-Soviet accord, in any case, made it possible to wrap both fears in one package.

The Hatch Act of 1939, regulating civil service workers, made loyalty to the United States a legal condition of employment for the first time. Its Section 9A prohibited federal employees from belonging to "any political party or organization which advocates the overthrow of our constitutional form of government." The original Civil Service Commission investigations carried out under the law limited themselves to character and competence; a screening of political affiliation was formally added in 1940. Since, however, agents of the Federal Bureau of Investigation (FBI) frequently carried out the examinations, questions of political association were actually considered from the beginning. And in 1940 Congress authorized the Secretaries of War and the Navy and the Secretary of the Treasury (for the Coast Guard) to dismiss summarily any employee who might be a possible "security risk."[12]

The Smith Act of 1940, an avowedly anti-Communist measure, made subversion and the advocacy of subversion federal crimes. This law, generally unapplied during the war years, nevertheless established federal supremacy in the field of anti-subversive legislation.[13]

Anti-Communism was now a distinct aspect of patriotism, even in many liberal quarters. The Nazi-Soviet Non-Aggression Treaty and the rape of Finland, following hard upon the horror of the purges, had facilitated Stalin's promotion to the rank of full devil. The ventilation of his former role in the forced collectivization of Ukrainian agriculture and his supposed part in the murder of Kirov enlarged recent impressions and exposed him as quite as monstrous as Hitler. His new stature in the public demonology was unchallenged.

When Roosevelt joined Winston Churchill in embracing the devil after the German invasion of Russia, June 22, 1941, another turnabout of public opinion was set in motion. The struggle against Nazism submerged popular reservations about the new victim. Stress in the public print began to be laid on, if not exactly the goodness, then at least the bluff straightforwardness of "Uncle Joe" Stalin. Some Kremlinologists discovered that the purges had been, after all, a necessary, if harsh, means of saving the Soviet state from Nazi subversion. The invasion of Finland became a strategic maneuver essential to bolstering Soviet defenses against Germany. The unquestionably heroic resistance of the Soviet forces, after the first shock of the German assault, received full attention here and in Great Britain. The long Russian countermarch that began the spring after Stalingrad was eagerly described in the American press as a march of liberation. That Stalin proved a trying associate and a tricky negotiator, even while the Soviet armed forces were heavily dependent on American matériel, was not revealed to the Western peoples; coalition diplomacy is difficult enough at best.

Serious substantive differences at Yalta between the Anglo-American Powers and the Soviet Union were papered over for public consumption. Stalin was clearly determined to hold all Eastern Europe in fief despite the protests of his Western partners. He observed, less than a month after the Yalta Conference, "This war is not as in the past; whoever occupies a territory also imposes on it his own social system. Everyone imposes his own system as far as his army has power to do so. It cannot be otherwise."[14] In an unfortunate effort to maintain the façade of allied unity, Roosevelt and Churchill formally conceded to Stalin what he already had in his hands and plainly intended to keep. The reservations in respect to the Polish government were precise but unenforceable except by the exercise of arms. Moral suasion would not have restrained the Soviet dictator; there was no need, all the same, to substitute sanction for censure. How far Stalin originally intended to go along the path of expansion is not clear, but his appetite seems to have grown in the eating and he dined rather too well at Yalta. The Potsdam Conference partly tore away the mask, although President Truman, still feeling his way and mortgaged to Roosevelt's commitments despite his own rising doubts, was not ready to acknowledge the dissolution of the Grand Alliance.

By the fall of 1946, however, the issues dividing the Soviet Union from the West threatened to become lasting. The thorny question of German reparations, the status of Berlin, and relations among the occupying powers had shoved the prospects of a final treaty between Germany and her conquerors into an indefinite future. Communist political victories, won under the aegis of Soviet armies of occupation, apparently ending any real hope of full independence for Poland, Hungary, Rumania, and Bulgaria, together with a full-scale Communist uprising in Greece, spelled for the United States and Great Britain a Soviet concept of security both excessive and dangerous. But the Soviet government construed Western resistance to its program as a direct menace to its safety. Both sides appealed to recent history—as each understood it—and neither would give way.

At the same time, the United States had undertaken to demobilize, as rapidly as possible, the huge military establishment that had brought victory and had cancelled Lend-Lease operations. Possessed of unprecedented power, we appeared to have taken the remarkable step of giving up the substance and keeping the shadow. Soviet assertiveness posed a special problem under the circumstances, and increasing numbers of Americans came to doubt that the Truman administration was coping with it effectively. This impression resulted partly from the President's and Secretary of State Byrnes's insistence on the free election formula devised at Yalta to dispose of the Eastern European question[15]—a formula that now highlighted both Soviet intransigence and the lack of an effective American answer to it. And the Soviet Union's free use of its veto in the Security Council of the United Nations to protect its supposedly ill-gotten gains heralded for not a few Americans the final failure of the principle of collective security. Certainly many former isolationists had supported the United Nations in the hope that it would guarantee forever American freedom from overseas entanglements—a hope surely not diminished by the administration's "hard sell."

Because of the popular desire for both demobilization and security (hardly restricted to the fabled man in the street),[16] more and more political leaders and would-be leaders came to "realize" that the Communist challenge was not external, but internal. The conspiratorial clique that had withdrawn from the struggle against Imperial Germany, preached worldwide revolution, and sent agents abroad to foment that revolution, had found a worthy successor in the dictator who tried to evade the fight against Nazi Germany and who was now launched upon a campaign of imperialism by subversion. The "godlessness" of communism, moreover, reinforced the fears of a public that had rediscovered churchgoing and formal piety during the war.[17] If only, then, the United States could successfully defend itself against its internal foes, any threat from the Soviet Union would dissolve.[18]

NOTES

1. This chapter generally follows the interpretations in John Higham, *Strangers in the Land: Patterns of American Nativism, 1860–1925* (New York: Atheneum, 1965) , chap. 8, and Harold M. Hyman, *To Try Men's Souls: Loyalty Tests in American History* (Berkeley and Los Angeles: University of California Press, 1959) , pp. 316–322.

2. Higham, *Strangers in the Land,* p. 210.

3. Cited in Hyman, *To Try Men's Souls,* pp. 268–269.

4. For an excellent discussion of World War I's amateur spy-hunters, see ibid., chap. 11.

5. Cited in Higham, *Strangers in the Land,* p. 229.

6. Cited in George F. Kennan, *Russia and the West Under Lenin and Stalin* (New York: Mentor Books, 1962) , pp. 196–197.

7. For an analytic consideration of this question, see ibid., pp. 187–188.

8. The available evidence on Communist cells in the federal government before World War II is well covered in Earl Latham, *The Communist Controversy in Washington: From the New Deal to McCarthy*

(Cambridge, Mass.: Harvard University Press, 1966) , chaps. 4 and 5.

9. No less a left-wing Socialist than Aneurin Bevan later warned against the dangers of alliance with Communists: "The Communist Party is the sworn inveterate enemy of the Socialist and Democratic Parties. When it associates with them it does so as a preliminary to destroying them. There is an old German aphorism which says: 'To cast an enemy out it is first necessary to embrace him.' That is what the Communists mean when they ask for cooperation and alliance with the Socialists." *The Curtain Falls*, ed. Denis Healey (London: Lincolns-Prager, 1951) , p. 6.

10. Cited in Robert K. Carr, *The House Committee on Un-American Activities, 1945–1950* (Ithaca, N.Y.: Cornell University Press, 1952) , pp. 14–15.

11. Ibid., p. 18.

12. Latham, *The Communist Controversy*, pp. 362–363 and n.

13. Hyman, *To Try Men's Souls*, p. 328 and n.

14. Cited in Milovan Djilas, *Conversations with Stalin*, trans. Michael B. Petrovich (New York: Harcourt, Brace & World, 1962) , p. 114.

15. Secretary of War Stimson warned against this policy, observing that "we have to understand that outside the United States, with the exception of Great Britain, there are few countries that understand free elections; that the party in power always runs the elections, as I well know from my experience in Nicaragua." Cited in David S. McLellan and John W. Reuss, "Foreign and Military Policies," in *The Truman Period as a Research Field*, ed. Richard S. Kirkendall (Columbia, Mo.: University of Missouri Press, 1967) , p. 47.

16. Secretary of the Navy Forrestal thought that the President was acting entirely on the advice of his political advisers in pushing for rapid demobilization. Walter Millis, ed., *The Forrestal Diaries* (New York: Viking Press, 1951) , pp. 89–90, 128–129.

17. Even skeptics and agnostics tended to be horrified by the Soviet Union's suppression of organized religion.

18. For one view of the significance of this outlook, see Norman A. Graebner, *The New Isolationism: A Study in Politics and Foreign Policy Since 1950* (New York: The Ronald Press Company, 1956) , p. 25.

3

Contra Infideles
Establishment of the Government
Employee Loyalty Program

THE reality of the internal threat was amply demonstrated during 1945, the last year of the war.

An accidental discovery by the security officer of the Office of Strategic Services (OSS) in February of that year led to OSS and FBI investigations discovering the presence of hundreds of government documents, many of them classified, in the New York offices of a minor magazine, *Amerasia*.[1] In consequence, the FBI arrested six persons: Philip Jaffe and Kate Mitchell, the listed editors of *Amerasia*, Mark Gayn, a writer for *Collier's* magazine, John Stewart Service and Emmanuel Larsen of the State Department, and Lieutenant Andrew Roth of the Office of Naval Intelligence (ONI). The Justice Department was uncertain of how to proceed, nevertheless, partly because much of its most conclusive evidence was inadmissible in court and partly because it feared diplomatic consequences.

The situation was reported to Secretary of the Navy Forrestal on May 28. He was told at the same time that the FBI wanted to place Lieutenant Roth under surveillance at once. But, wrote Forrestal,

> I pointed out that the inevitable consequence of such action now would be greatly to embarrass the President in his current conversations with Stalin, because of the anti-Russian play-up the incident would receive out of proportion to its importance. . . .
>
> I asked Captain Vardaman [Naval Aide to the President] to see to it that the President was informed in this matter and I then called Mr. Edgar Hoover and suggested that he advise Mr. Tom Clark [then an Assistant Attorney General] and have him also see that the President is in full information of all the facts in the matter as well as their implications.[2]

Since Secretary Forrestal, no friend of the Soviet Union, feared that opening up the espionage implications of the *Amerasia* case would disrupt current diplomatic exchanges, it is little wonder that lesser officials hesitated to push ahead. The chief of the Internal Security Section of the Criminal Division of the Justice Department made more than one false start at initiating prosecution. On May 29, 1945, he wrote a note saying, "Matter may be held up by Navy. Mr. Forrestal called Mr. Clark."[3] At the same time, there was a belief in the State Department that Captain Vardaman had ordered a halt on behalf of the White House. Vardaman later denied that he had, but the confusion was general. Finally, Acting Secretary of State Joseph Grew and Assistant Secretary Julius Holmes cleared up the muddle by seeking Mr. Truman's intervention and getting a presidential order to proceed.

A federal grand jury eventually returned true bills on Jaffe,

Larsen, and Roth, and no bills on Mitchell, Gayn, and Service. This was rather interesting because John Stewart Service, a prominent foreign service officer and well-regarded Far Eastern expert, admitted having passed to Jaffe secret information on American military dispositions in China, simply because he wanted them! No intent to commit espionage or subvert the interests of the United States, however, was proved against Service.

Lieutenant Roth was discharged from the Navy June 5, the day before his arrest, to avoid the embarrassment of a court-martial. Later his prosecutors felt that the evidence against him would not sustain a charge of espionage—no charge of *conspiracy* to commit espionage was brought to indictment—and the Justice Department entered a *nolle prosequi* on February 15, 1946. Jaffe and Larsen were let off with relatively light fines, although the conviction cost Larsen his job.

The *Amerasia* case just fizzled out, but it necessarily left doubts behind it. Even if one accepts the assurances of Jaffe's and Larsen's prosecutors that no disloyalty was involved, despite the former's close relations with the Soviet consul in New York, the State Department's security procedures must look inadequate. Whatever the motives of those who transmitted copies of government documents to the *Amerasia* offices, they had far too easy a time in doing so.

In the late summer of 1945, two former Communist agents, Elizabeth Bentley and Whittaker Chambers, approached the FBI with dramatic tales of Soviet espionage and intrigue in the United States. It took some while for FBI officials to credit these stories but eventually they were convinced. Director J. Edgar Hoover of the FBI wrote the President, November 8, warning him of Soviet espionage in this country. This letter, based on the Bentley-Chambers evidence, named, among others, Assistant Secretary of the Treasury Harry Dexter White and Lauchlin Currie, a former adviser on Far Eastern affairs to President Roosevelt. A full memorandum on the subject was prepared for the President and presumably sent to the White House on December 4. By the time the President had seen this material, early the following February, White had been appointed United States Director of the International Monetary Fund.[4] On February 6, 1946, Mr. Truman conferred hastily with Secretary of the Treasury Fred Vinson and other interested officials.[5] Since there was not enough concrete evidence against White to justify withdrawing his nomination and firing him from government service, it was decided to keep him under constant FBI surveillance. On the same day, the Senate confirmed his new appointment. White resigned in April, 1947, to enter private business, the question of his fundamental allegiance remaining unresolved. The case, however, caused the President to order the FBI to give top priority to the search for subversion.

Another blow fell in June, 1946, when the Canadian government reported the sensational disclosures of espionage made by Igor Gouzenko, a code clerk in the Soviet Embassy at Ottawa. Information obtained from Gouzenko led to the arrests of Klaus Fuchs in England and Julius and Ethel Rosenberg and their associates in the United States for turning over atomic secrets to Soviet authorities.

Pressure on the President to fight the presumed Communist fifth column mounted during the summer of 1946. Representative John Wood of Georgia, chairman of the House Committee on Un-American Activities,[6] wrote Mr. Truman in June, asking him to authorize the use of FBI agents in HCUA in-

200887

LIBRARY
MURRAY STATE UNIVERSITY

vestigations, an extraordinary request.[7] Wood's purpose was probably to embarrass the President and to lay the ground for an argument that his administration was insufficiently concerned with the Communist threat to take exceptional measures against it. On July 16, ex-Representative Martin Dies wrote that he gathered from a recent speech that Attorney General Tom Clark agreed with his old committee's findings.[8] Dies went on to urge such measures as registration of Communist organizations, punitive action against unions with Communist officers, denial of public employment to Communists, and revision of the immigration and naturalization laws to the disadvantage of Communists. A more currently authoritative expression of similar sentiments came from Jennings Randolph, then chairman of the House Civil Service Committee. Representative Randolph transmitted to the President on July 25 a subcommittee report urging that a commission be appointed within the executive branch, and

> that this commission make a thorough study of existing laws and the adequacy of existing legislation; that it study the problems raised by this report concerning the standards, procedures, techniques, needed funds and personnel necessary to protect this government from disloyal employees or prospective employees, and to present to the Congress at the earliest time practicable, and not later than the convening of the 80th Congress, a complete and unified program that will give adequate protection to our government against individuals whose primary loyalty is to governments other than our own.[9]

Pressure was also put on Mr. Truman from within the administration to institute some kind of program to provide more intensive screening of government employees. No completely unbiased evidence as to the source of pressure exists, but it was most likely the Justice Department, specifically the Attorney General's office.[10] The following summer, in fact, Mr. Clark did urge the President to broaden the permitted use of wiretapping by federal agents, giving the demands of internal security as his primary reason. Mr. Truman responded by authorizing an extension of such methods of detection, stressing the need in his turn to combat fifth-column activities.[11]

Plans to establish a commission along the lines suggested by the House Civil Service Subcommittee were set on foot during the late summer and fall of 1946. At that time—in the heat of an off-year election campaign—the administration was being accused, on the one hand, of "softness" toward Communism and, on the other, of tardiness in completing demobilization and in liquidating the remaining domestic controls and restrictions occasioned by the war. The results of the canvass, giving the Republicans control of both Houses of Congress for the first time in sixteen years, could not have reassured Mr. Truman and his associates as to the electorate's frame of mind. The vote, indeed, may have spurred the White House to provide an early answer to campaign charges.[12] In any case, the executive order creating the President's Temporary Commission on Employee Loyalty had been prepared by November 20 and was issued on November 25. The commission, an interagency group,

> composed of one representative, each, of the Justice, State, Treasury, War and Navy Departments, and the Civil Service Commission, under the chairmanship of the Department of Justice representative, [was] to inquire, on behalf of the President, into the

standards, procedures, and organizational provisions for the investigation of persons who are employed by the United States Government or are applicants for such employment and the removal or disqualification from employment of any disloyal or subversive persons.[13]

The commission held its first meeting on December 5.[14] Attorney General Clark appeared to give a background talk to the members, although the permanent Justice Department representative, and commission chairman, was to be A. Devitt (Gus) Vanech, Special Assistant to the Attorney General.[15] Other members of the commission were Under Secretary of the Navy John L. Sullivan, Under Secretary of War Kenneth C. Royall, the President of the Civil Service Commission, Harry B. Mitchell, Assistant Secretary of State Donald S. Russell, and Assistant Secretary of the Treasury Edward H. Foley, Jr. They were accompanied by aides who could serve as alternates in their absence.

The first meeting was principally occupied with an inconclusive discussion of the scope of the commission's competence; one has the impression that some commissioners were not quite sure what was required of them. By the second meeting, however, Chairman Vanech was able to express the view that the commission was supposed to determine minimum loyalty standards for the whole government.[16] He was also able to report that the Attorney General had determined, after a conversation with the President, that the commission was to restrict itself to matters concerning civilian personnel. This decision was more than satisfactory to the commissioners, who felt that military selection, recruitment, and loyalty standards constituted so different a problem that, if considered at all, should be taken up by another group. At this meeting, too, an agenda subcommittee (composed of the commission alternates) was appointed, to prepare an agenda and, possibly, to aid in special studies relevant to the work of the parent body.

One question plaguing the commission for more than six weeks was that of the scope of the problem: that is, the degree of the threat to the government represented by disloyal or potentially disloyal employees. There was even sharp disagreement as to whether this matter was a concern of the commission's. It was generally conceded that the problem had been *recognized* both by the Congress and by the President—by the Congress (through the House Civil Service Committee) in recommending that a commission be appointed, and by the President in his executive order establishing the commission. The subcommittee then proposed that both Herbert Gaston, chairman of the Interdepartmental Committee on Employee Investigations, and J. Edgar Hoover appear before the commission to discuss the nature and scope of the loyalty problem.[17]

On January 14, 1947, Assistant Director D. M. Ladd of the FBI testified in place of his chief. Ladd spoke principally of the investigative work already being done by his agency, notably the screening of applicants to the FBI itself and of prospective federal judges, United States Attorneys, et al. He estimated that five or six FBI applicants were rejected each year on loyalty grounds, more on other grounds. If, for example, an FBI applicant were revealed to be a member of the Washington Co-operative Bookshop or turned out to be, on a file check of the HCUA, on the "active list" of the American League for Peace and Democracy, he would be refused employment without further investigation. On the other hand,

Ladd did not remember ever having rejected an applicant on grounds of membership in the Ku Klux Klan or a so-called native fascist society.[18] The Assistant Director also expressed the opinion that all applicants for government employment should be carefully investigated—not just screened or file-checked. Operating under the Hatch Act, which vested legal responsibility for loyalty investigations of government personnel in the FBI, that agency had been responsible for the removal of about sixty persons[19] throughout the government service since 1940. Ladd further stated, in response to a direct question, that Communists in the government presented a substantial problem—without, however, offering any factual information in support of the claim.

The agenda subcommittee, meeting later in the day, unanimously voted a request to Chairman Vanech to have Ladd appear before it to furnish facts as to the scope and seriousness of the loyalty problem. Next day, Vanech denied the request on the grounds that Ladd was too busy to make such an appearance, but if the commission proper wished to interview him again, that could be arranged. Joseph C. Duggan, Assistant United States Attorney, Boston,[20] chimed in that the President had indicated the existence of the problem by establishing the commission, which body was thus precluded from looking into its extent. This statement, and the manner in which it was made, apparently struck a majority of the commissioners as so arrogant and antagonistic that they voted to have Ladd appear before them again.

The FBI's Assistant Director was somewhat more informative in his second appearance (January 17), although he offered no quantitative data. He now reported that the Communist party had set up a special branch called the "Government

Group" for the purpose of increasing its infiltration of the federal service, and that, since the elections of November, 1946, Communists in government employ had been instructed not to carry their party cards or other forms of political identification. Commenting further on the urgency of the problem, Ladd referred the commissioners to a United States Chamber of Commerce pamphlet on Communism. He also brought up the *Amerasia* case, although it had already fizzled in the courts. It was quite proper, of course, to point out the security failure indicated by the affair, even if Service really had believed Jaffe to be a reputable editor and loyal citizen.[21]

Inquiry was then made concerning the number of persons listed in the FBI subversive files, the number in government service (by agencies) in those files, and what put an individual on the subversive list. Messrs. Royall, Sullivan, and Foley were insistent on answers to these questions. Ladd could not provide an answer without authorization (or without checking), so he concluded his testimony by flatly repeating his earlier assertion that a record check was no good, that a full investigation was essential in loyalty cases.

The commission wound up the meeting with a request that the subcommittee prepare a list of questions for Mr. Hoover, whose appearance was still anticipated. The list was to be cleared with the Attorney General and given to the FBI Director a day or two before he was called.

When the subcommittee sat down to draw up questions for Mr. Hoover, the Department of Justice representative tried to argue that information as to the size and character of the FBI subversive files was no concern of the State or Treasury Departments or the Civil Service Commission. Such matters, he said, were exclusively for the consideration of the counterintelligence agencies—the monopoly of Justice, War, and Navy. Stephen Spingarn, the Treasury representative, retorted that whatever might be the proper concern of the departments so excluded, as separate departments, that as members of the President's Commission they were entitled to information necessary to reach reasoned conclusions. Mr. Goodrich of the State Department concurred. The Justice Department, in effect, was taking the position that the loyalty problem was a major one, while refusing to determine just how big it was. The subcommittee had already agreed to report to the commission that existing loyalty procedures were "inadequate to protect either against the employment or continuance in employment of disloyal or subversive persons." But in view of the attitude now adopted by Chairman Vanech and his deputy on the subcommittee, dissenters from the Justice position on examining the extent of the danger could no longer, without embarrassment, agree to support such language. The whole procedure, moreover, followed by Justice in general and the FBI in particular gave rise to a serious doubt that Mr. Truman himself had ever received a thorough and detailed briefing on the subject.

Despite all doubts and reservations, however, work proceeded on drafting questions to be asked of Mr. Hoover; subcommittee members had to agree they had been assigned the task. By January 20, twenty-two original questions had been pared down to eleven. The presumed purpose of the trimming was to avoid wasting time in raising points involving classified information, as well as to eliminate too closely overlapping questions.

All this effort proved partly futile. On January 23, Attorney General Clark appeared before the commission in executive

session, as a substitute for Mr. Hoover.[22] The effect of the Attorney General's appearance was, according to all the commission members, greatly to "dehydrate" the seriousness of the
picture as previously presented.[23] This more moderate outlook
was reinforced the next day by the testimony of Herbert Gaston. Outlining his committee's work, he reported that 729
cases had been handled, 453 employees exonerated, 24 dismissed as subversive, and 3 dismissed for other reasons. Sev-
enty-five cases were pending. Queried as to the seriousness of
the problem, Mr. Gaston replied that it depended on what
one meant by "serious." He saw no danger of violence or revolution in the foreseeable future; such a danger would arise
only in the event of a breakdown of government. He argued,
in addition, that the loyalty question involved a counterintelligence, rather than a personnel, problem, and the President
had sufficient power to act in this field without further legislation.

The first rough draft of the commission's final report was
circulated on January 28. It proved to be most unsatisfactory
in a number of respects to various members of the commission
and of the subcommittee. Notwithstanding the Clark and Gaston statements, for example, the draft report's estimate of the
seriousness of the loyalty issue rested entirely on a letter presented by the FBI. This letter, couched throughout in the
most general terms, urged that "statistics on the number of
cases investigated (primarily under the Hatch Act) conclusively affirms both the existence of a serious loyalty problem
and an extent thereof large enough to warrant the apprehension of those concerned with the matter of internal Government security." The FBI, moreover, had the field almost to
itself so far as this kind of formal presentation went, since

Military Intelligence did not even offer a letter.[24] The report further noted that Ladd had appeared before the commission only to give evidence of subversive techniques and FBI countermeasures, when in fact he was supposed, as Mr. Hoover's vicar, to offer substantial data on the scope of the problem.

Curiously enough, the draft report had nothing to say either about the nature of the Attorney General's remarks on January 23 (subsequent to the presentation of the FBI letter), or—having observed that he was called before the commission to give it "the benefit of his views"—about what Mr. Gaston's views were.

In other respects, too, the draft report strove to guarantee that the "proper" inferences would be drawn. It mentioned, for instance, only the date of authorization of the House Civil Service Committee investigation of federal employee loyalty and the date of the committee report (of which a great deal was made). The investigation was authorized by resolution in January, 1945, and the committee report was issued on July 20, 1946. One might assume, on this basis, an exhaustive inquiry lasting a year and a half. In reality, the investigation began some time after July 2, 1946, the Communist issue having by then become politically promising, and was concluded on July 16.

The draft, in a similar vein, implied an extensive examination by the commission of the nature of the problem before it. The commission actually sent out only a few routine letters to executive agencies (without drawing particularly useful replies) and heard only three witnesses—Ladd of FBI, Attorney General Clark, and Herbert Gaston. Indeed, Chairman Vanech and his deputies from the beginning took the debatable line that the presidential mandate required the commission to assume the problem, not study it. The draft report, drawn up under the chairman's supervision, thus represented exclusively the "hard line" position within the Department of Justice.[25]

Since the draft proved so controversial (so much so that it was almost useless, even as a basis for revision), and since the executive order creating the commission had given it a life of about two months, an extension was requested from, and granted by, the President.[26] The major issues thus remained open.

Representatives Rees, now chairman, and Combs of the House Civil Service Committee appeared before the commission on February 14. They had been members of the subcommittee that looked into the loyalty question the previous July and were anxious to present their views. Both men stressed the brevity of the hearings they had conducted and the consequent inadequacy of their investigation. Combs added that dealing with the problem seemed to him an executive rather than a legislative task.

Attorney General Clark spoke to the commission again the same day. His appearance was of considerable importance, since he voiced the formula that solved the "scope and seriousness" of the problem issue. Mr. Clark expressed his opinion that the disloyalty problem was not as serious as it once was, but that *any* disloyalty was a serious matter. Members of the commission and the subcommittee who had opposed the Justice-FBI line on this question had largely come around to the Attorney General's position on their own. Government employment is, after all, a privilege rather than a right, and any government is entitled to the loyalty of all its employees. There had been, as was well known, Communists and Communist sympathizers in the federal service since the days of

the Coolidge administration, the Department of Agriculture
having been the original point of infiltration. The Gouzenko
revelations and the Chambers-Bentley confessions had very
recently indicated the possible hazards of such a situation. Obviously, groups of Communists or other disloyal persons "nest-
ing" in certain departments or agencies could help each other
up the ladder of preferment, and might offer some embarrassment to the government in a serious national crisis.

From the beginning of the discussions, however, proponents
of the anti-Communist "hard line" had confused the issue by
confounding loyalty and security criteria. The FBI was particularly culpable in this respect. By advocating detailed investigation of federal employees, as if all government workers,
whatever their positions, constituted an equal threat to the
safety of the United States, and by insisting on the use of the
vague term "subversive," which might cover anything from a
crank opponent of a current administration to a trained sabo-
teur, it helped mightily to muddy the waters. For while loyalty is in some sense merely one aspect of the larger question
of security, it is also, on a practical level, a distinctly different
problem requiring different criteria.[27] The Attorney General's
position of February 14 was a reasonable one that his department had previously managed to evade. It is one thing to treat
a serious problem seriously and another to manufacture a crisis in order to justify emergency procedures smacking of
panic.

Beyond this, the overt political attitudes of some of the
"hard liners" were alarming. Admiral Inglis of the Office of
Naval Intelligence drew up a letter for the commission, dated
January 8, 1947, that, like the FBI letter, urged the serious-

ness of employee disloyalty in the most general terms. It began, however:

> As early as 1933, the "progressive swing to liberalism" which characterized the "socialized planning" of the next decade in American History, resulted in the introduction into the Federal system of large numbers of individuals whose concepts of democratic institutions had been developed abroad. At the same time, foreign-born "special consultants" were brought into the Federal Service in order to advise not only on problems of relief and rehabilitation but also on related topics such as money and banking, labor and race relations, and government control of the instruments of production.[28]

And in the course of a subcommittee discussion on January 20, Lietuenant-Colonel Randolph of Military Intelligence (G-2), one of the War Department alternates, asserted, "A liberal is only a hop, skip, and a jump from a Communist. A Communist starts as a liberal." No wonder, then, if proponents of a sane understanding of the loyalty question had for so long to fight out the issue on the ground taken up by their adversaries—that of an immediate security problem.

Many members of the officer corps of the armed forces and of the permanent civil service, of course, shared the conservative view that the New Deal had been a radical departure from traditional ideals and practices. Professionals in the law enforcement field were simply dubious of any deviation from standard opinion that might make their work more complicated. And their suspicions were fanned in the immediate postwar period by the uncritical way in which many American liberals, professedly seeking a balanced position, defended the policies of the Soviet Union against those of their own country. The rhetorical adventures of Henry Wallace showed, too, how close this self-conscious pro-Soviet sentiment could come to the seat of power.[29] Basically, however, the obvious errors that Roosevelt had made in dealing with the Russians seemed to make his whole program open to question. Anti-Communist liberals on the President's commission (as elsewhere) thus had great difficulty debating with their cocksure conservative colleagues.

Arguments over loyalty standards and procedures were briefer and more readily resolved than those over the nature of the problem, although here again compromises in language and a certain confusion of objectives seemed unavoidable. It was agreed quite early in the proceedings, by December 17, that the commission should confine its study and recommendations to standards and procedures that could be applied generally throughout the government, and that agencies with special security problems should develop their own standards and procedures over and above those generally adopted. There was not serious disagreement, either, in arriving at a basic uniform standard, that "[t]he underlying standard for the refusal of employment or removal from employment in loyalty cases should be that on all the evidence, reasonable grounds exist for believing that the person involved is disloyal."[30]

It proved a more difficult and prolonged task, however, to invent acceptable phraseology for the criteria to be used in applying the loyalty standard. But while it may be said that those most concerned with employee rights favored the most precise language in defining evidence of disloyalty, there were no disputes that could not be compromised. Several of the criteria for disloyalty developed by the subcommittee, and approved by the commission, were surprisingly short and clear:

acts of espionage or sabotage, or attempted espionage or sabotage; knowing association with spies and saboteurs; incitement to, or advocacy of, treason or sedition in writings or public utterances; intentional unauthorized disclosure of a treasonable nature to any person of nonpublic documents or information obtained as a result of employment; attempting to perform official duties, or otherwise acting in such a manner as to serve the interests of another government. Such comparative conciseness was not possible in all cases, of course, and the effort to accommodate all views could produce a definition like this:

> Membership in, affiliation with, or sympathetic association with any foreign or domestic organization, association, movement, group, or combination of persons, designated by the Attorney General as totalitarian, Fascist, Communist, or subversive, or as having adopted a policy of advocating, or permitting the commission of acts of force or violence to deny others their Constitutional rights, or that seeks to alter our form of Government by unconstitutional means.

Questions of style aside, it is clear that these criteria are not exclusively concerned with identifying disloyal employees but also impinge upon the question of security risks. The commissioners and their alternates assumed, for example, that the criteria covered the case of an employee having family relationships[31] that peculiarly subjected him to pressures inimical to the government. So covered, too, were the homosexual, the notorious womanizer, the man with a drinking problem, all presumably vulnerable to blackmail and thus persons who *might* be forced into the service of a subversive agency. Such persons are, of course, potential security risks, but no grounds exist for automatically impugning their loyalty. Weakness of character *may* lead *some* homosexuals, "chasers," or what have you, to agree to betray their country rather than hazard exposure, but many others will not be so persuaded. Nor need we believe that a person thus coerced into subversive actions in any sense *wishes* the overthrow of the United States government.

The plain truth is that absolute security is impossible. In ordinary sanity, then, no one ought to be considered a serious security risk, for any cause, unless he occupies a position that is at least somewhat sensitive. At the same time, a loyalty program should concern itself with the question of loyalty, which is a political attitude, not with the potential failings of a person whose loyalty, as such, is not in doubt. A reasonable *security* program will keep him out of a sensitive job. We all recognize that Senator McCarthy's fantasies about conspiratorial cleaning women lurking about classified files at night were absurd, but their credibility in the public mind was not impaired by an administration program that scrambled loyalty and security standards. And no matter how much the administration later claimed that the loyalty and security programs were separate, they were merged in practice, thanks in part to the indications provided by the President's Temporary Commission—so much so that the hopelessness of disentangling them had at last to be recognized.[32]

Serious discussion of the problem of securing a fair hearing for challenged employees began on December 30, and the subcommittee was able to arrive at a basic formula by January 14. One paragraph (then designated 3c) of the proposed executive order establishing an employee loyalty program read:

a. An employee who is charged with being disloyal shall have the right to a hearing before a loyalty board [of his own agency]. He may appear personally accompanied by counsel or representative of his own choice, with witnesses and present any evidence in his own behalf.[33] Each department or agency shall prescribe regulations for the conduct of these hearings.

b. A written notice shall be served on such employee so charged containing:

   1. A statement of the charges preferred against him. The specification of such charges to be as complete as security provisions make possible.

   2. A statement that he has a right to reply to the charges in writing within a reasonably stated period of time.

   3. A statement as to his opportunity for a hearing if he so desires, at which he may personally appear with counsel or representative of his own choice, and witnesses and present evidence in his own behalf.

c. When a loyalty board recommends removal, there shall be a right of appeal under provisions prescribed by the head of each department or agency.

d. Since these procedures provide for due process in all loyalty cases, and insure protection to the veteran, it is unnecessary to have special procedures for any particular class of persons, therefore, legislation should be secured which will exclude from Section 14 of the Veterans' Preference Act of 1944, appeals in cases involving charges of disloyalty.[34]

e. The rights of hearing, notice and appeal shall be accorded to all employees irrespective of tenure, manner, method or nature of appointment.

These were the provisions that, with amendments of form and language (unless otherwise noted here), went into the executive order, and they are still, at over twenty years' remove, not particularly comforting to the civil libertarian. The first draft report of the commission, it should be noted, emphasized the conclusion of the House Civil Service Committee "that all doubts relative to employee loyalty should be resolved in favor of the Government." Mr. Spingarn, for one, did not find this consistent with the commission's thinking, but it must have coincided with the Justice Department's view; and that department, both generally and through the agency of the FBI, would of course have much to do with the application of the program. Much, too, would depend on the judicial experience—or temperament—of loyalty board members. A great deal would be determined by the nature of the appeal process actually established; in all probability, more could be hoped for from departmental than from regional boards. How wide was the investigative net to be cast? How were hearings to be conducted in practice? Answers to these questions could well govern the extent of encouragement given to false accusation.[35]

The guidelines for hearings laid down by the commission suggested strongly that it was up to the employee to prove his loyalty, at least to a greater degree than it was incumbent upon his accuser to demonstrate "reasonable grounds to suspect disloyalty." The general standard, it is true, put a special burden on the accused, but the regulations established in the executive order increased that burden. This was the more true since it was perfectly clear that the accused could not hope for a confrontation with his accuser. The tradition of the Civil Service Commission and the settled practice of the FBI—on the perfectly good police grounds of protecting informers—made that point quite obvious. Modifications of language fought for by liberals on the commission, to provide that accusers appear "as frequently as possible," or if they themselves so wished, were essentially empty even of promise.

The problem, it would seem, was again one of the commission's falling between the two stools of loyalty and security. In evaluating a potential security risk, the burden of proof is necessarily on the employee, since the resolution of the case must be in the government's favor. Indeed, an intelligent suspicion in this regard may be enough, in certain instances, to justify peremptory dismissal or rejection of application. In the determination of the political attitude of loyalty, however, reasonable grounds to suspect disloyalty ought to be built upon substantial evidence. The commission's recommendations, unfortunately, opened the door for loyalty boards to act, in practice, upon general suspicion rather than upon reasonable grounds, solidly established.

It is very easy, of course, to criticize the commission for want of clairvoyance, but the uniqueness of the situation it faced cannot be overemphasized. The problem, both real and imagined, was new in American history and the commissioners had no sure precedents to guide them. They were obliged to establish a network of administrative boards with quasi-judicial functions, which meant that the quality of justice dispensed would depend entirely upon the temper and discretion of its administration. The commission, however, could furnish only verbal guarantees of due process. To the extent to which its language, the product of necessary compromise, was subject to broad interpretation, there existed a threat to civil liberties—but in 1947 the outbreak of another "Red Scare," such as that which had succeeded World War I, did not seem inevitable.

The subcommittee had agreed, for example, on January 9,

that the Attorney General should keep the Civil Service Commission furnished with current information on subversive organizations, as an aid in administering loyalty criteria. Such information had been so obtained, for similar purposes, during World War II. The query was now raised in the subcommittee as to whether this information would be published in the *Federal Register,* one strongly expressed view being that any publication should be limited to that outlet. The commission later ruled that publication should be left to the discretion of the Attorney General, without, of course, having any inkling of the extraordinary possibilities of the Attorney General's "list." It was also decided that the general card file kept on employee loyalty matters should not include the results of completed investigations. This step, one suspects, was taken largely in the interest of holding down administrative costs, there being no sure way of foreseeing that a federal employee changing agencies would be subject to a new investigation with each move.[36]

One important phase of the question of assuring administrative competence and propriety in carrying out the proposed executive order centered around the debate on whether or not there should be a central loyalty board. State and Treasury representatives wanted such a body "to give advice, opinions and assistance on loyalty matters." The idea was rejected in subcommittee, however, on January 8. The Justice Department, originally opposed to the idea, subsequently underwent a change of heart, and Chairman Vanech made persistent efforts to have the issue reopened. Attorney General Clark strongly seconded this position in a memorandum of February 12. Under Secretary Royall argued that since the commission had decided against a central loyalty board, it would be confusing to include Mr. Clark's recommendation in the final report. Eventually it was agreed to let the matter pass for the moment, so that the Attorney General might discuss it with the commissioners.

The subcommittee reopened the question February 14 with a motion by Mr. Johnson of the War Department that there be *no* central loyalty board. This was rejected by a standoff 3-to-3 vote. Mr. Goodrich, speaking for the State Department, moved that *if* there were to be such a body, it be purely advisory. That motion was defeated, 3 to 2 (with Navy abstaining), since Justice supported a board with final removal authority. Inconclusiveness in the subcommittee thus left the decision to the commission proper.

Chairman Vanech presented the views of his department on February 17. The Civil Service Commission president, Mr. Mitchell, responded that if a central authority were set up, the employee as well as the agency should have the right of appeal to it. Vanech agreed to this important amendment on the condition that an employee's appeal not include the right to a personal hearing, but only the right to submit affidavits and other written material in his behalf. Under Secretary Royall feared that so powerful a body might be used, on a change of administration, to purge the civil service on "loyalty grounds" and so renew the spoils system. When Mr. Clark reiterated his appeal for the board during a luncheon with members of the commission and subcommittee, discussion made it clear that Justice, State, and Treasury strongly favored the proposal. The War Department was just as strongly opposed. Navy was leaning in favor of the idea, while the Civil Service Commission simply took the position that it would oppose any such board outside its own jurisdiction.

The State Department, however, had serious doubts about establishing any review authority within the agency charged with investigations.[37]

The debate ended in the usual compromise, but this time a rather negative one—that least unsatisfactory to all concerned. A Loyalty Review Board was established within the Civil Service Commission, to be manned by "impartial" Commission personnel, having indeed a power of review but without even a semiautonomy that would have given it some useful freedom from association with the Civil Service Commission's investigative machinery. The Review Board, moreover, was entitled to offer only advisory recommendations in cases before it on appeal, although it was the confident expectation of the President's Temporary Commission that such recommendations would be followed by the responsible officers of the various departments and agencies.

The general conclusions reached by the commission in its final report were, on the whole, temperate.[38] The potential sources of trouble were to be found in the methods of procedure recommended, and—as was to be seen in due course—in the manner in which they were administered. Executive Order 9835, establishing the Federal Employee Loyalty Program, proved to be not an end but a beginning.

The creation of the loyalty program, indeed, exposed the administration to a "two-front war." Neither supporters nor critics of the President greeted it with enthusiasm. Friendly circles outside the government found it too great a concession to alarmists. A serious, and politically significant, complaint came from Philip Murray, President of the CIO.[39] He was fearful that adequate due process would not be accorded persons accused of disloyalty:

As carefully as I have read this Order, I cannot find clear guarantees of due process, whether with respect to specific charges being made available, or to the opportunity to confront accusers and cross-examine witnesses, or to any of the traditional protections afforded all our citizens under the laws of the Nation.

Murray went on to wonder what grave emergency had rendered the existing laws against treason and sedition obsolete, since these laws had apparently afforded sufficient safeguards in wartime. "What sudden threat," he wrote, "can warrant our throwing overboard the democratic principles of fair hearing and fair trial? . . . " He was also afraid that "the open expression of opinions on public issues may be listed by the Attorney General as subversive or disloyal."

Some of Murray's criticisms were exceedingly acute, even if others were overdrawn. His own attitude of surprise, for one thing, reflected the very poor preparation the administration had made for springing this program on the public.[40] Its apparent suddenness indicated the existence of a "grave emergency" of which the administration had confidential knowledge—and demonstrated for many citizens, no doubt, that HCUA and other Communist-fighting organizations had been right all along in their estimate of the immediate threat to American security. And the rather drastic means provided for rooting out disloyalty, despite the existence of statutes covering treason and sedition (for Murray was not willfully blind in his failure to discover any substantial guarantees of due process to accused employees), could not but heighten the sense of crisis. Murray foresaw, too, better than had many members of the commission, that the program could—quite possibly would—be administered in such a way as both to injure innocent employees and to stimulate public fears.

At the same time, influential persons in and out of Congress were attacking the President for not doing enough to check Communism. The subversion not merely of government but of the whole society became a popular theme of such people.

J. Parnell Thomas, the New Jersey Republican who was then chairman of the HCUA, addressed Mr. Truman on April 23, 1947, to report that he had written the previous fall

> to Attorney General Tom Clark, urging him to "immediately crack down on the Moscow-directed fifth column operating in the United States." . . .
>
> The Communist menace in America is serious. It is no myth, and it is no "bugaboo." As a member of the Committee on Un-American Activities for eight years, and as its present Chairman, I am convinced of this, just as is Mr. J. Edgar Hoover, the Director of the Federal Bureau of Investigation. It is a menace that is so serious, that unless it is dealt with by the law enforcement agencies of the Federal Government, the time may well arrive when the very security of our country will be impaired by this fifth column in our midst. . . .
>
> It will be sheer folly to spend $50,000,000 to purge the Government of communists, or $400,000,000 to stop the communists in Greece (in accord with the recently enunciated "Truman Doctrine"), if our Department of Justice is not going to face this issue squarely at home. The immunity which this foreign-directed conspiracy has been enjoying for the past 15 years must cease.[41]

Political necessity—that is, the hope of getting congressional support for any administration programs—dictated that the President pay special attention to this latter sort of criticism, despite the gratuitous insult here offered him and President

Roosevelt. Views like Thomas's were being used by the more sophisticated conservative Republicans of the congressional leadership to provide a popular base for attacking the administration. Thus, when the necessity arose for the United States to take over British commitments in the struggle against Communist rebellion in Greece (despite a recent American loan to the British to enable them to carry out the task), Senator Vandenberg advised Mr. Truman that his only real choice was to "scare hell out of the country."[42] The Truman Doctrine, the first public statement of the policy of "containing" the Soviet Union,[43] accordingly identified the USSR as the enemy and took an almost ideological anti-Communist line. Agitation against the presumed Communist threat at home increased in proportion. In order to bring a foreign threat under control, therefore, the administration was obliged to make at least verbal concessions to a domestic force over which it seemed to have no control.

A parallel line of reasoning governed the implementation of the loyalty program. Mr. Truman was obviously advised that public confidence in the program would be stimulated by appointing as its supervisors conservatives, men in no way associated with the administration. The problem, clearly, was to avoid placing any identifiable "liberals" in charge of loyalty operations. This was a major concession to the fanatical anti-Communists in the battle for public support. The President's appointment policy in this area could have served to confirm for the unthinking citizen, smitten by HCUA headlines, that the difference between a liberal and a Communist was indeed trivial; or, at least, that our traditional concepts of free speech were not valid in the crisis of subversion. Many fiscal conservatives, to be sure, were staunch defenders of civil liberties, but

these were not the men set at the levers of the loyalty program.

The first chairman of the Loyalty Review Board was Seth
Richardson, described by the President as a prominent conservative Republican.[44] Richardson was an honest, decent man
made extremely cautious by his experience in the federal service, inclined to resolve all doubts in favor of authority, very
literal in his understanding of directions. Hardly the man
HCUA supporters would have had as a first choice for the job,
he was yet not one to strive seriously for some balance between accuser and accused.

At the departmental and regional levels—there were 150 loyalty boards in operation by the end of 1948—the situation was
much worse.[45] Regional boards in particular were staffed by
social conservative of narrow vision who frequently treated
any deviation from the status quo as indicative of disloyal
tendencies. More than once, private prejudice was translated
into a public standard. The regional boards of the Post Office
Department, which employed numerous members of minority
groups, seemed especially prone to this failing. Thus, Walter
White, Executive Secretary of the National Association for
the Advancement of Colored People, felt impelled to write
President Truman on November 26, 1948:

> The National Association for the Advancement of Colored People
> is greatly concerned about an increasing tendency on the part of
> government agencies to associate activity on interracial matters
> with disloyalty. Thus, various investigating agents have been ask-
> ing white persons whether they associate with colored people. Col-
> ored people have been asked whether they have entertained white
> people in their homes. In addition, there is considerable evidence

before us that many colored government employees, who are now being charged with disloyalty, have such accusations brought against them because they have actively opposed segregation and discrimination in their places of employment or in their communities.[46]

The Post Office Loyalty Board in St. Louis was one of White's chief villains, but his complaints were not restricted to that agency or area. In like vein, Representative Andrew Jacobs, Democrat of the Eleventh District of Indiana, wrote a few months later to ask why 128 of 139 postal employees questioned by loyalty investigators in his constituency had been Jews and Negroes.[47] Appointments Secretary Matt Connelly replied for the President that there was no discrimination,[48] but the complaints did not cease. On October 8, 1949, George D. Kells, then Illinois Democratic Chairman, wrote Senator Scott Lucas to protest apparent discrimination against Negroes and Jews in Post Office loyalty investigations. The chairman of one Illinois Loyalty Board, according to Kells, was a southerner, and southerners predominated on that board.[49] The letter was passed on to the White House, and on November 1, David K. Niles, Mr. Truman's administrative assistant in charge of minority group affairs, replied to Majority Leader Lucas that the matter was being looked into.[50]

In an effort to determine political attitudes on a larger scale, employees were queried as to their views on such subjects as the peacetime draft, prewar lend-lease, the Truman Doctrine and aid to Greece and Turkey, the Marshall Plan, how to break the Berlin blockade, war and peace before and after the Nazi-Soviet Pact, and the possibilities of coexistence.[51] Obviously, an investigator or board member of very conservative bent would have a ready-made interpretation of the answers to such questions. In one well-attested case,

> [a] confidential informant, stated to be of established reliability, who is acquainted with and who has associated with many known and admitted Communists, is reported to have advised as of May, 1948, that the informant was present when the employee was engaged in conversation with other individuals at which time the employee advocated the Communist party line, *such as favoring peace and civil liberties* when those subjects were being advocated by the Communist party.[52]

When such "derogatory information" could be taken as decisive, one of the President's basic aims in establishing the loyalty program—the protection of employees against unfounded charges of disloyalty—was in grave danger.

No particular relief was forthcoming from the top. Seth Richardson, for instance, believed that

> the Government is entitled to discharge any employee for reasons which seem sufficient to the Government, and without extending to such employee any hearing whatsoever. We believe that the rights of the Government in that respect are at least equal to those possessed by private employers. We also think that the Government, if necessary, may conclude that any suspicion of disloyalty whatsoever, however remote, might, in view of the dangerous possibilities involved, suffice to warrant employee dismissal without hearing.[53]

Not only did the chairman of the Loyalty Review Board seem to confound loyalty with security criteria, but, taken literally, his statement would have rendered the hearings provided for by Executive Order 9835 farcical. He did, however, assume that some concessions to accused employees were advisable, although he strictly limited them. In an exchange of correspondence with Assistant Secretary of the Interior C. Girard Davidson,[54] he agreed that "embarrassment and prejudice to loyal employees should be prevented *if administratively possible*,"[55] and regretted that "in a few instances" loyalty boards had pursued apparently irrelevant lines of inquiry, although he himself had never seen any "horror" stories. In short, there was to be no Review Board disciplining of inferior bodies.

One paragraph of a letter of Richardson's is worth quoting in full, as a demonstration of the frame of mind prevailing in the administration of the loyalty program:

> With reference to the assertion that the loyalty program prevents "persons of liberal views, originality, and initiative" from entering the Federal service because of objection to an F.B.I. investigation, here again the difference between us arises from the difference existing with respect to the wisdom of the President's order, with which you as well as I am [sic] fully bound, and both of us should endeavor, in my opinion, to aid and help it to the extent of our abilities as Executive employees. From my standpoint, in view of the aroused public opinion with respect to espionage in the government service, I think it is exceedingly debatable whether the rules governing a loyalty check should be eliminated for the benefit of any person who would like to get into the Federal service but who fears the result of an F.B.I. investigation. I think a fair observance of our duty to the government in such times as are now about us would warrant the most careful investigation of any applicant who was afraid of an F.B.I. investigation, regardless of his reasons, embarrassments, or fears.

Apart from the indication that the neutral civil servant

shared the FBI's view of the "scope and seriousness" of the loyalty problem, what is important here is that Richardson completely misconstrued Davidson's plaint. While perhaps exaggerating his position, what Davidson was referring to was the man who disliked—not feared—the idea of an FBI investigation and who was concerned, in the light of the behavior of some loyalty boards, that government service might be a condemnation to a life of routine opinion and bland expression. Richardson, evidently, could not imagine anyone's objecting to an FBI investigation unless he were positively afraid of the results; that is, unless he were in fact secretly disloyal. This is made the clearer by the suspicion that Richardson had difficulty in believing in the innocence of any person once accused. Earlier he had written Davidson that "some misgivings" might be properly entertained in respect of employees who had been cleared after investigation. That would suggest that a clearance should never be allowed entirely to obliterate the "derogatory information" that had provoked the investigation. This attitude, coupled with the highly personal interpretation of loyalty standards employed here and there within the program and the publication of the Attorney General's list of subversive organizations, which permitted its use to deny private employment, could hardly have reassured the public as to the number of Communists abroad, or as to *who* were Communists.

Richardson believed, in effect, that an accused employee could not safely be given the means to present a reasonable defense. If it was one thing for the FBI to insist on safeguarding the identity of its confidential informants to preserve their usefulness, it was quite another for the chairman of the Loyalty Review Board to argue that a person accused by information so received had no right to knowledge of that information.[56] The accused, then, had to prepare his defense without knowing the basis of the accusation. J. Edgar Hoover, to the contrary, stated in reply to a reporter's question, "While the F.B.I. does not approve its reports being made public, it expects the contents of the reports to be used, and it has no objection to a loyalty hearing board confronting an individual with charges based upon the contents of its report."[57] Richardson apparently thought the loyalty program ought to be operated along lines more stringent than the FBI thought were required.

The effect of such outlook and procedure on the quality of the federal service is not hard to imagine. One careful observer of the whole postwar loyalty picture, the Executive Secretary of the President's Committee on Civil Rights, observed of the program:

> It is clear that the emphasis that has been placed upon loyalty and orthodoxy among public employees has served to encourage mediocrity in the public service. Federal workers have learned that it is wise to think no unusual thoughts, read no unusual books, join no unusual organizations, and have no unusual friends. What this has cost the government in terms of loss of independence, courage, initiative and imagination on the part of its employees is impossible to say, but it is clear that the cost has been great.[58]

NOTES

1. There is a brief, clear account of the *Amerasia* case in Earl Latham, *The Communist Controversy in Washington: From the New Deal to*

McCarthy (Cambridge, Mass.: Harvard University Press, 1966), chaps. 4 and 5.

2. Walter Millis, ed. (with the collaboration of E. S. Duffield), *The Forrestal Diaries* (New York: Viking Press, 1951), pp. 65–66.

3. Cited in Latham, *The Communist Controversy*, p. 208.

4. Cabell Phillips, while noting that Mr. Truman fudged a little, in later years, in recounting the White case, states flatly that he received the Hoover memorandum in February, 1946, and reacted immediately. *The Truman Presidency: The History of a Triumphant Succession* (New York: The Macmillan Company, 1966), pp. 358–359. Latham, *The Communist Controversy*, p. 183, supplies the December 4 date for the transmission of the memorandum and contents himself with the observation that Mr. Truman *says* he did not see it before February.

5. Phillips, *The Truman Presidency*, pp. 358–359, identifies the President's counselors as Vinson and Attorney General Clark. According to Latham, *The Communist Controversy*, they were Vinson and Secretary of State Byrnes. It is likely that all three met with Mr. Truman on this matter, as all had an interest in it, although Vinson's was, departmentally, the most urgent.

6. The establishment of the Un-American Activities Committee as a *standing* committee of the House was the fruit of a minor parliamentary coup of Representative John Rankin of Mississippi in January, 1945. Robert K. Carr, *The House Committee on Un-American Activities, 1945–1950* (Ithaca, N.Y.: Cornell University Press, 1952), pp. 19–21.

7. June 12, 1946, Papers of HST, Official File 10–B.

8. Ibid., Official File 263.

9. Ibid., Official File 252–I.

10. It was widely believed throughout the executive departments that the Attorney General not only recognized the problem of subversion as a real one, but that the activities of Congress had caused him to suffer panic. Interview with Stephen J. Spingarn, March 17, 1962. See also the memorandum for the President from Charles S. Murphy and Stephen J. Spingarn, May 16, 1950: "Justice policy on internal security legislation normally originates in the security branches of the Department, the FBI and the Immigration Service. . . . They are inclined to resolve all doubts in favor of security." Papers of HST, Official File 2750.

11. Referring to a memorandum, dated May 21, 1940, on the use of wiretaps in investigations of subversives and suspected spies, sent to Justice by President Roosevelt, Mr. Clark wrote the President, "It seems to me that in the present troubled period in international affairs, accompanied as it is by an increase in subversive activities here at home, it is as necessary as it was in 1940 to take the investigative measures referred to in President Roosevelt's memorandum." In Roosevelt's words, "It is too late to do anything about it after sabotage, assassination and 'fifth column' activities are completed." The President approved an extension

of wiretapping on this basis, July 17, 1947. Much later, however, Administrative Assistant George Elsey (in a memorandum of February 2, 1950) told Mr. Truman that he had approved the Attorney General's request without having been informed of FDR's caveat that wiretapping be limited "insofar as possible" to the investigation of aliens. How far Roosevelt seriously expected this restriction to be observed is, of course, another question. Papers of Stephen J. Spingarn (now at Harry S. Truman Library).

12. Several Republican candidates had tried out the Communist issue in the 1946 congressional campaigns. One advertisement for young Richard M. Nixon, seeking a seat in the House of Representatives from Los Angeles County, declared: "A vote for Nixon is a vote against the Communist-dominated PAC with its gigantic slush fund." The candidate was thus an underdog fighting a powerful conspiracy. Earl Mazo, *Richard Nixon: A Political and Personal Portrait* (New York: Harper & Bros., 1959), p. 46.

13. James E. Webb, Director of the Bureau of the Budget, to the Attorney General, November 20, 1946, Papers of HST, Official File 252–I.

14. The description of the creation of the loyalty program is taken from memoranda of commission and subcommittee meetings by Stephen J. Spingarn, together with the recorder's minutes of such meetings. The dates of these documents run from December 5, 1946, to March 17, 1947. Papers of Stephen J. Spingarn. Mr. Spingarn was then Assistant General Counsel of the Treasury Department (in effect, the attorney for the Secret Service) and departmental alternate on the President's Temporary Commission on Employee Loyalty.

15. Vanech, a career man who had risen in the Department of Justice through the Lands Division, was regarded by some persons acquainted with him as an excellent routine administrator without conspicuous legal talent. Private information.

16. In practice, the commission's competence was limited to employees of the Executive Branch.

17. The suggestion had been made, on December 16, that the commission's final report indicate that the views of outside groups had been considered. It was decided, however, because of the short deadline and of the divergent opinions that would result, that such views would not in fact be solicited.

18. We have no record, of course, as to whether the occasion arose.

19. Subsequent to the meeting, Ladd upped this figure to 101.

20. Duggan and David Edelstein, Assistant United States Attorney, Southern District of New York, had been called in to help Chairman Vanech write the commission report.

21. See p. 200-221 and n. 12.

22. Whether Mr. Hoover was concerned to preserve an air of mystery and special power, or whether he really was busier than his superior

(by no means an impossibility) , must be left to speculation.

23. Because the commission met in executive session, we have no record of Mr. Clark's precise words.

24. Colonel Randolph of Military Intelligence said he accepted anything the FBI told him without further investigation.

25. Justice "hard-liners" did have the support of counterintelligence services generally. And Mr. Spingarn felt that the War and Navy Department and Civil Service Commission representatives on the subcommittee did not accurately reflect the views of their principals, who took a moderate position.

26. It would have been most embarrassing, obviously, for the commission to have had to confess that it had arrived at conclusions based on inadequate study.

27. For a more extended discussion of this question, see pp. 37–38, 41.

28. Under Secretary Sullivan secured the deletion of the first two paragraphs of this letter, as it was to be an attachment to the final report.

29. Wallace, then Secretary of Commerce, delivered a speech before a Soviet-American friendship rally in New York on September 12, 1946. The United States and Great Britain should keep hands off Eastern Europe and stop rearming, while the American monopoly of atomic energy ought to be abandoned. "I am neither anti-British nor pro-British; neither anti-Russian nor pro-Russian," he concluded. "And just two days ago, when President Truman read these words, he said they represented the policy of his administration."
The President had indeed thumbed through the speech while nodding to Wallace's assurances that it would be more critical of the Soviet Union than anticipated, but he had hardly read it. Then, at a presidential press conference just three hours before the speech was delivered, reporters (who had seen the advance text) asked if it indeed reflected the administration policy. Mr. Truman said it did.
There was an explosion from the American delegation to the Council of Foreign Ministers meeting in Paris. Senator Arthur H. Vandenberg, the symbol of bipartisanship in foreign policy, complained that he could serve but one Secretary of State at a time. The present incumbent of the post, Mr. Byrnes, after fuming in private over this apparent undercutting of his position, cabled the White House asking that a choice be made between Wallace and himself. On September 20, the President, who had not changed positions, asked for Wallace's resignation. The incident was, after a fashion, closed. Phillips, *The Truman Presidency,* pp. 150–153.

30. It was agreed that uniform standards should apply to both job-holders and applicants.

31. For example, an employee with close relatives in a Communist country.

32. After a radio appearance by House Majority Leader McCormack,

the White House felt the need to prepare a statement to the effect that the loyalty program did not deal with security. Memorandum for Charles S. Murphy from Donald Dawson, February 11, 1949, Papers of HST, Official File 252–K.

More than two years later, however, John A. Danaher, member and spokesman of the Nimitz Commission, complained that "in various departments and agencies there may be confusion between problems involving security as distinguished from those involving loyalty." Letter to the President, July 17, 1951, Papers of J. Howard McGrath, Correspondence of the Attorney General. Finally, it had to be admitted that confusion of application and administration had become so great that uniformity could probably be secured only through merger of the loyalty, security, and suitability programs. Memorandum for Martin L. Friedman from Donald A. Hansen, June 4, 1952, Papers of HST, Files of Martin L. Friedman.

33. It was decided on February 4 that affidavits might be included.

34. This recommendation was later deleted. The due process "guaranteed" was perhaps not sufficient to warrant clashing with a politically powerful force.

35. In the course of his January 28, 1947, report to Assistant Secretary Foley on the first draft of the commission report, Stephen Spingarn commented, "Any vindictive person can bring the loyalty of any Federal employee into serious question by going to or writing to the FBI and stating that he is a Communist or otherwise subversive."

Even when the loyalty program was functioning properly, so to speak, this danger was acute. In the case of Dorothy Bailey, first federal employee dismissed under the program, the Chairman of the Loyalty Review Board, Seth Richardson, insisted on classifying the statements of unidentified informants as "evidence," over the protest of Miss Bailey's attorney, Paul A. Porter. And in reply to a direct question from Mr. Porter, Richardson said he did not think the statements had been made under oath. Phillips, *The Truman Presidency*, pp. 351–352. The question of whether this procedure involved a denial of due process was left hanging by a 4-to-4 *per curiam* decision by the Supreme Court that had the effect of upholding the verdict against Miss Bailey. The decision has been attributed by Thurman Arnold, former federal district judge and Solicitor General of the United States, and senior counsel to Miss Bailey, to the insistence with which Justice Frankfurter adhered, even under great stress, to the doctrine of judicial restraint. Interview with Judge Arnold, June 7, 1967.

36. Individual politics are subject to change, surely, but the possibilities for harassment in such a procedure are enormous.

37. This objection was diminished in force after it was decided that the FBI should handle the investigations, on grounds of greater competence. Memorandum of the Attorney General, May 1, 1947, and

memorandum of Clark M. Clifford, May 7, 1947, Papers of HST, Official File 252–K.

38. "1. Although the vast majority of federal employees are loyal, some are subversive or disloyal. Because of the secretive manner and method of their operation, it is difficult to assess the numerical strength of the disloyal group. Whatever their numbers, the internal security of the government demands continuous screening, scrutiny and surveillance of present and prospective employees.

"2. The presence within the government of *any* disloyal or subversive persons, or the attempt by *any* such persons to obtain government employment, presents a problem of such importance that it must be dealt with vigourously [*sic*] and effectively.

"3. In addition to the emphasis properly placed on Communist and Communist front organization activities, attention should be directed to the resurgence of native Fascist movements.

"4. Even if all the specific recommendations contained in this report are adopted and effectuated, there is still a distinct need for agressive [*sic*] and uninterrupted counter-intelligence, particularly in its counter-espionage phases. A clear example of that need is presented in the recent widely publicized Canadian experience with Communist espionage activities. It would be unrealistic to assume that foreign powers are not maintaining intelligence networks in this country.

"5. A guarantee of full and complete protection to the government is a commendable objective, but is rendered difficult of achievement by the fact that public funds are not unlimited and must be made available for many other necessary and vital purposes.

"6. There are compelling reasons for authorizing the Secretaries of the State, War and Navy Departments and the Atomic Energy Commission to remove summarily any employee in the interest of national security. These more sensitive agencies require this specific authorization to safeguard the government from the destructive influence of disloyal or subversive persons."

The Report of: The President's Temporary Commission on Employee Loyalty. "General Conclusions," pp. 27–28. Papers of HST, Official File 252–I.

39. Letter to the President, April 14, 1947, Papers of HST, Official File 252–K.

40. Taken as a whole, the President's staff lacked at this time the administrative experience that characterized it from 1948 to 1953. Of those who made the difference, only the shrewd and sensitive Clark Clifford was at all well established in 1947, but he had not been long in office and his was not the only voice to which the President listened.

41. Papers of HST, Official File 263.

42. David S. McLellan and John W. Reuss, "Foreign and Military Policies," in *The Truman Period as a Research Field,* ed. Richard S. Kirkendall (Columbia, Mo.: University of Missouri Press, 1967) , p. 56.

43. It is ironic that George F. Kennan, the reputed father of the containment policy, objected to the tone of the President's message. The commitment given, he feared, was so sweeping and the anti-Communist rhetoric so broad that future policy might be mortgaged to present necessity. George F. Kennan, *Memoirs, 1925–1950* (Boston: Little, Brown and Co., 1967) , pp. 319–322.

44. Harry S. Truman, *Memoirs* (Garden City, N.Y.: Doubleday & Co., 1956) , vol. 2, *Years of Trial and Hope,* p. 281.

45. Dr. John S. Dickey, President of Dartmouth College (and a former officer of the State Department) put the matter bluntly: "[Attorney General] Clark appeared before this Committee, and if you want my frank opinion, Clark was singularly naïve with respect to the operation of this problem in the federal government. He said that no Cabinet Officer wants to persecute any individual down the line, but the fact is that the Cabinet Officer has to delegate this authority to an Assistant Secretary, and the Assistant Secretary delegates it to an administrative assistant, and that administrative assistant is so scared by this responsibility that is imposed upon him by the Cabinet Officer that he chases any dissident individual up a dark alley, or some of them do, and I can name names if need be, and simply asks for their [*sic*] resignation on unspecified grounds." Papers of HST, Records of the President's Committee on Civil Rights, p. 627.

46. Papers of HST, Official File 252–K.

47. Ibid., March 25, 1949.

48. Ibid.

49. Ibid. For other indications of the operation of the loyalty boards, see Eleanor Bontecou, *The Federal Loyalty-Security Program* (Ithaca, N.Y.: Cornell University Press, 1953) , pp. 137–140. Additional material may be found in Walter Gellhorn, *Security, Loyalty, and Science* (Ithaca, N.Y.: Cornell University Press, 1950) , pp. 153–154.

50. Papers of HST, Official File 252–K. By this time, the White House was taking such complaints seriously.

51. Bontecou, *The Federal Loyalty-Security Program,* pp. 136–137.

52. Gellhorn, *Security, Loyalty, and Science,* pp. 152–153. Gellhorn's emphasis.

53. Cited in Edward S. Corwin, *The President: Office and Powers, 1787–1948,* 3d ed. rev. (New York: New York University Press, 1948) , pp. 131–132.

54. The correspondence in question covers December, 1948, and January, 1949. See especially, however, Richardson's letter of January 3 and Davidson's unsent reply of the same month. Papers of HST, Official File 252–K.

55. Emphasis supplied.

56. Corwin, *The President,* pp. 132–133.

57. Cited in ibid., p. 133.

58. Robert K. Carr, *The House Committee,* pp. 456–457.

4

War on Two Fronts
The Communist Issue in the
Campaign of 1948

THE primary purpose of the federal employee loyalty program was to ensure the allegiance of government workers. The problem to be solved was administrative. It was a reasonable hope, however, that some political benefit to the Truman administration could be secured as a by-product. The Republican opposition was already charging that the President was indifferent to the domestic challenge of Communism and that, in consequence, the executive departments were careless in checking the political affiliations of their employees and job applicants. The loyalty programs would demonstrate that the administration was by no means "soft on Communism," to use the expression later popularized by Senator Joe McCarthy, and that it was taking the lead in the fight against subversion.

The House Committee on Un-American Activities announced an eight-point program of activity at the beginning of the Eightieth Congress in January, 1947:

1. To expose and ferret out the Communists and Communist sympathizers in the Federal Government.

2. To spotlight the spectacle of having outright Communists controlling and dominating some of the most vital unions in American labor.

3. To institute a countereducational program against the subversive propaganda which has been hurled at the American people.

4. Investigation of those groups and movements which are trying to dissipate our atomic bomb knowledge for the benefit of a foreign power.

5. Investigation of Communist influences in Hollywood.

6. Investigation of Communist influences in education.

7. Organization of the research staff so as to furnish reference service to Members of Congress and to keep them currently informed on all subjects relating to subversive and un-American activities in the United States.

8. Continued accumulation of files and records to be placed at the disposal of the investigative units of the Government and armed services.[1]

The first goal was neither achieved nor even attempted in 1947. Hearings were conducted on the activities of four prominent or supposedly prominent Communist leaders, Communist influence in the labor movement, and Communist infiltration of Hollywood. These last hearings, which provided an October circus, generated intense heat but only an uncertain light. HCUA successfully indicated that a number of Communist sympathizers had obtained employment as script writers, but it was not really able to demonstrate that they had been able to turn out any obvious propaganda films. All this, of course, was far from the issue of Communists in government.

It might be giving the loyalty program too much credit to argue that it deflected HCUA from looking into the federal service for a year, but Chairman Thomas's April 23 letter to the President[2] suggests that this was the case. Thomas's principal concern was the impact of Communism on the society at large, and he seemed willing to give the new, expensive program "to purge the Government of communists" a chance to work. The initiation of the program, at any rate, did not offer a reasonable opportunity to attack the administration on this issue.[3]

Public sensitivity on the question of possible Communist infiltration of the government was, nevertheless, too great for the White House to feel easy. Even while the Temporary Commission was hammering out the loyalty program, a major presidential appointment was being subjected to hostile scrutiny in the Senate, the degree of the candidate's tolerance for Communists being a major consideration. David Lilienthal, Chairman of the Board of the Tennessee Valley Authority, had been named to the chairmanship of the newly created Atomic Energy Commission—a crucial appointment that was sure to be carefully screened in any event. Although Mr. Lilienthal had the reputation of a successful administrator, he was held suspect by conservative members of Congress as the head of the New Deal's most "socialistic" agency. The friends of private power were therefore likely to oppose him on principle. His air of intellectual superiority and his seeming impatience with contrary opinion, moreover, were not characteristics designed to endear him to legislators. The opposition of the powerful, if erratic, Senator Kenneth McKellar to this appointment could be taken for granted. The Tennesseean, an inveterate foe of Roosevelt, had never accepted the invasion of his bailiwick by public power, and he had maintained a running feud with the TVA's chairman.

Hearings on the appointment were held before the Senate members of the Joint Congressional Committee on Atomic Energy. McKellar brought before the committee a number of witnesses to make random charges against Mr. Lilienthal, while the Senator himself pursued the appointee with questions about his loyalty, his ancestry, his administration of TVA, and charges that Communists had infiltrated the organization.[4] Chairman Lilienthal bore this harassment with unusual patience; at one point, a taunt about his "leftist" affinities provoked him not to anger, but to an affirmation of his democratic faith.[5] The committee subsequently voted, 8 to 1, with only Senator John W. Bricker of Ohio in opposition, to recommend confirmation. The struggle seemed to be over, but in fact it was just beginning.

At some point during McKellar's performance, the Republican leadership of the Senate decided that the Lilienthal appointment was vulnerable and ought to be opposed. Majority Leader Wallace H. White and the party whip, Kenneth S. Wherry, a Nebraskan who was rising rapidly as an instrument of the leadership, announced that they would work against the appointment. The real leader of the party, Robert A. Taft of Ohio, chairman of the Republican Policy Committee and "Mr. Republican" to the press, announced his opposition on the grounds that Mr. Lilienthal was soft toward Communists.[6] The President, on the other hand, was determined to have the appointment confirmed[7] and would certainly try to make a party matter of it—an effort sure to be aided by the Democrats' minority status in the Senate.[8] In the circumstances, the po-

tentially decisive voice was that of Arthur H. Vandenberg of
Michigan, the second most influential Republican in the Senate and the symbol and chief support of bipartisanship in foreign policy. If Vandenberg could be brought to support Mr.
Lilienthal, just enough Republican "internationalists" might
follow him to ensure confirmation.

Vandenberg was not impressed by the arguments urged by
his colleagues. "I am willing to say to you," he wrote an old
friend on February 17, "that the charges of 'communism' (or
anything like it) against Lilienthal are a fantastic fabrication
highly remindful of the 'lynch law.' This leaves only the general prejudice growing out of his philosophical attachment to
the New Deal and his interest in 'public ownership,' as opposed to 'private enterprise.' "[9] Congressional conservatives, or
at least a considerable number of them, did indeed share the
notion of conservatives in the military and law enforcement
agencies concerning the proximity of liberalism to socialism,
and of socialism to communism. Add the personal element—
the self-conscious reformer was also a stiff-necked administrator whose taste in pronouns ran to the first person singular—
and suspicion of Mr. Lilienthal tended to harden into cer-
tainty.

While the Lilienthal appointment was before the Senate,
Vandenberg was largely engaged in working for the passage of
the Greek-Turkish aid bill. Under Secretary of State Robert
A. Lovett, the Senator's old friend and confidant and the administration's bridge to congressional Republicans disposed
to support its European policies, was in regular touch with
Vandenberg during the fight over the Truman Doctrine. The
question of the AEC chairmanship was raised, and Vandenberg concluded that it would not be consistent to cooperate

with the administration in the field of foreign policy while rejecting a major appointment relating to national security without sufficient reason for so doing.[10] Having voted for recommendation of Mr. Lilienthal in committee, the Senator now decided to make a strenuous effort to secure his confirmation. Vandenberg took his public stand on April 3:

> After weeks of testimony, I find no basis for this charge [that Lilienthal had "either sympathy toward communism or too easy toleration of it"]. I hope my own record plus the fact that I am in the top bracket of all communist blacklists all round the world, demonstrates that I am not calculated to be "soft" on such a subject. But I do not want to emulate the intolerance of communism itself. . . .
>
> [W]e solemnly and unavoidably decreed that government ownership and management, no matter how much we dislike it in other aspects of our national economy and life, is an indispensable public necessity for the sake of national security in respect to the control of atomic energy. . . . Therefore one of the most available men to run it is the successful manager of the greatest existing comparable example of public ownership and management. Whether we like it or him or TVA, this sequence leads logically to David Lilienthal's door. . .
>
> I have no quarrel with those who disagree. I know there is a deep-seated prejudice against Mr. Lilienthal in many earnest and sincere minds. I have no quarrel whatever with those feelings. But for myself, in the presence of the evidence, I have no alternative except to say to my colleagues that I have no doubt that in the interest of the national welfare and for the sake of a square deal, Mr. Lilienthal is entitled to be confirmed.[11]

Seventeen Republican senators thereafter followed Vandenberg in voting against a motion to recommit the nomination to committee. The vote against the motion was 52 to 38, so that this Republican support was decisive for the administration. Lilienthal was then confirmed, but the President had had a close call. On the other hand, undemonstrated charges of Communist sympathies against a presidential appointee, while gathering adherents, had failed to prevent his confirmation. The shape of the future might have been seen in the ease with which Mr. Lilienthal's association with TVA and his advocacy of public power were taken as presumptive evidence of alien political affiliation by some Senators; yet it was not foolish to hope that reason could continue to command the majority in matters of national interest. The successful operation of the employee loyalty program was expected to help guarantee that reason—as the administration saw it—would always find the forty-ninth vote.

Clark Clifford's now famous memorandum of November 19, 1947, setting forth a political strategy for 1948, took an optimistic view of the effects of the program.[12] Mr. Clifford, then Special Counsel to the President, assumed that the Republicans would try to make headway with the Communists-in-government issue, but he believed that Mr. Truman had stolen "their thunder by initiating his own government employee loyalty procedure." Catholic voters, the memorandum assumed, were predominantly motivated by a visceral opposition to Communism, and should be won over in handsome numbers by the President's record of having set himself against Soviet pretensions in Europe and the Middle East and having taken forthright action—exemplified by the loyalty program—against Communists at home.

Mr. Clifford, indeed, was less afraid that votes would be lost to Republican anti-Communist appeals than that liberal and left-wing followers of the New Deal would be seduced by the stand for peace taken by Henry A. Wallace. The former Vice-President was seen as running against Mr. Truman on a third-party ticket, with the President's foreign policy as his chief issue. An extensive program of domestic reform would help hold Roosevelt supporters to their Democratic allegiance, while well-known liberals and progressives in the Truman camp systematically exposed the support—even direction—given to Wallace by the Communist party. That Wallace's notions of peace required the United States to reach an accommodation with the Soviet Union on the latter's terms would give pause to many antiwar elements who were, after all, patriotic Americans.

Numerous people throughout the executive establishment seem to have been alert to the Wallace problem. On July 19, 1948, Walter Thurston, United States Ambassador to Mexico, wrote to Secretary of State Marshall, enclosing an alleged correspondence between Wallace and former President Lázaro Cárdenas of Mexico, which had been published in the "anti-American and Communist-inspired" newspaper *El Popular*.[13] Thurston apparently believed the letters, which seemed to have been written the preceding May, to be genuine.

General Cárdenas, who was openly anti-American and increasingly radical, even by the standards of the institutional Mexican Revolution, charged the United States government with pursuing a policy of world domination and with oppressing its own farmers and workers. Wallace replied, in part:

I am deeply concerned by the imperialist trend which the Democratic-Republican leaders are endeavoring to give to the international policy of my country. To attempt to dominate the world, by oppressing and starving the peoples in the interests of those favored by fortune, is not the way, in my opinion, to ensure the peace, the liberty, and the economic improvement of the common man.

This information was passed on to the White House for its use. By that time, the President's staff had long been alive to the danger from Wallace. Gael Sullivan of the Democratic National Committee had prepared a confidential memorandum over a year before, outlining the sources of Wallace's strength.[14] A friendly reporter, Ed Lahey of the *Chicago Daily News,* had observed that "[t]he Wallace phenomenon can only be explained on the theory that . . . the people see in this country a clear and pious conviction that the Truman administration has booted the ball and is heading the nation toward an anti-Soviet war." The Wallace meetings then being held, Sullivan asserted, were stage-managed by Communists; yet, although most of the crowds were made up of rabid left-wingers, a good number of isolationists and conservatives were also turning out. They feared that the Truman policy meant war. The feeling was so strong in California that James Roosevelt, eldest son of the late President, offered a resolution at a meeting of the State Democratic Committee to "greet Wallace with open arms." The resolution was defeated only by a narrow 44-to-38 vote.

The Sullivan memorandum stressed that the popular fear of war blinded many people to Wallace's Communist associations. Don Montgomery of the United Automobile Workers, an anti-Communist protégé of Walter Reuther, was reported as saying that although Wallace followed the "Commy line," he made a strong appeal to the people. The average American was uneasy about military aid to Greece and Turkey; he could understand sending food and machinery, but not arms, and Wallace played on this confusion.

The late summer of 1948 presented a distinctly different picture. The Democratic party had split off on the right as well as on the left, and the States'-Rights Democrats, popularly known as Dixiecrats, had their own presidential ticket in the field. This fragmentation, caused by Southern hostility to the President's program of civil rights for Negroes and, most immediately, by the success of some young liberals in forcing the National Convention—against the wishes of the White House—to adopt an advanced civil-rights plank for the party platform,[15] meant that President Truman needed every vote he could scratch up outside the South. Thus, while Henry Wallace's Progressive party was less formidable in the life than it had been in prospect, its pockets of strength, notably in California and New York, seriously weakened Democratic prospects. The Truman campaign was therefore compelled to find means of avoiding defections to Wallace on the peace issue without courting losses to the Republicans on the domestic Communist issue. A graceful strategy was almost out of the question.

Events beyond the President's control affected the impact any opposition appeal to anti-Communism might have had in 1948. The establishment of a Communist government in Czechoslovakia on February 25, under threat of intervention by the Red Army, was used by some Republicans to belabor Mr. Truman. Although the coup hardly represented a triumph of the techniques of subversion, it was so described by antiadministration leaders. It was also condemned, more plausibly, as a late consequence of the Yalta agreements which left Russian forces supreme in Eastern Europe.

Another European crisis, however, was turned to the administration's credit. On April 1, the Soviet Military Government in Germany, in an effort to force the United States, Great Britain, and France out of their occupation sectors in the western half of Berlin, closed all land access routes to the city. The President and his European allies stood firm, and British and American aircraft undertook—with dramatic success—to supply West Berlin by air. The Soviet authorities did not risk interference with the air corridors, and the essential aim of the blockade was thwarted. The White House was able to claim in good faith that prompt and determined action had balked an aggressive Soviet maneuver without provoking war.

What was even more important from the political standpoint, however, was that the HCUA finally addressed itself to potential Soviet espionage activity within the government. It began in March by an attack on Dr. Edward U. Condon, director of the National Bureau of Standards, who was then being checked for a security clearance—subsequently granted on July 15—as "one of the weakest links in our atomic security."[16] Dr. Condon was taxed for his connection with the American-Soviet Science Society and for his social contacts with members of the Polish Embassy (although the FBI found these innocent). HCUA also found the Czechoslovakian ancestry of his American-born wife suspicious. This investigation eventually petered out, the committee allowing silence to cover its embarrassment and its retreat in the face of articulate and convincing opposition.

Chairman Thomas and his colleagues persisted in their work, nevertheless, and were soon on a more promising trail.

The self-confessed former Communist agents, Elizabeth Bentley and Whittaker Chambers, who had unburdened themselves to the FBI nearly three years before, appeared before HCUA during the summer of 1948, Chambers testifying for the first time on August 3. He quickly accused Alger Hiss, a former second-line officer of the State Department, of having committed espionage for the Soviet Union during the 1930s. Since Hiss had been a member of the American delegation to the Yalta Conference and had been secretary general of the United Nations Charter Conference in San Francisco, the charges created an instant sensation. On August 5, President Truman summarily dismissed HCUA's labors:

> The public hearings now under way are serving no useful purpose. On the contrary, they are doing irreparable harm to certain people, seriously impairing the morale of Federal employees, and undermining public confidence in the Government.
>
> And they are simply a "red herring" to keep from doing what they ought to do.[17]

Asked at his next press conference a week later if he still thought the investigation was a "red herring," the President replied, "Yes, I do. The first—the strongest type you can smell."[18] The following week's press conference elicited from Mr. Truman a strong defense of the loyalty program, a defense that was also a challenge to HCUA:

> I can say categorically that [the loyalty program] has [protected us against subversion]. All the things that have been presented to these committees have been [in] FBI files and have been presented to the grand jury long before that. And the only two people who were in the Government employ who have been accused of disloy-

alty—which hasn't been proven on them by any means—have been
placed on indefinite leave, before the committee ever started any
hearings. It has had no bearing whatever on the loyalty of Government employees that are now on the payroll. . . .
[The program] has been very successful. It has been entirely
successful, I might say.[19]

The logical defense against Republican insinuations based
on the HCUA investigations was to insist on the efficacy of
the loyalty program. The President's "red herring" remarks
were not incompatible with a tough stand against Communists at home. There was then nothing against Hiss except
Chambers's allegations, and, in any event, he had left the federal service prior to the inauguration of the loyalty program.
It is probable, too, that Thomas's motives would not have survived a purity test. All the same, Democratic strategists feared
the possible effects of HCUA's charges. Senator J. Howard
McGrath of Rhode Island, Chairman of the Democratic National Committee, urged the President to treat the Communist issue more definitely, so as to forestall the opposition,
while at the same time advising caution on taking a strong
stand for civil liberties.[20]
One major question was what the GOP would make of the
issue. The Republican candidate for President, Governor
Thomas E. Dewey of New York, tried to turn the loyalty program to his own account: "This administration asked Congress for $25,000 to spot and fire the Communists whom
they themselves put in office. I have a better way to handle the
Communists—and a cheaper one. We won't put any Communists in the government in the first place."[21] But Governor
Dewey, who was following the "high road" on what he—along

with most politicians and reporters—believed was a sure trip to the White House, went no deeper into demagogy. His major speech on the Communist issue, delivered September 24 in Los Angeles, was measured and reasonable throughout. What was sauce for the candidate, however, was not necessarily sauce for his supporters.

The Republican National Chairman, Representative Hugh Scott of Pennsylvania, charged on September 25 that the President was careless about domestic Communism because the Communist party had endorsed him for Vice-President in 1944.[22] The next day Senator Homer Ferguson of Michigan telegraphed Mr. Truman, challenging him to "discuss the extent to which Communists, or others, whose loyalty to the United States is open to question, have been allowed to retain federal government positions."[23] And Lieutenant Governor Joe R. Hanley of New York, never a master of understatement, claimed that with Governor Dewey's election, "no one will be exempted from scrutiny as to their [sic] loyalty to the country. No one will be so high that they [sic] cannot be brought down and no one so hidden that they [sic] cannot be uncovered. We will have Americanism in the highest meaning of the word when Mr. Dewey becomes President."[24]

How was the administration to respond to these attacks? Outside the White House itself, the inclination was to take up a defensive position. Attorney General Clark stated in a speech of September 22 that "[t]he President's program has not ended with the investigation of Federal employees. Thirty-four persons have been convicted in the Federal Courts in Washington, D.C., since July 1, 1945."[25] Mr. Clark was in effect adopting the stance of a politically conscious district attorney whose public reputation must rest on his conviction record. By emphasizing the legal pursuit of subversives, Mr. Clark could underline the hardness of the administration's anti-Communist position. This, of course, was a proper view for the nation's chief law enforcement officer, but would any other be taken by the President's spokesmen? The day after the Attorney General spoke, William L. Batt, director of the Research Division of the Democratic National Committee, wrote Charles S. Murphy, then an administrative assistant at the White House, citing Walter Winchell's recent broadcast on the efforts of Senator Ferguson and others to get J. Edgar Hoover fired and arguing that the President had a chance to put "himself and Hoover on the side of the angels."[26] Many in the executive departments and the party leadership were indeed ready to lay all stress on the police problem and the effectiveness with which it was being solved.

The White House staff was anxious that President Truman make a major address on Communism, one that would not only highlight his record in opposing Soviet aggression abroad and subversion at home but would also make a plea for cool judgment and continued respect for traditional civil liberties. When it was decided that such a speech should be given, both its content and location became matters for concern. Oklahoma City was selected as the most appropriate site because it was in the Central Time Zone, thus guaranteeing a maximum of listeners for a nationwide radio broadcast, and because it was in the heart of that section of the country where the fear of Communism seemed to be stimulating the greatest concern.[27] Factual information for the speech was gathered early, and successive drafts produced by staff members in Washington were sent to the President's aides on the campaign train for a searching review.[28] Owing to the controversial nature of the issue, unusual care seems to have been taken with this speech. A late draft was submitted to President Mitchell of the Civil Service Commission for comment, and he offered a number of suggestions. He complained, for one thing, that the speech gave the impression that Mr. Truman was against making labor leaders sign anti-Communist affidavits; for another, he objected to "what seem exaggerated references such as 'the rich,'" observing that the President seemed too much given to this sort of thing.[29] The staff, of course, felt that the voters should be reminded of the administration's program of domestic reform at the same time they were assured of its hostility to Communism; the fight against subversion could not be allowed to look like a cover for standing pat. And the easiest way to achieve this goal was to give some free play to the President's natural populism. At the same time, the necessity that this speech be crisp and dignified in tone was evident.

The speech as delivered on September 28 laid emphasis on the administration's struggle against Communism overseas, and insisted that the FBI had proved it could combat subversion at home without amateur aid. The President went on the offensive to lambaste congressional investigating committees, especially HCUA, now under Republican control:

I charge that the Republicans have impeded and made more difficult our efforts to cope with communism in this country. . . . I charge that they have not produced any significant information about Communist espionage which the FBI did not already have. . . . I charge them with having recklessly cast a cloud of suspicion over the most loyal civil service in the world. . . . I charge that in all this they have not hurt the Communist party one bit. They have helped it.[30]

Late in the campaign, as the underdog came snarling and scrapping to the wire, the tone was a little shriller. Mr. Truman's charges were rather less to the point, if very close to the gut. "There are some Republicans," he asserted in Boston on October 27,

> who have been trying to make you believe that your government is endangered by Communist infiltration. That is just a plain malicious lie. All of this Republican talk about Communism . . . is in the same pattern with their appeals to religious prejudice against Al Smith in 1928. They are afraid to go before the American people on the merits of the policies they believe in. So they try to distract the people's attention with false issues. I want you to get this straight now. I hate communism.[31]

This was demagogy, a blatant appeal to the emotions of Catholic voters on a point of doubtful relevancy. Yet it probably did little violence to the man's true feelings. There *was* a very great deal of plain "smear" in the "soft on Communism" charges made against him by prominent Republicans. Many of these charges, moreover, were totally disingenuous; those making them knew the truth to be something else. The President lashed back, and the crowds loved it.

Such was the way devised to deal with conservative assaults on the Communist issue. Some other means was required to win back potential Wallace voters whose sentiments and interests demanded quite another appeal. What was the best way to deal with the problem? Where should it be tackled? During Mr. Truman's first major campaign swing, a well-disposed and trusted journalist convinced the White House staff—who in turn convinced the "boss"—that it would be a mistake not to speak about the Third Party (the Progressives) in California, where it was assumed to be exceptionally strong. Because of that strength, however, it appeared unwise to make an all-out attack on Wallace so early in the campaign. Accordingly, a fairly mild deprecation of the Progressives was added to the President's Los Angeles speech of September 23:

> There are . . . a small number of people with true liberal convictions, whose worry over the state of the world has led them to lend support to the Third Party.
>
> To these liberals, I would say in all sincerity: Think again.
>
> The fact that the Communists are the main influence behind the Third Party shows that this is not a party which represents American ideals.
>
> But there is another and very practical reason why it is folly for any liberal to stake his hopes on the Third Party. The Third Party has no power in the Government, and no chance of achieving power. The simple fact is that the Third Party cannot achieve peace because it is powerless. It cannot achieve better conditions here at home, because it is powerless.
>
> The Democratic Party is the party which really expresses the aspirations of American liberalism and which has power to fulfill those aspirations. We have worked for peace, in a difficult international situation, and we shall continue with all our strength to work for peace. . . .
>
> All that can result from a vote for the Third Party is to play into the hands of the Republican forces of reaction, whose aims are directly opposed to the aims of American liberalism. . . .
>
> I say to those disturbed liberals who have been sitting uncertainly on the outskirts of the Third Party—don't waste your votes! A vote for the Third Party is a vote for reaction. A vote for the

Democratic Party is a vote for the true purpose of American democracy.[32]

This is a standard plea to voters contemplating support of a minor party: since it cannot win, the vote cast for it is lost, and it may be more than lost; it may produce the worst possible result from the voter's standpoint. President Truman labored this argument at some length, while obliquely reminding his hearers that Wallace was a "spoiler," that the greater his vote, the greater the likelihood of a Republican victory. And a Republican victory would mean the triumph of the leaders of the Eightieth Congress, who would dearly love to undo the social legislation of the Roosevelt and Truman administrations. A vote for Wallace was therefore a vote for reaction. The reference to the Communist underpinnings of the Progressive party was brief and not pursued; there was to be no aggressive attack on the third party yet. In a sense, of course, that sentence was addressed to another audience, to countless concerned anti-Communists waiting for a slip.

Although the increasingly obvious Communist mantle thrown about Wallace might alienate the isolationists and conservatives fearful of war who had been originally attracted to the third-party movement, it might not serve to drive off those whose overriding concern was with what they called peace and who were suspicious of American foreign policy. To chip away at the hard core of Wallace's support, the Truman campaign would have to capture the peace issue for itself. Because of the problem on its other flank, however, it would have to do so without making serious concessions to the Soviet position.

Mr. Truman, with the aid of two speechwriters brought in

for the campaign, Albert Z. Carr and David Noyes, hit upon a solution to the dilemma—he would send a trusted friend, Chief Justice Fred M. Vinson, to Moscow as the President's private emissary to Stalin.[33] The President later described himself as trying to break a logjam in Soviet-American relations. He explained to Vinson his hope that this "off-channel approach to Stalin" would improve the Soviet leader's understanding of American attitudes and hopes. The chance "to talk with our own Chief Justice" might be decisive, he believed.[34]

Mr. Truman laid his commands on Vinson the evening of Sunday, October 5. The same day he had instructed his Press Secretary, Charles Ross, to arrange free radio time to announce the mission, and he ordered the State Department to secure the necessary clearances from Stalin to receive Vinson. These preparations were undertaken without the President's having notified either Secretary of State Marshall, then in Paris for a United Nations meeting, or any congressional leaders of either party of his plans.

On the morning of Tuesday the fifth, Ross called in representatives of the major networks to ask for time for the President on Thursday evening. He explained the purpose of the talk in strict confidence. At the same time, Mr. Truman was using the White House teletype to inform General Marshall of the project. The Secretary's response was prompt, firm, and negative. The Western European associates of the United States, then largely unarmed, would suspect the President of doing a deal with Stalin behind their backs. They greatly feared a bilateral solution of the Berlin blockade question that would ignore their interests. Under Secretary Lovett then strongly supported his chief's objections to the Vinson mission.

President Truman, rather shaken, agreed to postpone action and asked Marshall to come home for a thorough discussion of the problem. He also invited Vandenberg, as chairman of the Senate Foreign Relations Committee, and Tom Connally of Texas, as the ranking Democratic member of that committee, to come to the White House for a secret consultation. Vandenberg was surprised in restrospect that the Vinson mission was never discussed at all;[35] however, Connally, who had arrived at the White House earlier, was so adverse to the proposal that Mr. Truman decided not to mention it to the Republican leader.[36] The arrangements for the mission were cancelled, Ross calling the networks to inform them that the requested time would not be needed, and to swear them again to secrecy.

There was a leak all the same, and the the story broke on Friday, October 8. The President explained the following day, after conferring with Secretary Marshall, that he had not intended to bypass America's allies, but had only hoped to create an atmosphere in which fruitful negotiations could take place. He was subjected to a storm of press criticism, nevertheless, his irresponsibility being lavishly denounced. Second-line Republican campaigners seized on the openings thus afforded them. Governor Dewey, however, judging himself to be well ahead in the race, did not exploit the apparent opportunity, preferring to polish the image of statesmanship. And while many of the President's aides regarded the incident as a politically deadly fiasco, he himself reassured them, "I don't think it's that bad."[37] He had demonstrated his devotion to the cause of peace, his willingness to go the extra mile, at no real cost at all. While the episode may have exposed Mr. Truman's failure to understand Stalin, having displayed a naïveté in this regard as great as Roosevelt's, it must be remembered that the Vinson mission was originally conceived as the answer to a domestic problem. Seen in that light, it cannot be dismissed as a total failure.

One last, important raid on the source of Wallace's strength occurred as the campaign drew to a close. At Chicago, on October 25, the President charged that Governor Dewey was a front man for reactionary, antidemocratic forces, recalling for his listeners the support given Hitler and Mussolini by German and Italian industrialists. Clearly aiming at the minorities supposedly attracted to the Progressives, he referred to "a new outcropping of demagogues among us. Dangerous men, who are trying to win followers for their war on democracy, are attacking Catholics and Jews and Negroes and other minority races and religions."[38] The message was clear: Republican victory would bring these "dangerous men" close to power, and a vote for Wallace would contribute to a Republican victory. It was Mr. Truman's most free-swinging speech of the fall, and he did not return to its theme. For many observers, this Chicago speech and the Boston speech two days later were a measure of the President's desperation; in a dying effort, he had resorted to risky tactics.

The miracle of November 2 obliterated all questions about the Truman strategy. Whether the President had been right in detail or not, he had won. So far as the Communist issue and the Wallace candidacy went, things worked out very much as Clark Clifford had hoped might be possible in his year-old memorandum on strategy. Catholic voters did return to the Democratic fold in large numbers after Wallace, in effect, purged it of fellow travelers, while the Dixiecrat revolt not only fixed the bulk of Negro voters in the Democratic ranks but also did invoke memories of Al Smith among some Catholics, as the President had suggested in Boston.[39] Of course, other issues were important, generally more important than Communists-in-government in 1948. In the Middle West, falling hog prices stirred more hearts than rumors of rising subversion. The fear of another depression (and memories of the Republican handling of the last one) cut deep everywhere. And, despite sporadic outbursts, the Communist issue was not exploited as much by the Republicans as had been anticipated. The loyalty program was, to be fair, pretty much proof against anything the GOP could allege in the summer and fall of that year.

What clear effect the Communist issue had in 1948 was to the President's advantage. It accounted for the dramatic evaporation of "Gideon's Army," which, like that of Byron's Sennacherib, melted like snow. The purification of the Truman candidacy occasioned by Wallace's defection in the first place, and the return of potential Progressives to the Democrats after the new party's Communist support became evident, may have made the difference between victory and defeat. It is true that Wallace, getting about half of his unexpectedly low 1,150,000 votes in New York, threw that state into its governor's column, but in California, where every breed of elector known to political science and science fiction flourishes in the sun, the President's campaign (helped greatly by the public performance of the Progressives themselves) touched just enough nerves exciting old loyalties to eke out a plurality. Fortunately for Mr. Truman, the California example was more "catching." On the morning of November 3, the Communist

5

Talismans of the Opposition
Chiang Kai-shek and Alger Hiss

VICTORY, as it turned out, brought only a short respite for the President. The year 1949 was one of political ill-omen for the administration, largely because of a series of events all somehow related in the popular imagination to the issue of subversion: the "loss" of China to Communist revolutionary forces, the detonation of the first Soviet atomic device, and the trials that eventually ended in Alger Hiss's conviction on a charge of perjury (for having denied under oath that he had performed acts of espionage for the Soviet Union in the 1930's). The first and third of these developments were primarily responsible for launching the extravagant career of Senator Joseph McCarthy. The Communist victory in China provided the essential background for most of his charges against the State Department. The conviction of Hiss created the atmosphere that made the charges credible to many.

More than a century of missionary activity in China, and the perpetual hope of a future great market there, had given very many Americans a sense of sentimental attachment to the former Celestial Empire. China was regarded as a special protégé of the United States—it was our mission to make her great—and so was after a fashion ours to "lose." Unquestionably, the China policy of the Roosevelt administration played a major role in the outbreak of war between the United States and Japan in 1941. And during the war Roosevelt made a major rhetorical investment in the Kuomintang government —without, however, having the forces or funds to do very much to advance it. Broad elements of the public, including a number of congressional leaders, therefore understood our commitment to be an important one. When Communist rebellion following the victory over Japan turned into a civil war that engulfed the Kuomintang, they were aghast at the Truman administration's failure to do something about it.[1] The rationale for the position of antiadministration forces, in respect to the Far East, as Norman Graebner has argued,

> flowed logically from two assumptions: that the decline of American security had resulted from erroneous policy . . . ; and that diplomatic defeats of such magnitude could not have stemmed from conditions in the Orient and therefore must have been self-inflicted. In a bitter memorandum of August, 1949, Senators Styles Bridges, William Knowland, Kenneth Wherry, and Pat McCarran termed the China White Paper [of the State Department] "a 1,054-page whitewash of a wishful, do-nothing policy which has succeeded only in placing Asia in danger of Soviet conquest." United States policy failed, in short, because it has pursued the goals, not of this nation, but of the Soviet Union.[2]

It has to be doubted, nevertheless, that the senators would have advocated a truly forward policy, in any physical sense, issue no longer menaced the Truman administration; indeed, it seemed to have been turned to the President's account.

NOTES

1. Robert K. Carr, *The House Committee on Un-American Activities, 1945–1950* (Ithaca, N.Y.: Cornell University Press, 1952), pp. 37–38.

2. See p. 46.

3. Representative Thomas did write in *Liberty* magazine "stating that Oak Ridge was just crawling with Communists, and that there was nothing but a fence between saboteurs and the plants; [and] that Russia could get all the information about the atomic bomb she wanted, and was doing so, by copying patent applications." David E. Lilienthal, *The Journals of David E. Lilienthal* (New York: Harper & Row, 1964), vol. 2, *The Atomic Energy Years, 1945–1950*, 190.

4. Ibid., p. 141. Arthur H. Vandenburg, Jr., ed. (with the collaboration of Joe Alex Morris), *The Private Papers of Senator Vandenberg* (Boston: Houghton Mifflin Co., 1952), p. 353.

5. Vandenberg, *Private Papers*, p. 353. Lilienthal, *The Journals*, pp. 141–142.

6. Vandenberg, *Private Papers*, p. 353.

7. Clark Clifford reported that the President was in the fight to the finish, that he was willing to carry the issue of this appointment to the country. Lilienthal, *The Journals*, pp. 143–144.

8. So long as there had been Democratic majorities in Congress, conservative Democrats, especially southerners, had been willing to trade votes with the Republican leadership, in order to defeat administration measures repugnant to their constituents. With the Republicans now in a majority, and with the GOP leaders consequently seeking to make a party record, conservative Democrats were no longer so willing to give a *quid* for a *quo*.

9. Vandenberg, *Private Papers*, p. 354.

10. Private information.

11. Vandenberg, *Private Papers*, pp. 355–357.

12. Papers of Clark M. Clifford.

13. Ibid.

14. Ibid. June 2, 1947.

15. The best available account of the battle over the civil rights plank is to be found in Irwin Ross, *The Loneliest Campaign: The Truman Victory of 1948* (New York: The New American Library, 1968), pp. 120–126.

16. For a detailed account of the Condon investigation fiasco, see Carr, *The House Committee,* pp. 131–153.

17. *Washington Post,* August 6, 1948.

18. Papers of HST, Press Conference 153, August 12, 1948, Files of the White House Official Reporter.

19. Ibid., Press Conference 154, August 19, 1948.

20. Papers of J. Howard McGrath, Files of the Democratic National Chairman. The view is the more interesting since McGrath became Attorney General the following year.

21. Cited in Ross, *The Loneliest Campaign,* pp. 197–198.

22. Ibid., pp. 199–200.

23. Papers of HST, Official File 252–K.

24. Eleanor Bontecou, *The Federal Loyalty-Security Program* (Ithaca, NY.: Cornell University Press, 1950) , pp. 102–103.

25. Cited in a letter to the President from J. Parnell Thomas, September 29, 1948, Papers of HST, Official File 320–B.

26. Ibid., Files of Charles S. Murphy.

27. Memorandum for Clark M. Clifford from Stephen J. Spingarn, September 16, 1948, Papers of HST, Files of Charles S. Murphy.

28. Stephen J. Spingarn to Attorney General Clark, September 9, 1948, Papers of Stephen J. Spingarn. Spingarn to Murphy, September 20, 1948, Papers of HST, Files of Charles S. Murphy.

29. Letter to Spingarn, September 23, 1948, Papers of Stephen J. Spingarn.

30. Cited in Ross, *The Loneliest Campaign,* p. 203.

31. Cited in ibid., p. 236.

32. Spingarn to Clifford, September 22, 1948, Papers of HST, Files of Charles S. Murphy.

33. Albert Z. Carr, *Truman, Stalin, and Peace* (Garden City, N.Y.: Doubleday & Co., 1950) , pp. 111–120. See also Ross, *The Loneliest Campaign,* pp. 212–215, and Truman, vol. 2, *Memoirs,* pp. 213–219.

34. Truman, vol. 2, *Memoirs,* pp. 214–215.

35. Vandenberg, *Private Papers,* p. 458.

36. H. Bradford Westerfield, *Foreign Policy and Party Politics: Pearl Harbor to Korea* (New Haven: Yale University Press, 1955) , p. 318.

37. Cited in Ross, *The Loneliest Campaign,* p. 214.

38. Cited in ibid., p. 235.

39. Samuel Lubell, *The Future of American Politics* (New York: Harper & Brothers, 1951) , pp. 205–214.

In 1923 the Communists joined Sun Yat-sen's party of national regeneration, the Kuomintang. After Sun's death, Chiang Kai-shek, then a promising military commander, resolved to assume leadership of the party and purge it of its Communist elements. This was accomplished by force in 1927, large numbers of Communists being massacred. Stalin judged Chiang to be the predominant force in China and refused to involve the Soviet Union in the fate of the Communist brethren.

The Kuomintang began a five-year campaign in 1930 to wipe out what remained of the Chinese Communist party. During this time, the Communist remnant, under the leadership of Mao Tse-tung, abandoned their base in the south of China and trekked along the periphery of the country to relative safety in the fastnesses of Yenan in the northwest. Following the kidnapping of Chiang in December, 1936, by a young war lord who had been in negotiation with the Communists, a superficial accommodation was reached between the contending forces. The basis of the agreement was the need for national unity in the face of renewed Japanese aggression, then believed imminent. For a year or more after the Japanese invasion of July, 1937, there was in fact some effective cooperation between these rival Chinese parties.

By 1943, at the latest, however, the past had reasserted itself, and the hostility between Kuomintang nationalists and Communists had once again become the dominant political reality of China. Neither side was at that time equipped, materially or psychologically, to participate decisively in the struggle against Japan; each therefore concentrated on working for a postwar world that would be brightened by the elimination of the other. "The National Government was counting on

American victory to secure the ultimate defeat of the Communists. The Communists were counting on the Soviet Union to assure their survival, and in good time their victory."[6]

After the Japanese attack on Pearl Harbor had brought the United States into the war, the Roosevelt administration cast about for means to establish effective liaison with the Chinese government and to support it in its military endeavors. Lieutenant General Joseph W. (Vinegar Joe) Stilwell was sent to Chungking, the Chinese provisional capital, to be Chief of Staff to Generalissimo Chiang, concentrating on the retraining and reequipment of Chinese forces, and to command American troops in the Far East under the authority of the Generalissimo. The mission was destined to be a difficult one, in any event, since American strategy was committed to a policy of dealing with Germany before Japan, and could spare the China theater only promises, reassurance, and such little surplus equipment as might be available. It eventually became impossible because of a clash of personalities between Chiang and Stilwell.

For over two years, Stilwell tussled with a variety of demons. He complained to his superiors in Washington about the promised men and matériel that never came. He fought for the Generalissimo's ear with Kuomintang officials and Nationalist commanders interested in their own fortunes—some in regular contact with the Japanese or Communists. He squabbled constantly with the British theater commander, trying to prod the British into a major action in Burma, against Churchill's judgment. Above all, he resented Chiang's reluctance to commit troops to action in sufficient numbers to ensure proper results, and he could not comprehend the "G-mo's" insistence on reserving his best divisions for the task of for the United States in the Far East. The Republicans had been attacking the Democrats as a "war party," while antiadministration leaders generally insisted on budget-cutting. The expenditure of men and money that would have been required to save the Chinese Nationalists would have betrayed their only secure base of popular support. And, it should be remembered, the Chinese issue was widely agitated only *after* Chiang Kai-shek had been conclusively defeated. One is reminded of the position that Senator McCarthy later took toward the Korean War, that "the program for military aid to South Korea was sabotaged to the extent that only $52,000 worth of wire out of the [$112,900,000] appropriated [in 1949] was sent to Korea with which to stem the threatened onslaught of Communist planes, tanks, artillery, etc."[3] If it had not been for subversives in the State Department, South Korea could have defended herself alone, and we could have had our security on the cheap. If it had not been for those same saboteurs, Chiang Kai-shek could somehow have been enabled to vanquish his Communist enemies. Treachery in the State Department accounted for all our Far Eastern troubles—just as if it had not been for the Rosenbergs and their associates, Alan Nunn May, and Klaus Fuchs, the Soviet Union would never have developed nuclear weaponry. Thus ran the argument embraced by McCarthy and his followers.

In good part, a large cross-section of the American public simply could not stand the stress of living in the postwar world. After World War I, Europe had "gone away"; now it not only showed no signs of vanishing, but the administration was committed to prevent its going away. We were settling down to a policy of permanent involvement with the other powers of the globe. Speaking of this popular feeling, then As-

sistant Secretary of State Dean Acheson found it significant
that Americans called their problems "headaches." Of ordinary headaches, he said, "You take a powder and they are
gone." But of our international commitments:

> These pains . . . will stay with us until death. We have got to
> understand that all our lives danger, the uncertainty, the need for
> alertness, for efforts, for discipline will be upon us. This is new to
> us. It will be hard for us.[4]

How more poignant an estimate of American response to
the international situation this became after the onset of the
"cold war"! With the Truman administration committed to
fighting what it perceived to be a danger without starting
World War III, the public wish for some escape grew even
more intense.[5] The sense of frustration was galling. Under
the circumstances, successes of foreign policy—the Soviet lift-
ing of the Berlin blockade under Western pressure, the smoth-
ering of Communist insurrection in Greece (with an assist
from Tito's newly anti-Stalinist regime in Yugoslavia), the
beginning of Western European rehabilitation under the
Marshall Plan, the development of the Atlantic alliance
(NATO)—counted for nothing against the supposed failures,
which were rubbed like a leper's sores.

In this atmosphere, what was known of American difficulties in China was readily exploited by the President's opponents. What was known was that American policy, which had
aimed at reconciling the recognized national government of
Chiang Kai-shek with the Chinese Communists, had apparently failed. The disintegration of Nationalist China began in
the fall of 1948 and proceeded apace through 1949, without
the United States' taking any steps to halt the disaster.

not the United States Army. In the long run, this was the most important result of the Wallace mission. Contact with the Communists, who put their best foot forward, served to increase official American disenchantment with the Kuomintang regime, and to convince Secretary of State Hull, as well as the President, that Chiang was unreasonably recalcitrant about seeking an accommodation with the Communists.

Roosevelt now decided to send Major General Patrick J. Hurley, a colorful and combative Oklahoma Republican who had been Hoover's Secretary of War, as a special emissary to Chiang. The appointment was pleasing to conservative Republicans, and may have been designed in part to boost their confidence in administration policy, yet it is hard to see what his qualifications as a diplomat were. He was to report directly to the President, and the latter may have intended to keep him in leading strings, an intention undermined by the pressure of more immediately urgent problems.

Hurley's assignment was to improve relations between General Stilwell and Generalissimo Chiang, to establish clearly Stilwell's command over Chinese troops (apparently including Communists, if the National government could be brought to accede to their use), and to clarify the military organization of the theater under Chiang's overall command. His instructions, however, could not have been completely clear, as Herbert Feis points out:

> Hurley was under the impression—which was never clearly contradicted—that the President and the Secretary of State (Roosevelt and Truman; Stettinius [Hull's successor in November, 1944] and Byrnes) agreed that it was essential to keep the Chiang Kai-shek regime in control of the government of China. But his mission

was disturbed by disputes as to whether this was or was not a primary and governing rule of American policy. And, paradoxically, in the course of his effort to arrange for military unification, he sponsored proposals which might have brought other elements to power.[11]

Hurley traveled to China by way of Moscow, where he was informed (as Wallace had been by Stalin), and seemingly convinced, by Foreign Minister Molotov that the Chinese Communists were not Communists at all.[12] His dealings with both Chiang and the Yenan group were to be governed by this assumption.

On his arrival in China, however, Hurley had to plunge immediately into a new crisis in the relations between General Stilwell and Generalissimo Chiang. A victory won in northern Burma by Chinese forces under Stilwell's command impressed Washington, and twice during the summer of 1944 Roosevelt urged the Generalissimo to place Stilwell in command of all Chinese troops. Chiang seemed to agree but he never made the appointment. When a new Japanese advance into the interior of China overran an American air base and appeared to threaten not only Chungking but the great American supply base of Kunming, the White House stepped up the pressure on its ally. Chiang, for his part, wished to withdraw the greater part of the Chinese forces in Burma unless Stilwell made a diversionary movement with a smaller army group. The latter wanted to press on with the Burmese campaign already under way and felt that Chiang should recall the crack units assigned to watching the Communists for the defense of his capital.

Roosevelt was then (in the middle of September) meeting

watching the Communists in Yenan. Many of the young American foreign service officers assigned to Stilwell's staff shared his doubts about the Kuomintang regime—indeed, they stimulated them—and thought that the United States might serve its purposes better by dealing directly with the Communists. The Communists were busy at this stage soliciting Western approval, and they assiduously advertised unprovable guerrilla victories over the Japanese. They did not, to be sure, give equal publicity to the fact that their own best units were occupied watching the Nationalists.

Not only Stilwell and his staff but their superiors, political and military, back home became convinced that only full-scale collaboration between the Nationalists and Communists could make China an important factor in the war. It accordingly became official American policy to reconcile these adversaries and yoke them together in harness for the final drive against Japan. When the war in the Pacific had ended, the same goal was maintained for the purpose of establishing political stability in China. The United States had committed itself, without much forethought, to raising up China to be the world's fourth great power. If that aim were to dissolve in revolution and anarchy, the American conception of the postwar Far East would vanish with it. The British, whose own standing as the third great power rested on no material base, objected to the investment of time and prestige in what they regarded as a hopeless cause, but the Americans persisted.

Three major presidential missions were sent to China to achieve this overriding objective of American policy. In June, 1944, FDR sent Vice-President Wallace to confer with Chiang and to try to win him over to a policy of conciliation. Wallace was accompanied by John Carter Vincent, who ran the

"China desk" at the State Department, and who sat in on—and took notes of—all three days of talks between Wallace and the Chinese leader. Professor Owen Lattimore of Johns Hopkins University, a specialist in Far Eastern affairs and then an adviser to the Generalissimo, participated in the conversations on two days.[7] Wallace reported the President as having said that "nothing is final between friends,"[8] in asking his Vice-President to urge Chiang to try once again to come to terms with the Communists. Whether Roosevelt seriously believed that there were any ties of friendship between the Kuomintang and the Chinese Communist party we cannot know, although many of his notions about east Asia seem to have been based on sentiment and nourished by misinformation. Chiang responded to this ill-advised platitude by denying that the common quality of being Chinese was enough to extinguish acute political differences. The Communists were not, he said, agrarian reformers, as was widely believed in the West; they were in fact more doctrinaire than their Russian preceptors. Wallace observed that in view of the patriotic attitude of the Communists in the United States, he could not understand the behavior of the Chinese Communists, as the Generalissimo described it.[9] Quite plainly, he thought Chiang either to be mistaken or lying. It is probable that he had accepted Stalin's evaluation as the literal truth: "The Chinese Communists are not real Communists. They are 'margarine' Communists. Nevertheless, they are real patriots and they want to fight Japan."[10]

Wallace succeeded in persuading Chiang to permit American observers to visit areas under Communist control, his host insisting only that they be accompanied by Nationalist officers and that they go under the auspices of his Military Council, hopes. A new basis for negotiation might be found in Chiang's announcement that the Communists would be recognized as a legal party as soon as their army and local administration had been brought under Nationalist authority. The Communists immediately rejected the plan as insincere and a betrayal of democracy, yet Hurley was not discouraged. As he saw it then, "two fundamental facts are emerging: (1) the Communists are not in fact Communists, they are striving for democratic principles; and (2) the one party, one man rule of the Kuomintang is not in fact fascist, it is striving for democratic principles."[16]

Since the Alice-in-Wonderland quality of this statement led to no challenge of Hurley's usefulness (he had been appointed Ambassador to China the previous December), he was free to pursue his plans for unification. Such was the general state of American policy in China when Roosevelt died on April 12, 1945, and Harry Truman became President in his stead.

The new President was, of course, quickly informed of the military and diplomatic arrangements to which the government was committed. The world was being turned upside down so rapidly in that hectic spring, however, that Mr. Truman just had not the leisure to give full attention to all the problems before him. He had very little choice but to carry forward his predecessor's policies, perhaps altering their application if circumstances demanded. In questions of supposedly less than immediate consequence, such as that of China, he could only let subordinates carry on as before in the hope that nothing might happen to force new decisions.

The principal object, in respect to the Far East, sought by the American delegation to the Yalta Conference in February had been the entry of the Soviet Union into the war against

Japan. At the same time, the Americans were resolved to resist claims to extravagant concessions at China's expense that the Soviets might advance as the price of their participation in the conflict. To grant such concessions would impair China's role as one of the world's "four policemen," to use the language of the Teheran Conference. By way of making China a great power, the United States was determined that she should recover all that she had lost to Japan over the past half century, notably Manchuria, called Manchukuo by the Japanese, and the island of Taiwan, renamed Formosa. It was also essential, in the American view, that the peaceful political unification of the country be accomplished as rapidly as possible.

What Stalin wanted, as it turned out, was substantial: the same operational control of the Manchurian railway system enjoyed by the Tsar's government prior to the Russo-Japanese War of 1904–1905 and leases on the ports of Dairen and Port Arthur, the latter having been also a holding of the tsarist imperium. Roosevelt objected to outright Soviet control of such valuable concessions. He suggested, as an alternative, the operation of the railroads by a joint Soviet-Chinese commission and the internationalization of the ports. The Russian dictator accepted these points as a basis for discussion, and, generally following Roosevelt's proposals, produced the formula that was adopted as paragraph 2 (b) and (c) of the "Agreement Regarding Japan" reached at Yalta:

> (b) the commercial port of Dairen shall be internationalized, *the pre-eminent interests of the Soviet Union in this port being safeguarded* and the lease of Port Arthur as a naval base of the U.S.S.R. restored.
>
> (c) the Chinese-Eastern Railroad and the South-Manchuria

in Quebec with Prime Minister Churchill and the Combined
Chiefs of Staff. On the advice of the Combined Chiefs, he sent
Chiang a virtual ultimatum, insisting on *reinforcement* of the
Burma forces and Stilwell's being placed in "unrestricted command" of all Chinese armies. The blow was softened by an
expression of genuine personal regard.[13] Again the Generalissimo agreed in principle to the new role for Stilwell, but—a-
gain—failed to act. The American commander believed that
Chiang hoped that the American offensive in the Pacific
would move fast enough to spare him any further sacrifice or
effort. On September 26, Stilwell reported bluntly to the War
Department, "I am now convinced that . . . the United States
will not get any real cooperation from China while Chiang
Kai-shek is in power."[14]

Chiang had in fact written the day before, capitulating to
Roosevelt's summons—with the exception that he could not
confer so great a responsibility on Stilwell. He asked for a new
commander. Hurley advised the White House that the clash
of personalities was now too bitter for reconciliation. To save
Chiang as a functioning ally, he argued, Stilwell must be replaced. As a political necessity, then, the President and the
War Department reluctantly agreed to Stilwell's recall. "Vinegar Joe" was replaced by an officer who proved more accord-
ant with the Generalissimo—Lieutenant General Albert C.
Wedemeyer.

Hurley was thus freed to go ahead with what he believed to
be his main task, the unification of *all* Chinese forces for the
final drive against Japan. His instructions offered him no
guide as to how the essential accommodation between Chiang
and Mao was to be achieved, so he was left to his own devices.
Like many Americans, Hurley obviously believed that politics

is politics, and that what works in the United States ought to work anywhere. His contacts with the "non-Communists" from Yenan convinced him they were reasonable people. The Communists, it must be noted, worked carefully to maintain the democratic façade of the Yenan regime; still is a precarious position, limited to a relatively remote corner of the country, they infrequently showed their true colors in the area they administered. Hurley, accordingly, carried what he considered a negotiable proposal for a coalition government to Chiang. The Generalissimo, as President of China, combined the principal political and military authority in his own person, and he feared that a retreat in the one area would sap his prestige in the other. Anything that looked like a viable coalition would be construed as a surrender by the Kuomintang, alerting the military commanders to protect themselves against a possible transfer of the "mandate of heaven." In a coalition, control of the armed services, the police, and finances are decisive. The Communist conception of a proper coalition would be intolerable to Chiang's supporters. What the Kuomintang could accept would be death to the Communists. A true coalition is simply impossible between hostile elements that have learned with good reason to distrust each other. Certainly Chiang was not going to let the Communists retain control of their troops; it was logical for him to insist on the incorporation of such forces into the National Army under the safe direction of Nationalist officers. General Wedemeyer was astounded by Hurley's apparent assumption that he was handling a simple arbitration.[15]

The Generalissimo's announcement on March 1, 1945, that a People's Congress would meet the following November to establish a constitutional government for China raised Hurley's

American policy, however, remained one of uneasy neutrality. As the conquerors of Germany met at Potsdam, and the hour of decision with Japan drew close, a number of persons concluded there would have to be a change. State Department representatives at Potsdam—Ambassador Harriman, Eugene Dooman, head of the Far Eastern Division, and John Carter Vincent, chief of the China Section, among them—were pressing the new Secretary of State, James F. Byrnes, to intervene on Soong's behalf in Moscow, lest all China's pretensions to great power status be bartered away under coercion. They were joined by Secretary of War Stimson, who warned the President that Stalin might try to close the Manchurian door to the rest of the world. In a consequent conversation, Mr. Truman thought that he had secured Stalin's promise that Dairen would be maintained as a free port under Soviet control, and he was anxious that Soong realize that the United States insisted on this point, lest the Chinese Foreign Minister himself make too many concessions.[20]

Before the Potsdam Conference ended, Ambassador Harriman pressed Secretary Byrnes to support the Chinese in their unequal negotiations with the Soviet leaders. Finally, while he was on the way home, Mr. Byrnes authorized the Ambassador to remind Stalin of the American interest in the "Open Door" in Manchuria and to point out that Soong could not be made to concede more than was determined at Yalta. Stalin was already demanding Soviet police control of the city and port of Dairen, administrative control of the port, and renewal of the tsarist leasehold on the Kwantung Peninsula to protect Dairen. Dairen would be included in the Kwantung military zone. Mr. Harriman advised Soong that his government considered the Chinese to have gone as far in their own offers as required by the Yalta agreement, and need not—or ought not—to go further. If, however, the Chinese made additional concessions—the Ambassador realized that Soong, and through him Chiang, were weakening under pressure—it would be only to secure special considerations of value from the Soviet Union.

A Sino-Soviet agreement was signed on August 14, 1945, the day the Japanese surrendered under the terror of atom bombing and six days after the Soviet Union had entered the war. Soong had conceded, contrary to his earlier position, the inclusion of Dairen within the Soviet military zone. Stalin promised in return not to exercise military authority in the city, port, or connecting railway system during time of peace. And the Chinese made substantial concessions on the management of the Manchurian railroads. What they got in return was a general Soviet commitment to support the National government and to withhold assistance from dissident elements, i.e., the Chinese Communists. The Soviet government also promised that the Red Army would act as the agent of the National government in accepting the surrender of Japanese troops and that Manchuria would be evacuated by Soviet occupation forces and turned over to Chiang's control as soon as possible.

Although Chiang seemed satisfied with the guarantees he had obtained, American authorities were suspicious of their real value. They arranged, for their part, for small American forces, largely marines, to be landed in the coastal areas of China to receive the surrender of Japanese troops in and near the ports. The Air Corps and the transport services were called upon to move National forces to the liberated provinces of North China. As a further precaution, Japanese officers were

Railroad which provides an outlet to Dairen shall be jointly operated by the establishment of a joint Soviet-Chinese company, it
being understood that *the pre-eminent interests of the Soviet
Union shall be safeguarded* and that China shall retain full sover-
eignty in Manchuria.[17]

Although it was agreed that the concurrence of Generalissimo Chiang was necessary to validate this disposition of the
ports and railroads, the United States had failed to obtain any
Soviet guarantee of cooperation with China. The Soviet Government proclaimed a "readiness to conclude with the National Government of China a pact of friendship and alliance,"[18] but nothing was decided at Yalta that might have restrained Stalin from putting an extortionate price on friendship. Above all, there was no precise understanding of what
might be subsumed under the mischievous heading of safeguarding the preeminent interests of the Soviet Union.

While the Chinese Foreign Minister, T. V. Soong, was in the
United States for the United Nations Charter Conference, he
had three interviews with President Truman and additional
conversations with Under Secretary of State Joseph C. Grew.
President Truman was friendly, optimistic about the future of
China, but very general in the terms of his conversation. He
was still catching up with what had been done before his coming to the office and was not, in truth, well informed on
Chinese affairs. After the Chinese were informed of the terms
of the Yalta agreement on June 15, they became uneasy, suspecting their ally's purpose in keeping those terms secret for
over four months. Mr. Truman told Soong in effect that he
would fulfill his predecessor's commitments, that he felt obliged to secure Chiang's concurrence with the agreement, but

that he was confident that Stalin would respect the interests of the National government and deal with it in good faith. The report made by Harry Hopkins, Roosevelt's old confidant, after a special mission to Russia, convinced the President that Stalin could be trusted in this matter. Soong was not wholly appeased, being still dubious as to how the "pre-eminent interests of the Soviet Union" might be defined, but he understood the President's assurances to indicate American support in the event of a dispute with Stalin. He went off to Moscow, therefore, to negotiate the general settlement the Soviet authorities professed themselves willing to make, with somewhat revived spirits.

It was official United States policy, nevertheless, not to interfere in the Sino-Soviet negotiations. At the highest level, American leaders were concerned only that some sort of agreement be concluded before Soviet entry into the Far Eastern war. Stalin, sensing his opportunity, raised the price for his support of the Kuomintang regime well beyond anything agreed upon at Yalta. He now insisted that the Manchurian railroads and the industries connected with them be exclusively owned by the Soviet Union, which would also have the deciding voice in their operation and be given control of a military zone including the ports of Dairen and Port Arthur and surrounding land and sea areas. A new naval base would be built in one of the Dairen bays for the exclusive use of the Soviet and Chinese navies (the latter being practically nonexistent). Stalin also demanded that China recognize the independence of Outer Mongolia.[19] Soong was naturally appalled, and our Ambassador to the Soviet Union, Averell Harriman, warned Washington that the Chinese government, out of national self-respect, could not accept such terms.

Chief of Staff of the Army and chairman of the Combined Chiefs, accepted this assignment as a duty and at once set about to prepare himself. With civil war in the making in North China and Manchuria, the President's instructions to Marshall were urgent: "The fact that I have asked you to go to China is the clearest evidence of my very real concern with regard to the situation there. . . . In your conversations with Chiang Kai-shek and other Chinese leaders you are authorized to speak with the utmost frankness." The Generalissimo was to be particularly reminded that "a China disunited and torn by civil strife could not be considered realistically as a proper place for American assistance."[25]

To help Marshall persuade Chiang, American marines would be kept in coastal North China to complete the disarmament and evacuation of the Japanese (that is, the marines would be a substitute for Chinese troops), and, while Chinese forces would be transported to the Manchurian ports for the same purpose, no more Nationalist units would be moved into North China, where they might interfere with the efforts to secure an internal truce. If the Communists refused to agree to a reasonable truce, then Nationalist divisions would have to be moved into North China. If the Generalissimo so refused, he was still to be supported, and his troops would have to be carried to North China, to avert the permanent division of the country and prevent the Soviet repossession of Manchuria.[26]

General Marshall soon found that accessions to American proposals by the one side or the other were not made in good faith. Both sides seemed to agree to his system of establishing and policing cease-fires in the areas of physical conflict; then one or another would charge a truce violation and fighting would recommence. The Chinese rivals were in fact using his presence to score propaganda points against each other. Marshall finally concluded that, under the circumstances, his presence in China would be of no further use. On October 5 he requested that he be recalled.[27]

Generalissimo Chiang, in an effort to prolong the mission, offered a ten-day truce and the beginning of serious talks. The Communists, however, rejected the truce offer formulated by Chiang, and supported by Marshall, and there was really nothing more to be done. The General felt that Communist intransigence was forcing Chiang into the arms of Kuomintang diehards, making any agreement next to impossible.

General Marshall was recalled on January 6, 1947, to become Secretary of State within the month. No further special missions were sent to China, and American policy there had been thwarted. Given the adversary relationship between Kuomintang and Communists (to speak of it softly), it seems highly doubtful that any accommodation was possible.

American policy, in the months following the failure of the Marshall mission, was one of offering political, economic, and military aid to the Generalissimo while seeking to avoid direct United States involvement in the civil war. It operated, in effect, on the realistic appraisal presented by General Wedemeyer in the closing days of the war. China, with a huge population submerged in illiteracy and the direst poverty, was not ready for democracy. The minimal needs of the people, under the circumstances, could best be met by some sort of dictator—and the political complexion of that dictator was not of great importance. Viewed from the standpoint of American interests, however, the general retained "the impression that the Generalissimo's leadership offers the best opportunity ordered to surrender only to qualified representatives of the Chinese National army, the Soviet occupation forces, or the American units in the Pacific ports. This last step was taken because General Wedemeyer feared that the Chinese Communists would actively seek to accept enemy surrenders in order to possess themselves of Japanese arms and equipment. The event proved the fear justified.

Throughout the spring and summer Hurley had continued his mission, and he carried on into the early fall. He had tried to establish his interpretation of American policy by forcing a showdown with the foreign service staff that General Wedemeyer had inherited from Stilwell. His quarrel was in particular with John Stewart Service and John Paton Davies, Jr. The dispute, interestingly enough, was principally over the tactics to be followed by the executors of American policy. Both Hurley and Service accepted the democratic professions of the Yenan group at face value and assumed the Communists could be understood in something akin to American political terms. Hurley concluded, therefore, that if the United States stood firmly by Chiang, the Communists would accept the inevitable and enter a coalition on the Generalissimo's terms. Service, on the other hand, reached the opinion that American interests would not be ill served if the Communists replaced the authoritarian Kuomintang. John Davies had no such idyllic picture of the Communists. He regarded their democratic posture as a device imposed by necessity, although he did assume they would remain gradualist out of the same deference to expediency. He also assumed that they represented a genuine popular forces, whose strength was nourished by the corruption of the Kuomintang. They had an excellent chance of coming to power, whether the United States liked it or not.

Hurley, on the contrary, felt that the Communists were a temporary phenomenon in Chinese political life, without real grass-roots support; they would die out soon after coalescing with the National government.

John Service was transferred to duty in the China Section of the State Department—the apparent basis of Hurley's later charge that his opponents in the service "were returned to Washington and placed in the Chinese and Far Eastern Divisions of the State Department as my supervisors."[21] Mr. Davies was recalled to Washington prior to being transferred to the Embassy in Moscow. On his departure he had to undergo an emotional attack by Hurley, who accused him of being a Communist who had sought the downfall of the Nationalists.[22]

When Hurley returned to the United States in October, the President asked him to continue as Ambassador. At first he agreed, but a little later he changed his mind and resigned on November 26, protesting that State Department career men were undermining American policy. "The professional foreign service men," he wrote, "sided with the Chinese Communist armed party and the imperialist bloc of nations whose policy it was to keep China divided against herself."[23] Yet a few days later he was still insisting that "Russia . . . does not recognize the Chinese armed Communist Party as Communists at all."[24] With the war ended, Hurley's mission, even if successful, had reached a logical end, and his conception of current Chinese realities had certainly terminated whatever usefulness he had had.

On November 27, 1945, the day after Hurley resigned, Mr. Truman appointed General of the Army George C. Marshall as his personal representative in China. General Marshall, who had but recently retired after long and arduous years as shall Plan might accomplish in Western Europe, that we had encouraged the Chinese Communists in the past and were now going to let them have Manchuria by default. It seemed to "Mr. Republican" that the fall of Manchuria would open Japan to the triumph of Communism and the United States ought, therefore, to render as much assistance to the National government of China as to the royal government of Greece to support its resistance of the red tide. He concluded bluntly, "I believe very strongly that the Far East is ultimately even more important to our future peace than is Europe."[31] Senator Vandenberg pursued a like argument, if gentler in his tone, in presenting to the Senate the recommendation of the Foreign Relations Committee for a large aid program for China. The proposed bill authorized an appropriation of $338 million in economic aid for China, as well as a grant of $100 million in military supplies, to be used at the discretion of the National government. The committee report made it clear that its intention was to strengthen the hand of Chiang's regime "without, at the same time, involving the United States in any additional commitments of a military nature."[32] The Republican leaders were still convinced that adequate aid would enable the Kuomintang to win its own battle.

The assistance sent to the Nationalists in 1948 proved of little avail; a great part of the military equipment ended in Communist hands, brought over by deserters—now commonly changing sides in regiments or divisions—or abandoned by National army units in flight. By early fall, the Generalissimo's forces were approaching collapse, their ability to resist further problematical at best. While congressional supporters of Chiang talked about emergency aid, the China experts of the State Department were speaking in terms of writing off the National government. They believed that the President and the Secretary of State should explain the deficiencies of the Kuomintang to the American people to demonstrate the futility of supporting the Nationalists any longer. Secretary Marshall, however, was convinced that such a step could only "administer the final coup de grâce to Chiang's government, and this, he felt, we could not do."[33] Mr. Truman supported him in this decision, and the commitment to Chiang remained publicly firm.

There is little question that numerous leading Republicans refrained from opening up a full-scale attack on the Truman administration's China policy because they believed that the Dewey administration would take a new, strong line. When the electorate decided on November 2, 1948, that there would be no Dewey administration, many such Republicans repented their restraint, and began to wonder, indeed, if it had not contributed to their defeat. Alfred M. Landon, former Governor of Kansas and GOP presidential candidate in 1936, complained that his fellow partisans had been "gulled" by the spirit of bipartisanship into keeping silent about a disastrous policy that was delivering China over to the Communists. Vandenberg reacted sharply to this point. He spelled out his reactions to Senator William F. Knowland of California, a vigorous advocate of more effective support for Chiang, on December 11:

> Mr. Landon may be of the opinion that we "gulled" Republicans should have yelled our heads off about China and the Generalissimo during the past year or two, but in my opinion it would only have precipitated and underscored a discussion of Chiang's weaknesses and would have nullified any remnant of his prestige.

at this time for stabilization in the area, political and economic.''[28]

Since the notion of Chinese unreadiness for democracy could not—for political reasons—be ventilated publicly, administration policy remained static on the surface. Chiang had indeed contrived to bring his non-Communist opponents into a coalition dominated by the Kuomintang, so appearances were in some sense improved. Unfortunately, the Generalissimo was surrounded with venal officials and untrustworthy commanders; his real position was deteriorating in strength. No reform of the administrative structure was possible. No gesture toward the economic uplift of the masses could be made. Less than zealous troops abandoned their equipment on the battlefield, and the Communists were outfitting themselves with American arms. There was even a serious question whether or not officers of the National government and the National army were selling such supplies to the enemy. When General Wedemeyer returned to China in July, 1947, to observe conditions for the President, he found

apathy and lethargy in many quarters. Instead of seeking solutions of problems presented, considerable time and effort are spent in blaming outside influences and seeking outside assistance. . . .

To gain and maintain the confidence of the people, the Central Government will have to effect immediately drastic, far-reaching political and economic reforms. Promises will no longer suffice. Performance is absolutely necessary. It should be accepted that military force in itself will not eliminate communism.[29]

In a certain sense, the question of China was beginning to cause the administration more trouble at home than in Asia.

The same Republicans who had opposed the "Europe first" strategy of World War II now entertained doubts about the wisdom of centering the fight against Communism in Europe. And they complained about the policy of fostering unity in China. Even so friendly a Republican as Senator Vandenberg attacked that policy in a public address, and he was clearly relieved when the policy was abandoned. Drawing upon recent history, he observed that he had never known "a Communist to enter a coalition government for any other purpose than to destroy it."[30] The President and Secretary Marshall would hardly have disagreed, but they took the view that the resources of the United States were not unlimited. If Communist rebellion in Greece were to be snuffed out, if the economic health of Western Europe were to be restored, to thwart Communist subversion and propaganda there, Nationalist China simply could not have all the assistance it might like. It seemed to the policy makers of the administration, moreover, that our investments in Greece and Western Europe promised a better return. Priorities, in any case, depended upon a determination of national interest, and Mr. Truman, like Roosevelt, was persuaded that Europe was the key to the mastery of the world.

For the Republican leadership, this judgment was erroneous. As Chiang's position weakened steadily in 1947, as desertions of his troops and defections of his commanders became so frequent as to stir alarm, the Republicans became convinced that the administration had left the back door unlocked while mounting guard at the front gate. Robert A. Taft, the acknowledged leader of the Senate majority in the Eightieth Congress, asserted on February 24, 1948, that the President's Far Eastern policy would undo anything the Maron the majority side. The very junior Arkansan, once characterized by the President as Senator "Halfbright," simply did not merit buying off. That the Republicans, with a similar majority in the Eightieth Congress, had claimed, at Vandenberg's insistence, only a 7 to 6 margin on the committee, increased resentment at this "raid." Because, too, Vandenberg's candidate for the expected sixth minority seat, Senator Wayne Morse of Oregon, was an advanced proponent of bipartisan cooperation, the maneuver seemed unnecessary.

The administration's political vulnerability was increased, as matters developed, by the retirement of General Marshall that same month and the appointment of Dean Acheson as Secretary of State. He had served as Under Secretary for Mr. Byrnes and (for six months) General Marshall, and had previously been Assistant Secretary for Congressional Relations, winning no personal following in that role, although genuinely respected as an advocate. Some Republicans felt that Mr. Acheson had advised too cautious a policy toward the Soviet Union in the past and that he had fostered anti-Chiang sentiment in the State Department by arranging the promotion of John Carter Vincent, a persistent supporter of coalition, to be head of the Far Eastern Division. Senator Vandenberg confessed that "Mr. Acheson would *not* have been my choice for Secretary of State."[36] Vandenberg, of course, regretted the loss of the broad confidence accorded General Marshall and of the excellent personal relations that had grown up between himself and Under Secretary Lovett, who retired with his chief. The new Secretary, unlike his two predecessors, was a foreign affairs specialist without a "power base" of his own, and

was at once identified as the President's man. His standing
with Congress would depend largely on Mr. Truman's.[37]

Secretary Acheson almost immediately touched the
"Chinese nerves" of the Republican leaders by moving to liq-
uidate a bad investment. At the probable instance of the State
Department, the National Security Council recommended
withholding $60 million worth of military supplies already
appropriated and earmarked for China. At a White House
conference on February 5, Senator Vandenberg and Vice-President Barkley argued against this drastic step. Vandenberg
took the position that the public would not understand the
callous abandonment of an ally in his hour of need. Foreign
opinion would certainly condemn such an action. The Senator admitted that Communist victory seemed inevitable, but
he added, "I decline to be responsible for the *last push* which
makes it possible."[38] The President acceded to this line of reasoning, but there were to be no new aid programs for China.

As the year wore on, congressional friends of Chiang pushed
for dramatic, all-out aid for his beleaguered regime. It was
even proposed that American officers be provided for Chinese
combat units. Moderate Republicans, like Vanderberg, reiterated with growing emphasis that our China policy was the
responsibility of the administration alone. But Communist ad-
vances underscored the futility of all such rhetorical last
stands. The fall of Peiping early in the year signaled the coming death of the National government.

The State Department was meanwhile preparing an apolo-
gia. It planned, with the President's approval,[39] to issue a
White Paper explaining the reasons for Chiang's disaster and
demonstrating why the United States had been unable to

It is easy to sympathize with Chiang—to respect him . . .—as I always have and still do. But it is quite a different thing to plan resultful aid short of armed American intervention with American combat troops (which I have never favored and probably never shall).

I think our China policy was wrong (and always said so) in striving to force a Communist coalition on Chiang. . . . I think we should have taken realistic steps long ago to sustain the Nationalist Government—but certainly it is now evident that this "realism" also involved an indispensable house-cleaning in Chiang's government. . . . When practically all of our American-trained and American equipped Chinese divisions surrender without firing a shot—where do you go from here? I am afraid I totally miss Mr. Landon's point when he volunteers to take Republican responsibility for these Democratic decisions which never were, and are not now, any part of the bipartisan liaison.[34]

China policy had in fact never rested on bipartisan consultation. One reason, clearly, was that China was not close to the top of the Truman administration's priority list. The President and the State Department thus concentrated on winning Republican votes for their European programs, Greek-Turkish aid and the Marshall Plan. Anti-European isolationist sentiment among congressional Republicans, particularly the followers of Senator Taft, required a concerted effort to line up Senator Vandenberg and other so-called Republican internationalists in support of these novel policies. Raising the question of China might have prompted a fatal diversion.

The administration also wished to avoid having its hand forced on China. The long-standing "Asia First" sentiments of the Taft Republicans, not to mention the strong pro-Chiang views consistently expressed by Vandenberg, made it possible, even likely, that bipartisan agreement on China could have been obtained only by the administration's committing more American resources and prestige to the Nationalist cause than it deemed wise. But the failure to establish any interparty liaison on the Far East exacted its own price. The apparent failure of whatever policy the United States had in China, coupled with the administration's assumption of the right of deciding what did, and what did not, require consensual decisions, led the more traditional Republicans to challenge the concept of bipartisanship.

Taft had always suspected Vandenberg's notions of a "national" program in foreign affairs. Since an opposition ought to oppose, he disliked the Republicans' binding themselves to policies they had not originated and had no responsibility for executing. Vandenberg, in his turn, feared that Taft, responding to electoral defeat in 1948, would exercise his paramountcy among Senate Republicans to insist on extending the principle of opposition across the board, scrapping bipartisanship.[35] This the Ohioan did not do, but neither did he foreclose his options in foreign policy.

The opening of the Eighty-first Congress in January, 1949, brought an affront to bipartisanship from the Democratic side. The Senate Democratic leadership decided to exploit its return to power by assigning the party an 8 to 5 majority on the Foreign Affairs Committee, giving the Republicans the smallest representation allowed them by law, given their numbers in the Senate. This decision was a concession to the importunate ambitions of Senator J. William Fulbright of Arkansas. It was not only regarded by the Republicans as a provocation, but it stirred unease among the southern grandees

bring about a happier result to events in China. Early in July, a draft of the proposed White Paper reached the White House for comment. Special Counsel Clifford had a number of stiff criticisms of the document.[40] It did not mention the Yalta agreement on China (because this had been a White House matter), it did not mention Stilwell's role in China (because this had been an army matter), it made much of Chinese-Soviet relations without discussing Soong's negotiations in Moscow in the summer of 1945, it argued that the policy of bringing together the Kuomintang and Communists was designed to aid the war effort—yet it did not consider what effect the end of the war had on this policy, and it set out the story of the Marshall mission in a rambling fashion, including some slanted judgments of persons that seemed out of place. These comments were passed on to the State Department at once, and two days later Secretary Acheson informed the President:

> Ambassador Jessup spent three-quarters of an hour yesterday discussing with Mr. Clark Clifford the latter's memorandum to you concerning the draft of the White Paper on China. Ambassador Jessup was able to explain to Mr. Clifford that many of the points noted had already been taken care of in the redrafting which was under way, and that every effort would be made to meet the other suggestions. On certain points, Mr. Clifford agreed with Mr. Jessup that problems of practicability would necessarily determine the extent to which all of the points noted could be fully covered.[41]

When the efforts of the State Department to limit its own liabilities in the China question had been corrected or better explained, the White Paper still did not prove convincing to administration critics. They could not draw the conclusion from the evidence that Mr. Acheson did:

> The unfortunate but inescapable fact is that the ominous result of the civil war in China was beyond the control of the government of the United States. Nothing that this country did or could have done within the reasonable limits of its capabilities could have changed that result; nothing that was left undone by this country contributed to it. It was the product of internal Chinese forces, forces which this country tried to influence but could not. A decision was arrived at within China, if only a decision by default.[42]

The publication of the White Paper on August 5 raised a storm of criticism. Senators Bridges, Wherry, Knowland, and McCarran, as we have seen, condemned it as a "whitewash" and accused the State Department of advancing Soviet interests in eastern Asia. Even Senator Vandenberg wrote that the White Paper amounted only "to a defense of Administration policy in China. . . . . I think we virtually 'sold China down the river' at Yalta and Potsdam and in our subsequent official demands for coalition with the armed Chinese Communists. . . . What we need is a 'new look' at China which can disclose the realities. We must *not* surrender the Far East to the Soviets."[43] Supporters of the Nationalists, the so-called China bloc, began a determined effort to include last-minute aid for Chiang in the general military assistance bill. This appropriation was intended to implement the new North Atlantic Pact, as well as to continue aid to other countries, imperiled by Communism, that had been brought under the American wing. China was not included, and some members of Congress found the omission sinister. But it was indeed too late. Secretary Acheson had been right; the civil war in China had found a result, and an ominous one.

Opponents of the Truman administration regarded as its only China policy the effort to bring about a coalition between Nationalists and Communists. This, however, was a mistake. There was another China policy, developed under the Marshall-Lovett regime in the State Department and advocated much earlier by General Wedemeyer, a policy of giving the Generalissimo material support while trying to compel his government, against its will, to reform itself root-and-branch to secure its popular base. Yet by the time General Marshall became Secretary of State, there was not enough time left to give the policy a fair trial. The position of the National government was worsening, and the corruption that permeated the Kuomintang and the National army was being transformed by the prevailing atmosphere of *sauve qui peut* into naked treachery. When Dean Acheson assumed the Secretaryship, there was little left to be done but to cut losses as well as possible.

Having been jolted by an intractable reality, the administration may have retreated too far into pessimism. The day before the publication of the White Paper, Mr. Acheson put out a memorandum anticipating the occupation of Formosa by the Chinese Communists. Diplomacy and economic aid could no longer guarantee the island's safety, and military means would not be used, although its strategic value was generally recognized. That this was also the professional view of the armed services appeared when the Joint Chiefs of Staff met on August 16. The Joint Chiefs of Staff, according to General Wedemeyer, who was then Deputy Chief of Staff of the Army, "reaffirmed their previous views that overt United

States military action to deny Communist domination of Formosa would not be justified."[44] Whether or not Mao had then the transport to carry an adequate force over open water remains an unresolved question. The result of this military-diplomatic decision, in any case, was to place Formosa in the center of the debate between the administration and its opponents.

While the administration persisted in the policy of nonintervention, even moderate Republicans began to ask for an American occupation of Formosa to forestall a Communist conquest. On December 8, the National government gave up the mainland and established its capital at Taipeh on Formosa. The State Department held firmly to its former position, pointing to the professional diplomatic and military consensus that Formosa would fall in 1950. About this time, however, Secretary of Defense Johnson raised questions about the established policy, and the JCS began to have second thoughts. The State Department insisted to the President, however, that only American armed intervention could save Formosa, and that the political position of the United States in the Far East would be undermined by such intervention. On political grounds, therefore, the President sided with State, and the National Security Council reached the same decision in its meeting of December 29. The Senate Democratic leadership was then called upon to make a party issue of nonintervention on Formosa. Since there was no chance of bipartisan agreement on this issue, the administration made no pretense of seeking it.

"There isn't any bipartisan foreign policy and there hasn't been any for the past year," Senator Taft asserted in a radio speech of January 8, 1950.[45] Taft went on to argue that Secretary Acheson had adopted a policy of not consulting Republican leaders. Under the circumstances, Republicans in Congress would feel free to question any part of the administration's foreign policy.[46] But the Senate Majority Leader, Scott Lucas, had rallied his forces so well that the President seemed safe from any adverse vote on the Formosa question.[47] Almost at that moment, however, the administration's front in Congress was breached by a bombshell—the conclusion of the Hiss case.

Although the charges made against Alger Hiss by Whittaker Chambers had not become an important factor in the campaign of 1948, HCUA pursued its investigation through the fall. Gradually, Hiss's confident defense broke down under the "able, discerning, and persistent" questioning of Representative Richard M. Nixon.[48] The young California Republican had approached the case with extreme caution. He discussed Chambers's testimony with Bert Andrews, a reporter for the *New York Herald Tribune,* who had written a book attacking the State Department's administration of its loyalty program as unfair, William P. Rogers, chief counsel for the Senate Internal Security Subcommittee, Representative Charles J. Kersten of Wisconsin, John Foster Dulles, then foreign policy adviser to Governor Dewey, his brother, Allen Dulles, Representative Christian A. Herter of Massachusetts, and C. Douglas Dillon, a prominent investment banker associated with the Dewey campaign.[49] Foster Dulles, greatly impressed with Mr. Nixon's sense of responsibility, urged him to follow up the case.[50] There was unanimous agreement among those consulted that Chambers knew Hiss, and that the latter's denial must be false. Hiss's denial that he had ever transmitted copies of classified material from the State Department files to

Chambers appeared also to have been exploded after patient investigation turned up incriminating evidence. On December 15, 1948, Hiss was indicted for perjury for having persisted in these denials under oath. The operation of the statute of limitations protected him against a charge of conspiracy to commit espionage.

Alger Hiss's first trial resulted in a hung jury in July, 1949. Representative Nixon, who was more responsible than anyone else for the indictment, attacked the conduct of Judge Samuel H. Kaufman, the presiding jurist at the trial, charging that he had been unfair to the prosecution. The Congressman hinted at impeachment proceedings, but nothing came of it.[51] The ambitious Californian had darts for greater targets, too. "I think the entire Truman administration was extremely anxious that nothing bad happen to Mr. Hiss," he said. "Members of the administration feared that an adverse verdict would prove that there was a great deal of foundation to all the reports of Communist infiltration into the government during the New Deal days."[52]

The second Hiss trial began on November 17, 1949, and ended with the conviction of the defendant on January 21, 1950. Four days after the verdict, Secretary Acheson, speaking of a human relationship, told the press, "I will not turn my back on Alger Hiss."[53] That statement came to some as a perfect illumination: the difficulties the United States had experienced with the Soviet Union, the disaster in China, were not the result of errors in policy; they had been the consequence of treason in high places. Representative Nixon, now planning on a campaign for the Senate, was ready to draw the lesson of Hiss's conviction:

Five years ago, at the time of the Dumbarton Oaks Conference in 1944, when Alger Hiss served as director of our secretariate [*sic*], the number of people in the world in the Soviet orbit was 180,000,000 approximately the population of the Soviet Union. Arrayed on the anti-totalitarian side there were in the world at that time, in 1944, 1,625,000,000 people. Today there are 800,000,000 in the world under the domination of Soviet totalitarianism. On our side we have 540,000,000 people. There are 600,000,000 residents of United Nations countries which are classified as neutral, such as India, Pakistan, and Sweden. In other words, in 1944, before Dumbarton Oaks, Teheran, Yalta, and Potsdam, the odds were 9 to 1 in our favor. Today, since those conferences, the odds are 6 to 3 against us.[54]

At that moment, however, there was waiting in the wings another junior Republican, who was to draw the lesson in even more spectacular fashion.

NOTES

1. It should not have to be repeated that American isolationism has been, and apparently remains, an anti-European phenomenon that has never precluded an active policy in Latin America, the Pacific, or the Far East.

2. Norman A. Graebner, *The New Isolationism: A Study in Politics and Foreign Policy Since 1950* (New York: The Ronald Press Company, 1956), p. 45.

3. Letter to President Truman, July 12, 1950, Papers of HST, Official File 20.

4. Address to the Harvard Club of Boston. State Department Press Release 377, June 3, 1946.

5. Graebner, *The New Isolationism*, p. 18.

6. Herbert Feis, *The China Tangle: The American Effort in China from Pearl Harbor to the Marshall Mission* (New York: Atheneum, 1965), p. 85.

7. Seven years later, after Wallace had almost completely reversed his position on international questions—and had, indeed, virtually repudiated his own campaign of 1948—he denied that either Vincent or Lattimore, most particularly the latter, had played any consequential role in his mission to China. Wallace to Truman, September 19, 1951, Papers of HST, Official File 1170.

8. Earl Latham, *The Communist Controversy in Washington: From the New Deal to McCarthy* (Cambridge, Mass.: Harvard University Press, 1966), p. 254.

9. Ibid.

10. Cited in Feis, *The China Tangle*, p. 140. The remark was made to Ambassador Harriman, who passed it on to Wallace when the Vice-President stopped in Tashkent en route to China. The Ambassador was inclined to be skeptical of the source (i.e., Stalin), Wallace, at that time, trustful.

11. Ibid., p. 179.

12. Ibid., p. 180. Latham, *The Communist Controversy*, p. 257

13. Feis, *The China Tangle*, pp. 188–189.

14. Cited in Latham, *The Communist Controversy*, p. 253.

15. Albert C. Wedemeyer, *Wedemeyer Reports!* (New York: Henry Holt & Co., 1958), p. 310.

16. Cited in Latham, *The Communist Controversy*, p. 259.

17. Feis, *The China Tangle*, p. 247. Feis's emphasis.

18. Ibid., pp. 252–253.

19. The Chinese could have accepted—if only because they had already endured it so long—the status quo in this area. This would have left Outer Mongolia as an autonomous province of the Chinese Republic, under de facto Soviet control.

20. James F. Byrnes, *Speaking Frankly* (New York: Harper & Bros., 1947), p. 205.

21. Cited in Latham, *The Communist Controversy*, p. 263.

22. Wedemeyer, *Wedemeyer Reports!*, pp. 318–319. Kennan describes John Davies as "a man of broad, sophisticated, and skeptical political understanding, without an ounce of pro-Communist sympathies, and second to none in his devotion to the interests of our government." George F. Kennan, *Memoirs 1925–1950* (Boston: Little, Brown and Co., 1967), p. 239.

23. Cited in Latham, *The Communist Controversy*, p. 263.

24. Cited in ibid., p. 260.

25. Truman, vol. 2, *Memoirs*, pp. 67–68.

26. Feis, *The China Tangle*, p. 419.

27. Truman, vol. 2, *Memoirs*, p. 87.

28. Cited in ibid., pp. 63–64.

29. Cabell Phillips, *The Truman Presidency: The History of a Triumphant Succession* (New York: The Macmillan Company, 1966), p. 282.

30. Arthur H. Vandenberg, Jr., ed. (with the collaboration of Joe Alex Morris), *The Private Papers of Senator Vandenberg* (Boston: Houghton Mifflin Co., 1952), p. 523.

31. Cited in William S. White, *The Taft Story* (New York: Harper & Bros., 1954), p. 160.

32. Vandenberg, *Private Papers,* pp. 524–525.

33. Cited in Walter Millis, ed. (with the collaboration of E. S. Duffield), *The Forrestal Diaries* (New York: Viking Press, 1951), p. 534.

34. Vandenberg, *Private Papers,* p. 527.

35. Ibid., pp. 466–467. Cf. White, *The Taft Story,* pp. 146–147.

36. Vandenberg, *Private Papers,* p. 469.

37. H. Bradford Westerfield, *Foreign Policy and Party Politics: Pearl Harbor to Korea* (New Haven: Yale University Press, 1955). Westerfield makes this point with considerable force (pp. 327–329). It can be carried too far, however. Although Mr. Acheson's political weakness undoubtedly made him a personally more tempting target than his predecessors would have been, it is hard to believe that either of them could have stayed the antiadministration forces from their attack in late 1949 and 1950. Senator McCarthy's later attack on General Marshall, among other things, argues the contrary.

38. Vandenberg, *Private Papers,* pp. 530–531. Senator Vandenberg's emphasis.

39. Testimony of Louis A. Johnson. 82d, Cong., 1st sess., United States Senate, Committee on Armed Services and Committee on Foreign Relations, *Hearings to Conduct an Inquiry into the Military Situation in the Far East and the Facts Surrounding the Relief of General of the Army Douglas MacArthur from his Assignments in that Area* (Washington: Government Printing Office, 1951), pp. 2668–2669 (hereafter cited as MacArthur Hearings).

40. Memorandum for the President, July 6, 1949, Papers of Clark M. Clifford.

41. Memorandum to the President, July 8, 1949, Papers of Clark M. Clifford.

42. Cited in Westerfield, *Foreign Policy and Party Politics,* p. 355.

43. Vandenberg, *Private Papers,* p. 536.

44. MacArthur Hearings, p. 2371.

45. *New York Times,* January 9, 1950.

46. Vandenberg's absence from the Senate after the summer of 1949, owing to illness, opened the door to Taft to take over leadership in foreign, as well as domestic, affairs. The widespread suspicion that Vandenberg's removal would be permanent reduced resistance to Taft.

47. *New York Times,* January 18, 1950.

48. Robert K. Carr, *The House Committee on Un-American Activities, 1945–1950* (Ithaca, N.Y.: Cornell University Press, 1952), pp. 230–233. Carr argues that without Mr. Nixon's pertinacity and ability, the case

would have been abandoned. The Californian's talents gave to HCUA's investigations a quality they had neither before nor after his service.

49. Richard M. Nixon, *Six Crises* (Garden City, N.Y.: Doubleday & Co., 1962) , pp. 20–21. Earl Mazo, *Richard Nixon: A Political and Personal Portrait* (New York: Harper & Bros., 1959) , pp. 58–59.

50. Mazo, *Richard Nixon,* pp. 58–59.

51. Carr, *The House Committee,* p. 234.

52. Cited in Mazo, *Richard Nixon,* p. 66.

53. *New York Times,* January 26, 1950.

54. Cited in Carr, *The House Committee,* p. 99. Hiss's conviction was a bonanza for the Republicans. As Hofstadter nicely put it, "Hiss is the hostage the pseudo-conservatives [Hofstadter's name for the extreme right] hold from the New Deal generation. . . . If he did not exist, the pseudo-conservatives would not have been able to invent him." Richard Hofstadter, "The Pseudo-Conservative Revolt," in *The Radical Right,* ed. Daniel Bell (Garden City, N.Y.: Anchor Books, 1964) , p. 92 n.

6

Enter Joseph R. McCarthy

THE intensely emotional quality of the Communist issue, and the readiness of the electorate to respond to it, are best illustrated by the leap of Joseph R. McCarthy from obscurity to national fame. After a hardscrabble rural upbringing and a painfully won education, including a law degree from Marquette University, McCarthy entered politics. He began his career as a follower of Franklin D. Roosevelt, although Wisconsin Democrats habitually ran third in the state to the La Follette Progressives and the Republicans. Having carefully observed this phenomenon, young McCarthy turned Republican and was elected to the state circuit court. His record on the bench appears to have been adequate, not outstandingly to his credit or discredit,[1] and his political future remained open. With American entry into the Second World War, he enlisted in the Marine Corps and came to serve as a ground officer in the Marine Air Intelligence Service.

McCarthy returned from service to find that "Young Bob"

La Follette, for a variety of reasons, had scrapped the old Progressive party and returned to the Republican fold. Because of his name—if nothing else—he was assumed to be safe both within the party and in the state at large. McCarthy, however, decided to challenge him in the 1946 senatorial primary. "Tail-Gunner Joe," as the newcomer brashly called himself, parlayed a service record and a postwar reaction against liberalism into an upset victory. Elected to the Senate the following November, McCarthy entered upon an apparently routine career. For three years he attracted no attention, voting loyally with the Republican leadership, except for deviations in favor of farm price supports and public housing legislation. If not a liberal, he was not clearly a conservative; but no one, apart from his Wisconsin constituents, cared much about his identity in this, or any other, respect.

McCarthy was introduced to the value Communism places on subversion by a distinguished priest-educator from Georgetown University, an authority on the subject, early in January, 1950. The Senator translated the issue into his own terms and decided, almost immediately, to do something about it. Whether he fully grasped the problem, or merely had a sense of its electoral possibilities, may never be known. The question of McCarthy's "sincerity" is as incapable of resolution as that of anyone else on an ambiguous issue, and it is not, in truth, of great historical or political consequence.

Senator McCarthy's unveiling as an authority on Communism came in the course of a Lincoln Day address before the Republican Women's Club of Wheeling, West Virginia, on February 9, 1950. Claiming as his authority a letter on the screening of State Department employees written nearly four years before by Secretary Byrnes, he warned of a massive Communist infiltration:

> While I cannot take the time to name all of the men in the State Department who have been named as members of the Communist Party and members of a spy ring, I have here in my hand a list of two hundred and five that were known to the Secretary of State as being members of the Communist Party and who nevertheless are still working, and shaping the policy of the State Department.[2]

Continuing his weekend speaking tour in honor of the Great Emancipator, McCarthy more modestly reported to an audience in Salt Lake City that he "had the names of 57 card-carrying members of the Communist Party" in the State Department.[3] At Reno the number 57 was maintained, but the delinquents were now described as "*either* card-carrying members *or* certainly loyal to the Communist Party."[4] Having created an overnight sensation with his shocking charges, McCarthy knew he would have to justify himself. He promised to take his cause to the floor of the Senate, and he did so on February 20. He would present to the Senate, he said, 81 "cases in which it is clear there is a definite Communist connection . . . persons whom I consider to be Communists in the State Department"—having previously brushed off a question by Senator Lucas on the relationship between the number 81 and the numbers 205 and 57. A "sizable number" of the persons in question, as it turned out, were no longer employed by the State Department. Several had never been. Two were identified as *anti*-Communists. In several cases the evidence cited was either inconclusive or irrelevant, while four cases were not presented at all. These, however, were the cases which McCarthy described, in hours of rambling discourse and involuted advocacy, spiced by countless—and increasingly ill-tempered—interruptions, sharp exchanges between the speaker and the floor, and plain double-talk, as being "of those I consider to be Communists in the State Department."[5]

There was certainly no immediate rallying to McCarthy's standard. The most vigorous and suspicious critics of the administration's foreign policy, the most single-minded trackers of Communist subversion, all shied away from their would-be champion. The Republican leaders of the Senate took no comfort in what Taft called "a perfectly reckless performance."[6] In the first flush of his new fame, McCarthy had turned to Richard Nixon for help and had been given competent advice—a case in this field ought always to be understated, not overstated; a claim of any number of card-carrying Communists in the State Department is unprovable; but a charge that available records disclose so many persons with Communist-front affiliations and associations is subject to proof.[7] McCarthy ignored this warning to follow a bolder course, but he came close to being finished before he had fairly started.

The Democrats, in a sense, recognized the possibilities of this free-swinging assault on the integrity of their administration before anyone else. If McCarthy were to go on, *some* people would inevitably believe him, and the Republican leadership might well reconsider its original negative response. In an election year it would be well to smother the danger in infancy. The Senate Democratic Policy Committee decided that McCarthy's charges would have to be investigated and discredited (to be fair, it should be remembered that the committee members believed investigation could have no other

result). The investigation was to be assigned to the Foreign
Relations Committee, and carried out through the agency of a
subcommittee headed by Senator Millard E. Tydings of Maryland. Tydings was a border-state man, a strict traditional
conservative, a diehard opponent of New Deal spending and
welfare policies, and a triumphant survivor of FDR's party
purge of 1938—qualifications to commend him to the confidence of southern members. The southerners, as a matter of
fact, whatever their record on domestic legislation, had firmly
supported Roosevelt's prewar and wartime foreign policies and
had given crucial support to President Truman's European
programs. Many had enjoyed friendly relations with the State
Department over a period of years. All Democrats, whether
labeled liberal or conservative, stood to be endangered by
McCarthy's line of attack.

McCarthy quickly proved to have one advantage that his
detractors and doubters had not considered—headlines. A
United States Senator charged—and said he could make it
stick—that there were 81 (or 205 or 57) Communists in the
State Department. Nothing so sensational could go unre-
ported, yet few, if any, newspapers could reprint the full texts
of his speeches. With the legal demonstration of Alger Hiss's
treason fresh in mind, and with the Communist powers apparently waxing mighty in Europe and Asia, it is little wonder
that many Americans assumed that there *must* be some real
fire behind the billowing smoke of McCarthy's claims.

Senator Taft, who had himself recently alleged that the
State Department "with its pro-Communist allies" had been
responsible for the Communist victory in China, now remarked, as the Tydings subcommittee hearings got under
way, that McCarthy should "keep talking and if one case

doesn't work out he should proceed with another."[8] Later he argued that "[w]hether Senator McCarthy has legal evidence, whether he has overstated or understated his case, is of lesser importance. The question is whether the Communist influence in the State Department still exists."[9] This was interesting language from the man who had courted unpopularity by questioning the legality of the Nuremberg trials and who successfully blocked, on constitutional grounds, a bill authorizing the President to draft striking workers when the national security was involved. All the same, "Mr. Republican" had switched to McCarthy's side.

The Tydings subcommittee hearings offered the Wisconsin Senator a kind of forum and he was determined to take advantage of it. Tydings asked McCarthy to be the first witness and invited him to lay his cases before the subcommittee for examination. Although McCarthy was still settled on eighty-one as the number of his cases, only nine were presented at the hearings. They appeared to be a random selection, the six persons named in the earliest phase of the hearings seeming to represent no pattern. But as time passed, the cases that caught and kept public attention could all be directly related to the administration's China policy. There is no reason to believe that McCarthy planned it that way, but he did recognize quickly what captured his audience. This emphasis, moreover, was most pleasing to his party leadership.

The second of McCarthy's first six cases was one Haldore Hanson—a man with "a mission to communize the world."[10] He was, in 1950, chief of the Technical Cooperation Projects Staff of the Point Four aid program. Previously, he had served for a brief time in a minor capacity with the Far Eastern Division of the State Department. A book written by Hanson in

1938, after spending four months as a correspondent with Chinese Communist troops, expressed some praise for the Yenan soldiers. This was cited as evidence of his "pro-Communist proclivities,"[11] the point being heavily belabored as no more recent evidence was introduced.

After the first six cases had been presented, the hearings gained in excitement. McCarthy turned next to the *Amerasia* case and the career of John Stewart Service, whose "Communist affiliations . . . [were] well known."[12] Service, at that time consul general at Calcutta, was described as one of the State Department's top policy makers on Far Eastern questions. Although McCarthy was on solid ground in pointing out the peculiarity (to say the least) of Service's behavior in the *Amerasia* affair, he had no evidence beyond that on which a grand jury had refused to indict, or that had compelled the State Department Loyalty Board to clear Service three times. On the score of the advice he had given to Generals Stilwell and Wedemeyer, there was nothing on the record against him except mistaken judgment.

McCarthy was able to use the hearings, however, to level spectacular charges against Ambassador-at-Large Philip C. Jessup—a man who had "unusual affinity for Communist causes" —and Owen D. Lattimore, director of the School of International Relations at Johns Hopkins University, "an extremely bad security risk" who had been "one of the principal architects of our far eastern policy."[13] The case against Jessup, which was made more on the floor of the Senate than before the subcommittee, rested on the use of his name as sponsor by Communist-front organizations, his association with the Institute of Pacific Relations, an organization with presumed left-wing connections, and his appearance as a character witness for Alger Hiss during the famous perjury trial. In a Senate speech, McCarthy also accused Jessup of being part of a State Department clique that had "delivered China to the Communists."[14]

Ambassador Jessup flew home from a mission in Pakistan to testify before the Tydings subcommittee. He made an excellent impression on his hearers in answering the charges against him, and he chided McCarthy for endangering the conduct of American foreign policy by making irresponsible accusations against its executors. Sensing the hostile mood of his audience, McCarthy did not pursue this antagonist but moved daringly in another direction by informing the press that he was going to name the "top USSR espionage agent" in the country.[15]

As the subcommittee met in executive session on March 21, Owen Lattimore was promoted from "bad security risk" to the guiding hand of the State Department espionage cell to which Alger Hiss had belonged—to the exalted rank, indeed, of "top Russian spy" in the United States.[16] McCarthy announced himself at this meeting "willing to stand or fall" on the case against Dr. Lattimore. The slugging Senator nevertheless wanted the judgment of the public as well as that of the subcommittee, and he made sure that newspapers of March 27 carried his sensational discovery in headlines.

Very shortly, however, McCarthy confessed to the Senate that he "may have perhaps placed too much stress on the question of whether or not [Lattimore] had been an espionage agent."[17] The top spy was quietly degraded back to the level of security risk in the State Department, but then it developed that at no time in his career had he been on the department payroll, never even having served as a consultant. On the other hand, having been sent by President Roosevelt as an adviser to Chiang Kai-shek in 1941, having served as a ranking official of the Office of War Information in China, and having been assigned, while with the OWI, to the Wallace mission to Chungking in 1944, it could hardly be said that he had had no association with Chinese affairs, and the likelihood that he had had some influence on American policy in China could not be dismissed out of hand. It developed, too, that Dr. Lattimore had associated with known Communists and that he had not repudiated those associations. The basic issue, however, was decided when the President made an extraordinary exception to standing regulations[18] and directed J. Edgar Hoover to make a summary of the FBI file on Dr. Lattimore available to the subcommittee. Senator Tydings afterward informed the accused man, who had appeared to make an extended defense against McCarthy's charges, that "there was nothing in that file to show that you were a Communist or had ever been a Communist, or that you were in any way connected with any espionage."[19] Even if Dr. Lattimore had been indiscreet in some of his associations, his loyalty could not be impugned. "Either Tydings hasn't seen the file, or he is lying," McCarthy commented briefly. "There is no other alternative."[20] He informed the Senate on March 30, in fact, that his investigations had revealed an important truth:

> It was not Chinese democracy under Mao that conquered China, as Acheson, Lattimore, Jessup, and Hanson contend. Soviet Russia conquered China and an important ally of the conquerors was this small left-wing element in our Department of State.[21]

"Tail-Gunner Joe," moreover, was no longer alone as he

slashed away at the State Department. After a meeting of the
Senate Republican Policy Committee on March 22, Taft an-
nounced that while support of McCarthy was not a party mat-
ter, Republican Senators would be giving him assistance.[22]
Three days later, a principal Taft lieutenant, Senator Styles
Bridges of New Hampshire, promised to expose Secretary
Acheson's failures.[23]

Mr. Truman had now the task of preventing the paralysis
of American foreign policy by a no-holds-barred partisan attack. Some of his friends were hopeful that the Tydings subcommittee would clear the air by showing Senator McCarthy's
charges to be the creation of a fantasist. Members of the
White House staff, however, were not sure that the subcommittee could accomplish as much as desired, no matter how favorable its report might be. This was especially true after the
President's order on March 15, 1950, to withhold government
loyalty files from the subcommittee. Although the decision
was taken on professional grounds, at the instance of Attorney
General McGrath and FBI Director Hoover,[24] it aroused a
new storm of criticism from McCarthy and his supporters,
who implied that the administration was covering its tracks.[25]
Senator Tydings himself, while a supporter of Secretary Acheson and his policies, was no friend of the Truman domestic
program, and there seemed to be some fear lest he try to use
his position to secure some modification of the latter.[26] There
was certainly legitimate doubt, under the circumstances, as to
what the subcommittee might achieve.

The President decided to appeal directly to certain Republican leaders, reminding them that the disruption of bipartisan unity in the face of a foreign threat might endanger
national security. There was a slim chance that the apparently

solid ranks of the opposition might be broken by such an approach. Mr. Truman wrote to Senator Bridges, a leader of the conservatives, and to Senator Vandenberg, whose removal from Washington by a serious (and, as it proved, mortal) illness had returned GOP policy-making in international questions to men intolerant of our new overseas commitments.[27] Both Senators were cordial in reply, but Vandenberg could no longer give practical help, while Bridges, in the pinch, was among those who believed that an opposition's duty was to oppose.[28] With no aid forthcoming from the Senate "club," the administration had to rely on winning public support for its case.

The White House staff consequently began casting about for a solution to that difficult problem.[29] Staff members came shortly to agree that Congress should create a commission of distinguished citizens, along the organizational lines of the Hoover Commission on Government Reorganization, to investigate the government employee loyalty program. Such a commission, it was felt, should not only look into the effectiveness of measures in force, but should also take the opportunity to examine the procedures of loyalty boards to determine whether employees' civil liberties were being infringed. It was time indeed for some balance to be restored to consideration of loyalty and security problems. Mr. Truman, being inclined to the proposal, convened a meeting of party leaders and advisers at Blair House on June 22, to talk over the possibility of establishing such a commission.[30] Those present included, apart from members of the White House staff, Vice-President Barkley, Speaker Rayburn, House Majority Leader McCormack, Senators Tydings, McMahon, and Green of the special subcommittee, Attorney General McGrath, and Clark Clifford, who had resigned as Special Counsel the previous February but remained a presidential confidant.[31]

The Vice-President and the Speaker reported themselves as inclined against the idea at just that time, but wanted to give the matter further consideration.[32] Mr. McCormack's opposition was unqualified. Senators Tydings and McMahon, on the other hand, were strongly for the proposal but expressed a preference for a commission appointed by the President to one created by legislation. Senator Green was against the suggestion, as was the Attorney General, who emphasized possible repercussions on legal action against Communists taken by the Department of Justice and appeal on such cases then pending in the courts. Additional support for the commission came from Mr. Clifford and all the White House staff men present, except for Dr. John Steelman, who offered no firm opinion one way or the other.

It is possible to re-create the arguments used for and against the proposed commission by those who attended the Blair House meeting.[33] The principal argument on behalf of the idea—nonpolitical in the narrow sense—was that people in democratic countries, during periods of international tension, become exceptionally anxious about national security. Public fear, under such circumstances, is often directed more toward internal than external security—perhaps because of a popular feeling that all politics is in some sense a conspiracy. Those who hope to gain from fishing in troubled waters can usually find a broad response to the insinuation that the enemy is boring from within. In 1950, of course, the success of Fascist and Communist "fifth columns" in Europe was a matter of very recent history and seemed to lend credence to charges like McCarthy's. The spy case involving Klaus Fuchs and his

American associates lent even stronger point to the argument, especially with the arrests of Harry Gold and David Greenglass coming so soon after the first Soviet nuclear explosion. It was therefore necessary to reassure the American people that their government was doing everything possible to secure the nation from the threat of subversion. In the climate of opinion then prevailing, such reassurance could be best provided by a bipartisan or nonpartisan commission of the highest caliber.

Other arguments emphasized the great amount of time devoted of late by members of the executive departments, as well as congressional leaders, to questions of employee loyalty—a burden that might be partially lifted from them by a special commission. The advice of a competent commission would surely be valuable in handling other thorny problems, such as the future course of the loyalty program and proposed internal security legislation pending in Congress—some of it drastically repressive. It was also recognized that the United States was in danger of entering upon a period of hysteria in which a premium would be put upon slander and delation, with the informer gaining something of the status he enjoyed in Soviet Russia and Nazi Germany. Honest liberals and reformers might be carelessly identified as Communists, to their own cost and that of the country.[34]

On the more obviously political side, supporters of the commission proposal felt that the report of the Tydings subcommittee would not effectively discredit Senator McCarthy. The two Republican members of the subcommittee (Henry Cabot Lodge of Massachusetts and Bourke B. Hickenlooper of Iowa) seemed sure to dissent, even if separately, from the majority report, and it was not completely clear that the majority re-

port would be sufficiently unambiguous to convince those who
were reluctant to believe in the administration's competence
and probity.[35] It appeared likely, therefore, that the "McCarthy business" would continue into 1952 and influence the
presidential election of that year, as well as the upcoming congressional contests, unless halted by decisive measures. Senator
Hickenlooper, Representatives George Smathers and Richard
Nixon, and Willis Smith, it was pointed out, had all challenged their opponents' attitudes toward Communism in the
course of successful senatorial primary campaigns. McCarthy's
tactics, therefore, invited expedient imitation by other enemies of the administration, and the whole Truman program
might thereby be placed in jeopardy.

Those against the commission, however, argued that its
mere establishment would allow McCarthy to claim that he
had been right all along, that the administration would never
have created such a body if his charges had been empty. The
anti-commission group believed, in any case, that McCarthy
was losing momentum, and that there was no point to the administration's giving him gratuitous assistance in this manner. In support of the view that McCarthy's accusations were
having increasingly less impact on the public, it was urged
that the past associations and utterances of Senators Pepper
and Graham made them peculiarly vulnerable to "red"
charges in their races against Smathers and Smith,[36] that Senator Hickenlooper had not run as well as previously in the
Iowa primary, and that Helen Gahagan Douglas, who had
been attacked in California as a fellow traveler (in part because she had opposed the Truman Doctrine), had won a re-
sounding victory in the senatorial primary there.

A major objection to the President's pushing the plan at

this time was found in the anxiety of Congress to adjourn. Petty spitefulness on the part of some members might decide the issue. Either the Republicans and their allies would so load the bill to create the commission with amendments that the President would have to veto it, or Congress would simply refuse to act on the proposal; whatever happened, Mr. Truman was inviting a rebuff. Opponents of the plan went on to reassure their hearers that the Tydings subcommittee report would put the lid on McCarthy, and that by publicly branding him as a constitutional liar and political opportunist McCarthyism could be defeated in November. It was also suggested, probably by Barkley or one of the congressional holdouts, that it might be all right to establish the commission the following January—after the elections.

It is difficult to avoid the impression that those opposed to the commission were playing Mr. Micawber, waiting for something to turn up. Fear of McCarthy's influence at the polls, coupled with a lack of confidence in the administration's ability to meet the challenge, appears in retrospect to have dominated their reactions. The insistence that no action be taken prior to the fall elections suggests, more than anything else, a desire not to provoke the enemy further. After all, several important Democratic Senators were facing narrow contests in November. It is probably correct to say, however, that, as of the moment, Congress would not have welcomed such a proposal. Still, that difficulty was hardly insurmountable; it could have been disposed of by adoption of the Tydings-McMahon suggestion of a commission appointed by the President. For the rest, no matter what hay McCarthy might have tried to make of administration action, inaction was, given the state of the public temper, the most dangerous of possible courses. The anti-commission arguments thus seem as lame today as they did in June, 1950, to advocates of the proposal.

The outbreak of the Korean War on June 25 killed plans for a second meeting on the proposed commission early the following month, the President having become too much engaged with the novel emergency. For a very brief time, the crisis rallied the nation in support of the administration, but the Republicans soon recovered the voice of opposition, and popular fears of internal subversion, instead of being allayed, were severely exacerbated.

NOTES

1. McCarthy appears to have had something of a reputation for the quick granting of divorces. Richard H. Rovere, *Senator Joe McCarthy* (New York: Harcourt, Brace & Co., 1959), pp. 91–93. Whether his procedures would have created any stir if he had not been a Roman Catholic is an interesting question.

2. Cited in ibid., p. 125.

3. Cited in ibid., p. 128.

4. Cited in ibid, p. 130.

5. Ibid., pp. 131–134. Although Rovere is biased against McCarthy, it would be difficult to argue that this speech was anything but a poor performance, probably the Senator's worst.

6. Cited in ibid., p. 135.

7. Earl Mazo, *Richard Nixon: A Political and Personal Portrait* (New York: Harper & Bros., 1959), pp. 140–141.

8. William S. White, *The Taft Story* (New York: Harper & Bros., 1954), pp. 89, 85.

9. Cited in ibid., p. 85.

10. 81st Cong., 2d sess., United States Senate, Subcommittee of the Committee on Foreign Relations, Hearings Pursuant to S. Res. 231, *A Resolution to Investigate Whether There Are Employees in the State Department Disloyal to the United States* (Washington: Government Printing Office, 1950), p. 82 (hereafter cited as Tydings Subcommittee).

11. Ibid., p. 74.

12. Ibid:, p. 131.

13. Ibid., pp. 92, 104.

14. Earl Latham, *The Communist Controversy in Washington: From the New Deal to McCarthy* (Cambridge, Mass.: Harvard University Press, 1966), p. 275.

15. *New York Times,* March 22, 1950.

16. Tydings Subcommittee, pp. 277 ff.

17. Cited in William F. Buckley, Jr., and L. Brent Bozell, *McCarthy and His Enemies: The Record and Its Meaning* (Chicago: Henry Regnery Co., 1954), p. 154.

18. See p. 134 and n. 24.

19. Tydings subcommittee, p. 484.

20. Cabell Phillips, *The Truman Presidency: The History of a Triumphant Succession* (New York: The Macmillan Company, 1966), p. 386.

21. *Congressional Record,* 81st Cong., 2d sess. (1950) 96: 4407–4408.

22. *New York Times,* March 23, 1950.

23. Ibid., March 26, 1950.

24. Memorandum for the President from Attorney General McGrath, March 17, 1950, Papers of HST, Official File 419–K. See an earlier letter of J. Edgar Hoover to the President's Military Aide, Brigadier General Harry Vaughan, June 19, 1946, Papers of HST, Official File 10–B.

25. *New York Times,* March 21, 1950.

26. Tydings wrote the President saying that the people backed his foreign policy because it gave them a sense of security, but they had serious reservations (as had Tydings himself) about the domestic program—especially deficit spending, the Brannan Plan for agriculture, some phases of FEPC, and Point 7 of the Health Program ("socialized medicine"). The Republicans, according to Tydings, made people believe their ultimate security, at least on the domestic scene, was threatened, and the Communist inquiry compounded such fears. Memorandum for the President, April 12, 1950, Papers of HST, Official File 419–K.

27. Truman to Vandenberg, March 27, 1950, Papers of HST, Official File 386. Truman to Bridges, March 26, 1950, Truman to Acheson, March 27, 1950, and Acheson to Truman, March 28, 1950, Papers of HST, Official File 419–K. On Vandenberg's role, see, e.g., John W. Spanier, *The Truman-MacArthur Controversy and the Korean War* (New York: W. W. Norton & Co., 1965), pp. 45–46.

Despite superficial appearances, it was logical for the President to appeal to Bridges. In Vandenberg's absence, he was the ranking minority member of the Senate Foreign Relations Committee, so it was a matter of protocol that Mr. Truman address him. What mattered more was that the two men were friends. When Bridges first came to Washington in 1937, Senator Truman, then beginning his third year of service, undertook to show him around Capitol Hill and the capital city. This unsolicited kindness laid Bridges under a debt of gratitude that no political differences ever quite extinguished. Interview with former President Truman, July 21, 1961.

28. Vandenberg to Truman, March 29, 1950, Papers of HST, Official File 386. Bridges to Truman, March 29, 1950 and Truman to Bridges, April 3, 1950, Papers of HST, Official File 419–K. On the Republican isolationists, see Norman A. Graebner, *The New Isolationism: A Study in Politics and Foreign Policy Since 1950* (New York: The Ronald Press Company, 1956) , p. 13.

29. Memorandum for the President from Charles S. Murphy and Stephen J. Spingarn, May 16, 1950, Papers of HST, Official File 2750.

30. The account of the meeting is taken from a memorandum for the files by Spingarn, June 23, 1950, Papers of HST, Files of Charles S. Murphy.

31. No Republican leaders attended this meeting, as is readily seen. Richard Nixon argued retrospectively (*Six Crises* [Garden City, N.Y.: Doubleday & Co., 1962], p. 65) that Mr. Truman's problems in this field arose from his failure to recognize "the need for bipartisanship in fighting Communism at home as well as abroad." It is perfectly obvious, however, given the behavior of the GOP leadership in backing McCarthy and in pushing drastic internal security legislation, that the President could have had this kind of bipartisan cooperation only on the Republicans' terms. Stalemate was better than surrender, from the administration point of view.

32. There was no question of Rayburn's feelings for McCarthy and his backers. He bitterly resented George Smathers's successful red-baiting tactics in the Florida senatorial primary, and, years later, reached out of his bailiwick to impose an authoritative veto on Smathers's prospective appointment as the Senate Democratic whip. Rowland Evans and Robert Novak, *Lyndon B. Johnson: The Exercise of Power* (New York: Signet Books, 1968) , pp. 109–110. It was at the same time (and for the same reason) that the Speaker acquired his strong distaste for Mr. Nixon, a feeling that led him to reverse himself in the advice he gave Senator Johnson in respect to the Vice-Presidency in 1960. Ibid., pp. 299–300.

33. Memorandum by Stephen J. Spingarn, June 26, 1950, Papers of HST, Files of Charles S. Murphy.

34. John L. Snell, "The Cold War: Four Contemporary Appraisals," *American Historical Review 68* (October, 1962) :69. For an indication of such thinking within the intelligence services, see above, pp. 34–35.

35. Division on this issue within Congress was now along party lines to a remarkable degree. Even the signers of Margaret Smith's Republican "Declaration of Conscience" would not go so far as to support the administration's position.

36. Lubell argues persuasively that the defeats of Graham and Pepper,

especially the former, were determined by the racial issue above every-thing else. The defeated Senators' identification with the President's civil rights proposals was their undoing. Samuel Lubell, *The Future of American Politics* (New York: Harper & Bros., 1951), pp. 100–108, 120–121.

7

Delusions of Security
The McCarran Act

THE Tydings subcommittee "done its damnedest," but Senator McCarthy emerged from his confrontation with it essentially undamaged. The clear partisan division between majority and minority reports, the rather casual procedures followed by the chairman, and the somehow affectionate tone adopted by the majority in clearing the persons accused, simply served to convince those elements of the public who had responded affirmatively to the McCarthy charges that the subcommittee had intended, and achieved, a whitewash. Senator Tydings certainly made it rather too obvious that he had prejudged the issue. The "indiscretion" admitted in the Service and Lattimore cases was not unreasonably open to a more sinister interpretation, even in the absence of substantive evidence. And while it was a cynical defense of Senator McCarthy to insist that the mandate of the subcommittee was to investigate the general problem of disloyalty in the State Department—rather than to confine itself to cases presented by the Senator—it served to demonstrate that the language of the enabling resolution was, at best, euphemistic. The real task assigned to the subcommittee was to "get" McCarthy, just as the Republican leadership judged his real job to be to "get" the administration.[1]

With McCarthy still "alive," the White House concentrated on what seemed the real danger of his activity. His onslaught, beginning the previous February, had not only tended to focus antiadministration sentiment on the Communist issue, but, by its concentration on the State Department, sought to discredit American foreign policy as sometimes treasonous, frequently derelict, and always inconsequential. No wonder that the President turned to two key opposition leaders to help sustain a responsible Senate position on international matters—unavailingly, as has been seen. Senator Bridges did meet with President Truman and Secretary Acheson,[2] presumably as a gesture of courtesy, but he had already bound himself to Taft's policy of down-the-line opposition and the exploitation of McCarthy.[3] McCarthyism provided a means of containing, if you please, the Truman-Acheson foreign policies by closing off certain avenues of development. Any exploratory tendencies toward compromise or toward a more diversified approach to the Communist powers—certainly when congressional approval was required—could be aborted by cries of "Sellout!" or "Sabotage!" And since 1948 had demonstrated the continuing inability of Republicans to compete with Democrats on pocketbook issues, GOP leaders were determined not to fumble this new chance so wondrously afforded them.

The furor created by McCarthy's charges also spurred the congressional coalition of Republicans and southern Democrats to further hem in the administration by imposing upon it new, drastic internal security legislation. The outbreak of the Korean War, by stimulating still greater public alarm over subversion, provided the impetus for a final, decisive effort. This was an area, however, in which the President could fight back with some hope of success.

The Justice Department, interestingly enough, was first to stake a claim in the field. Law enforcement experts felt that wartime experience showed a need for tightening existing antisubversive statutes. In 1947, accordingly, the Interdepartmental Intelligence Committee (composed of the Director of the FBI and the chiefs of the military intelligence services) prepared the draft of a bill that Justice undertook to sponsor.[4] As originally conceived, it was a very drastic bill indeed, and most of the agencies among which it was circulated by the Bureau of the Budget criticized it severely. The Treasury Department was particularly alarmed. Secretary John W. Snyder wrote to the Budget Bureau on March 23, 1948, that the draft bill would not "provide safeguards for adequate protection of civil rights of the people of the United States from infringement or abuse in the name of security." The Defense Department, in the person of Secretary Forrestal, the State Department, and the Federal Communications Commission agreed with virtually all of Treasury's criticisms and suggested revisions. In April, 1948, Charles S. Murphy, administrative assistant to the President, presented the file to Mr. Truman. After a weekend's deliberation, he ruled that the Justice Department should amend its draft bill in accordance with the Treasury Department's suggestions. The Bureau of the Budget then informed Justice that if the draft were so amended it could be cleared for presentation to Congress.

There were, in particular, three serious objections to the Justice Department draft. For one thing, it would have brought within the penalties of the Espionage Act of 1917 the transmission, written or oral, of any "information relating to the national defense" to a person not entitled to receive it. Treasury felt that this provision was a serious infringement upon free speech and a free press since it would penalize the passing of innocent information, even trivial information. It would, moreover, offer government officials a convenient excuse for suppressing or withholding information of almost any character.

The proposed bill, for another thing, would have given the FBI and the military services a blanket authorization to engage in wiretapping, with the evidence so obtained admissible as evidence in court cases to which the United States was a party. The investigative or intelligence agency involved, furthermore, was to be the sole judge of when and where wiretapping was to be conducted. The Treasury Department suggested, by way of amendment, that the head of the department (not of the investigative agency) concerned certify in writing in each case that wiretapping was essential, and that, in addition, an authorization be issued by a federal judge before any action was undertaken.

Finally, the Justice draft would have required registration under the Foreign Agents Registration Act of 1938 of "any person who had knowledge of, or who had received instructions about the intelligence services and tactics of a foreign government or a foreign political party." Treasury, however, insisted on the logical necessity of exempting former intelligence or security officers of the United States government.

The Department of Justice was not pleased with the modifications directed by the President and approached the Treasury to seek a withdrawal of the recommended changes. This maneuver proved fruitless, for the Treasury would not forthwith abandon a position of principle and Justice would not consider compromise or even discussion. Subsequently, there were conversations between Justice and Budget, resulting in both parties' somewhat relaxing their positions. The draft bill was then revised to include about 75 percent of the recommendations advanced by the Treasury Department. In regard to amendments to the Espionage Act, the new bill provided that the transmission of information to an unauthorized person had to be carried out in the belief that it would injure the United States (without requiring, however, a showing of intent to commit espionage) ; and it extended the statute of limitations from three to ten years. So far as the Foreign Agents Registration Act was concerned, the revised draft went the Treasury one better by exempting persons who acquired knowledge of a foreign regime or party as a result of academic or personal interest. Criminal penalties were also provided for violation of regulations established by the Secretary of Defense for the security of military installations and property. In this form the bill was submitted to the House in January, 1949 (H.R. 4703). It passed that body and a companion bill was later reported in the Senate (S. 595). In the late summer of 1949, the President's dramatic if shadowy consultant, Max Lowenthal, described the measure as worse than a sedition bill,[5] because of its dependence, in the first part, on determining what was in the accused's mind. Still, viewed in the light of its rivals for congressional approval, the bill was comparatively mild.

The congressional Communist-fighters were, of course, not

satisfied with the measure. The HCUA had been demanding
that the government root out the Soviet-sponsored conspiracy
wherever it existed, and this new proposal did not—from its
point of view—contain adequate provisions for exposure. Even
the fact that H.R. 4703 came as a Justice Department, not a
White House, bill did not prove sufficiently reassuring. In 1948
—the *annus mirabilis* of the Eightieth Congress—the House
had passed the Mundt-Nixon bill (H.R. 5852), and the Republican leadership was disposed to rest on it. This measure,
in the view of an authoritative scholar not generally friendly
to the HCUA, was a well-thought-out, carefully drafted bill, a
tribute to the precise mind and legal orthodoxy of Representative Nixon.[6] It required the registration of Communist organizations with the Attorney General, provided for a subversive activities control board to determine which organizations
might be Communist, denied members of such organizations
employment in the federal service or in defense industries,
withheld passports from such persons, and forbade the use of
the mails or mass media to designated organizations, except
for material or programs clearly labeled as Communist propaganda.

Senators Mundt, Ferguson and Olin Johnston (Democrat
of South Carolina) joined in introducing a new bill (S.
2311), essentially the same as Mundt-Nixon, into the upper
house on July 22, 1949. This measure, like Mundt-Nixon, not
only provided penalties for espionage and sabotage, but required the registration of the Communist party and Communist front organizations. A board was to be established to decide what organizations should be classified as subversive. The
Justice Department, which had doubts about the constitutionality of the Mundt-Nixon bill, particularly in respect to the

registration procedures, did not, except by implication, seem to suffer from the same scruples regarding S. 2311.[7] Justice's ambivalence about the measure, needless to say, was of small comfort to the White House.

No final action had been taken, nevertheless, by the opening of the second session of the Eighty-first Congress. In the spring of 1950, after McCarthy's opening salvos, the Senate Judiciary Committee reported favorably on the Mundt-Ferguson-Johnston bill by a twelve-to-one vote. The Korean War gave an added sense of urgency to the proceedings, and the Republican Policy Committee of the Senate put the bill on its "must list."

The White House, meanwhile, had been busy. Charles S. Murphy, who had succeeded Clark Clifford as Special Counsel to the President, and Stephen Spingarn, who had some time since come from the Treasury Department to be an administrative assistant at the White House, prepared an important memorandum for Mr. Truman on May 16, 1950.[8] It noted that congressional sources had produced a rash of ever more stringent internal security measures. "The tendency also," the staffers observed, "is to draft these measures in very broad, loose terms—to paint the whole barn in order to cover the knothole." It was essential that internal security laws be adequate to protect the country, but

> excessive security . . . can be as dangerous as inadequate security. Excessive security brings normal administrative operations to a standstill, prevents the interchange of ideas necessary to scientific progress, and—most important of all—encroaches on the individual rights and freedoms which distinguish a democracy from a totalitarian country.

Every proposal for new internal security laws, therefore, should be carefully scrutinized, not only from the standpoint of how much it will add to the national security but also from the standpoint of the other considerations noted above, and particularly the last.

Under the circumstances, the President was urged to call in the Attorney General and his Assistant and tell them (1) that he wished that internal security legislation be fully adequate, (2) that he equally wished a balance struck between internal security and individual rights, to avoid excesses in favor of the former, and (3) that, to this end, he wanted all internal security proposals to be carefully scrutinized by the civil rights section of the Justice Department as well as by security branches.

At the staff meeting of May 18, the memorandum was presented to President Truman, who fully concurred in its suggestions.[9] Matt Connelly, the presidential Appointments Secretary and political handyman, also referred to the question of the Hobbs bill (H.R. 10), an exceedingly severe measure for the deportation of presumably subversive aliens. Despite the President's specific instructions to the contrary, the Justice Department was still pushing this legislation. It was then agreed that Stephen Spingarn, bearing with him a brief memorandum from Mr. Truman stressing the evils of excessive security, should meet with Attorney General McGrath and discuss the whole situation with him.

During the course of this meeting, which took place the following afternoon, McGrath took the rather extraordinary step of reading over the President's memorandum and casually handing it back to Mr. Spingarn.[10] On the whole, however, the Attorney General was most accommodating. He remarked that he was fully aware of Mr. Truman's deep convictions on the subject of protecting individual rights, and, as for H.R. 10, that was a bill initiated by Tom Clark two years before.[11] McGrath said he had not heard of the President's position on the measure, so no doubt his people were still promoting it. He had simply assumed it was acceptable because his predecessor had sponsored it. McGrath promised to correct this situation and to follow the President's suggestions in all details. These cheerful assurances were certainly honestly meant; the question was as to how far they would be implemented by a somewhat nonchalant administrator.

Although it was recommended that the President support as "must" legislation, with minor revisions, the Justice-sponsored security bill,[12] the Senate Democratic leadership feared that, if it was brought up for a vote, the Mundt-Ferguson package would be tacked onto S. 595.[13] On August 8, however, President Truman followed his staff's advice by sending a message to Congress, urging the passage of a slightly modified version of H.R. 4703 (the Justice bill that had been passed by the House). This proposal was to face substantial competition since the congressional specialists in internal security had not been idle.

At the end of April and the beginning of May, HCUA had conducted hearings on "legislation to outlaw certain un-American and subversive activities." The committee took under consideration two bills referred to it by the House. One was H.R. 7595, known as the Nixon bill—an up-to-date edition of the Mundt-Nixon bill passed by the House in 1948. The other, H.R. 3903, called the Wood bill after the committee chairman, was a much shorter measure imposing criminal penalties on federal employees or national defense contract workers for membership in, or contribution of funds to, the Communist party or any organization designated subversive by the Attorney General. In August, HCUA reported out a compromise bill retaining the essential features of the Nixon draft, H.R. 9490. In the Senate it was assimilated to a measure sponsored by the inimitable chairman of the Judiciary Committee, Nevada's Pat McCarran. The Senator's contribution was to amend the immigration and naturalization acts to permit the barring or deportation, as the case might require, of suspected alien subversives, and a Title II providing for the detention of potential subversives in time of emergency. But the heart of the bill in Title I, including the registration requirements and a Subversive Activities Control Board to hunt out, expose, and recommend prosecution of Communists and their sympathizers, was neither more nor less than the Mundt-Nixon resolution. It was thus largely HCUA's creature despite the common appellation of McCarran bill.[14]

It was not until August 22 that Representative Emanuel Celler of New York, chairman of the House Judiciary Committee, introduced a bill embodying the President's proposals. By that time, the White House position had been somewhat embarrassed by the Justice Department, which clearly had not absorbed the message given it in May. In an effort to compete with congressional schemes, it was offering an amendment to the Foreign Agents Registration Act as a substitute for similar provisions in the Mundt-Ferguson bill.[15] For a beginning, the new Justice bill referred to subversive groups as "foreign aid organizations," thus inviting by confusion of terminology the discrediting of the administration's foreign aid program and the work of such charitable organizations as CARE. In place

ACME

President Truman *and Gen
eral* MacArthur *greet each
other upon meeting for the
first time on Wake Island.*

Below: *Attending the An
nual Dinner of the Fordham
University Club of Washing
ton, D.C., on Tuesday, April
15, 1947, at the Hotel May
flower were: seated (L to R)
Senator* Brien McMahon,
Former Senator James Mead,
Francis Cardinal Spellman
of New York, Senator Joseph
C. O'Mahoney, *Representa
tive* John W. McCormack;
*standing (L to R) Speaker
of the House,* Joseph Martin
Jr., *Senator* J. Howard Mc
Grath, *Senator* Scott W.
Lucas, *Senator* Joseph R.
McCarthy, *Very Reverend*
Robert I. Gannon, *S.J., Presi
dent of Fordham University.*

ACME

Portrait of Robert Taft.

Harry S. Truman *and* George Marshall.

Below: *Testifying on Communist control legislation before a subcommittee of the* House Committee on Un-American Activities, *Attorney General* Tom Clark *opposed proposals to outlaw Communist party, saying it would only make "martyrs" out of Reds and turn them into a hard-to-reach underground. With Clark are Representatives* Karl E. Mundt *and* Richard Nixon.

ACME

of setting up some sort of examining board, which had become the hallmark of HCUA bills, Justice proposed giving to
the Attorney General extremely broad powers to identify "foreign aid organizations." The drafters of the bill also apparently failed to distinguish between listing an organization as
subversive for the purposes of the loyalty program[16] and so la-
beling one as grounds for criminal prosecution. The stated
standard of evidence in the new bill was "reasonable grounds
for belief" that an organization was subversive—an open door
to all kinds of mischief. Finally, the key designation, "totalitarian political movement," was simply not defined. David
Lloyd of the White House staff considered this Justice contribution "worse than the Mundt bill. All the arguments against
a Political Purity Board apply with greater force against the
A[ttorney]. G[eneral]. as a political purifier."[17]

The basic problem, all the same, was what to do about the
McCarran bill. Senator Lucas seemed to feel that only fire
could fight fire in this case, and that he himself should offer a
registration bill. The President gave the Justice Department
permission to assist him in the drafting, with the understanding that the result would not be an administration measure
and could not be presented as such.[18] Although Lucas was the
administration's floor leader in the Senate, he was facing a
stiff fight for reelection in Illinois, a state where the McCarthy charges and adverse criticism of China policy had destroyed the President's popularity. Lucas's opponent, Representative Dirksen, was following the line suggested by McCarthy and developed by the Republican Policy Committee, that
the Communists within were compelling the government to
yield to the Communists without. His vote for a drastic anti-
subversive bill might help at home; his sponsorship of an ac-

ceptably tough measure might help even more. Lucas gave up the latter plan, partly because the Justice Department advised against it in the end, partly because the passage of the McCarran bill seemed a foregone conclusion. And since it was going to pass by a wide margin, his vote against it would not help the President. Understanding the problem, as a former Senator and former Democratic National Chairman, Attorney General McGrath wrote the Majority Leader on August 26, soliciting his opposition to the McCarran bill, lest his defection embarrass the administration.[19] The problem was becoming a sticky one for Democratic legislators.

Just how sticky, Under Secretary of State James E. Webb learned in the course of a telephone conversation with Carl Hayden, a highly respected member of the Senate and a virtual institution in Arizona:

> Senator Hayden informs me that the whole problem of foreign policy is being injected into the campaign in Arizona. He states that at a recent meeting of the American Legion, Senator McFarland had to utilize every effort to prevent the passage of a resolution condemning Secretary Acheson, and that he had to make the strongest arguments that this type of thing was Republican politics and that the Legion should stay out of politics. Hayden, himself, is being attacked as a Senator who votes for the confirmation of men who will not turn their backs on men convicted of perjury and treason. Hayden thinks that any material that will help him explain the Korean affair, and particularly that the attack was not caused by Mr. Acheson's drawing a line of American interest that did not include Korea, would be appreciated.[20]

If an officeholder as secure as Senator Hayden was worried, the outlook for the ordinary Democratic member of Congress was extremely uncertain. The President could understand such a man's being tempted to go along with the McCarran bill; he himself, it appeared, would have to decide whether to sign it or veto it. The measure clearly violated the concept of civil liberties that Mr. Truman and his staff had been contending for. It established peculiarly cumbersome administrative machinery. Its procedures, moreover, were a horror from the professional police viewpoint, since the investigative and public hearing features of the bill very probably meant the uncovering of confidential information and sources and the premature exposure of the extent of government information about subversive agencies.[21] It was feared that all "working" Communists would be driven completely underground.[22] And there remained doubts of the constitutionality of the registration procedure.[23] The President seemed to have little choice but to veto the bill; yet if he signed it, he might avoid serious political hazard.

He told Messrs. Murphy and Spingarn on September 13 that he wanted them to prepare a very careful analysis of the bill as a basis for his final decision.[24] Although all his public statements on the McCarran bill and its predecessors in the internal security field indicated his distaste for this type of legislation, Mr. Truman certainly wanted to make it clear that he gave full consideration to the bill. He may have been anxious to find some merit in it, to which he could point, in a veto message, as a guide to future action. He may have hoped to find enough of value in the measure to justify his approving it. Earlier in the week, he had been pressed by the Vice-President, the Speaker, and the Democratic floor leaders of both houses to sign the bill, and this was advice he could not brush off. The President, however, refused to make any commitment to the "Big Four," although he did promise them that, on receiving the bill, he would act promptly one way or the other.

Stephen Spingarn, the White House staff's "one man civil liberties union,"[25] was assigned to gathering the material for the necessary analysis and preparing a first draft of a veto message. A draft of a possible signing statement was also ordered. Since the McCarran bill was still in the hands of a House-Senate Conference Committee, the staff chose to work on the assumption that the conference would produce something very like the version passed in the Senate—an omnibus bill with something for almost everybody.

At his regular Thursday press conference the following day, the President, on being asked if he would veto the McCarran bill, replied that he could make no decision until he had seen and analyzed it. In view of his strong negative remarks only the week before, it seemed possible that he was contemplating retreat. Telephone calls began coming from the corporal's guard on Capitol Hill (seven Senators and twenty Representatives) who had voted against the bill. If the President now approved the bill, they would be in serious trouble with some of their constituents, who would brand them as supersoft on Communism. Mr. Spingarn reassured them as best he could, saying that he did not understand Mr. Truman's position of September 7 to have weakened.

Receipt of a confidential committee print of the conference agreement at the beginning of the next week enabled the staff to complete its analysis of the bill and to proceed apace with the revision of the message drafts. On Wednesday the 20th, Mr. Truman said to the staff that he had told Vice-President Barkley that he did not think he was going to be able to sign the bill. With this obvious indication that the President had made up his mind, the staff stepped up its efforts to hammer out a veto message. Both House and Senate approved the conference report (which conformed to the staff's expectations of it) that day, and it reached the White House early the next afternoon. The President, who had read the third draft of the veto message, participated actively in the preparation of the fourth.

At the Cabinet meeting on the morning of the 22nd, Attorney General McGrath personally handed the President his recommendation for a veto. The Defense Department, the CIA, and the State Department were also on record against the McCarran bill. After the meeting, Mr. Truman conferred with his aides for over two hours, making final changes in the fifth draft of his veto message. He then decided to add an unprecedented cover sheet note to each copy of the message, urging each member of Congress to read it carefully before deciding to sustain or override the veto.

The message went to the House about four that Friday afternoon. The Representatives, having decided the issue, wasted no time in overriding the veto by a vote of 286 to 48. One bastion had fallen—not unexpectedly—and there was every indication that the other might follow suit without much delay. The House had already passed a concurrent resolution to adjourn until after Thanksgiving, beginning at the end of its Saturday session. The Senate leaders had consequently decided on the strategy of staying in session through Friday night, until a few minutes after midnight, then passing the same resolution and departing. With the anxiety to adjourn so evident, it did not seem likely that the Senate would give the veto message the attention the President wished.

Although Mr. Truman was unwilling to give up without a fight, his position in the Senate was hardly promising. He had no majority leader on this issue, because Senator Lucas was committed to vote to override the veto. Voter sentiment in Illinois, he believed, left him no choice. Such a defection was remarkable, however, no matter what the circumstances. Even during the divisive battle over Roosevelt's court reform bill, Senator Joseph T. Robinson led administration forces as a matter of duty, despite grave personal reservations about the proposal. There were, to be fair, important differences between Robinson and Lucas. Robinson had been an extraordinarily able legislative tactician, a man of great personal prestige, and the possessor of a secure seat. When Robinson died, FDR, having to choose, picked loyalty over leadership, and secured the election of Alben Barkley as majority leader. After Barkley became Vice-President, Lucas, an amiable man, was selected to replace him because he had no outstanding enemies and because he would take the job. Since the majority leadership is unattended by much real institutional authority, he was able to marshal his "troops"—as he had done on the Formosa question the previous January—only when the interests of the administration and a majority of Senate Democrats happened to coincide, whether for the same reasons or not. The moderate to conservative southern delegations looked to Richard Russell or Harry Byrd for guidance. The northern liberals, preferring good deeds to good discipline, were commonly left with good consciences as a balm for lost legislation. Now the political fears generated by the controversy over loyalty and security had disintegrated whatever there had been of party fealty.

Forced to look elsewhere for a champion, the President found that he had no reliable second-in-command. Senator McFarland, the Democratic whip, had no positive commitments, but it was quite clear that he felt a vote to override would strengthen him in Arizona. There was nothing to do but take what leadership the moment offered. About eleven o'clock Friday night, after talking with Special Counsel Murphy, the President called several Senators known to favor sustaining his veto—including Senator Hubert H. Humphrey of Minnesota, the freshman who had taken charge of the floor fight, and Senator Harley M. Kilgore of West Virginia, a former New Deal wheelhorse. Mr. Truman suggested that the debate be continued well into Saturday to permit the press, radio, and public reaction to the veto message to have what impact on the Senate that it might.

The President's supporters carried on through the night, despite vicissitudes, holding the floor hours on end. At nine-thirty Saturday morning, Senator Humphrey's administrative assistant called the White House to say that the backers of the veto felt that if the debate were continued until about two, that would be enough. Whatever public reaction that could be brought to bear on short notice would have been felt by that time. Senator Humphrey and his colleagues feared to give the appearance of a filibuster to their efforts because that would undermine their position. The President said that if carrying the debate past midnight could avoid a vote, it should be risked; if not, his supporters should decide when to permit the vote.

President Truman then moved to bring his own influence

directly to bear. He telephoned Senator Dennis Chavez, the
patrón of the New Mexico Democracy, and Senator McFarland, the reluctant whip, asking frankly for support. Chavez
promised his vote to sustain the veto, and later delivered it;
McFarland agreed that if the vote were close enough to make
his vote important, he would give it to the President. Encouraged by these conversations, Mr. Truman asked his Special
Counsel to call the Democratic National Committee, to have
them put pressure on any likely Senators. The White House
staff, too, was set to work on the project. Here the difficulties
facing the administration became apparent. Mr. Murphy
talked with Lister Hill of Alabama, once considered radical
for his all-out support of the New Deal, only to discover that
the passage of time and the change of issues made his effort
futile. Senator Hill was sympathetic, but considered himself
bound to the McCarran bill. Mr. Spingarn learned that Brien
McMahon of Connecticut, shepherd of the administration's
atomic energy program, member of the recent Tydings subcommittee, and bitter foe of McCarthy, would not help sustain the veto. Senator McMahon indicated that the President's cause was hopeless. If ordinarily friendly Senators (and
good Democratic partisans) such as these could not be won,
the fight was over.

At about four-thirty the Senate voted to override the veto
by a vote of 57 to 10. The Internal Security Act of 1950 was
law.

Despite all his efforts, and the resources theoretically at his
disposal for influencing congressional decisions, Mr. Truman
had suffered a serious, even a humiliating, defeat. The number of members of Congress who voted to override his veto
was not the whole story, of course, nor was the very small

number voting to sustain it. The painful part of the story, from the White House point of view, was that the great majority of the Senators and Representatives who sided with the President on this issue chose to absent themselves rather than be recorded against the McCarran Act. The President's defeat, moreover, echoed through the congressional campaigns of the fall, and the elections showed that those administration supporters who had followed the lure of prudence had a sure sense of the public temper—though it proved unavailing to some of them.

NOTES

1. A perceptive, if partisan, criticism of the work of the Tydings subcommittee can be found in William F. Buckley, Jr., and L. Brent Bozell, *McCarthy and His Enemies: The Record and Its Meaning* (Chicago: Henry Regnery Co., 1954), pp. 62–191.

2. Statement by the President, April 18, 1950, Papers of HST, Official File 386.

3. See above, p. 135.

4. The history of this measure is taken from a memorandum for the President from Stephen J. Spingarn, July 14, 1950, Papers of Stephen J. Spingarn (now at Harry S. Truman Library).

5. Letter to Matt Connelly, attention Miss Barrows, n.d., Papers of HST, Official File 589.

6. Robert K. Carr, *The House Committee on Un-American Activities* (Ithaca, N.Y.: Cornell University Press, 1952), pp. 230, 279.

7. Memorandum for the Files, August 23, 1949, Papers of HST, Files of Clark M. Clifford.

8. Papers of HST, Official File 2750.

9. Ibid., Memorandum for the Files, May 20, 1950.

10. Interview with Stephen J. Spingarn, March 17, 1962.

11. Memorandum for the Files, May 20, 1950, Papers of HST, Official File 2750.

12. Memorandum for the President from Stephen J. Spingarn, July 14, 1950, Papers of Charles S. Murphy.

13. Memorandum for Messrs. Murphy, Dawson, and Elsey from Spingarn, July 20, 1950, Papers of HST, official File 2750.

14. Carr, *The House Committee,* pp. 193–194. See also a memorandum of August 23, 1950, Papers of HST, Official File 2750.

15. Memorandum for Spingarn from David D. Lloyd, August 10, 1950, Papers of HST, Files of David D. Lloyd. For the President's requests of August 8, see Truman, vol. 2, *Memoirs,* pp. 283–284.

16. There were those, of course, who felt that the department was far too careless in this respect.

17. Memorandum for Spingarn from Lloyd, August 17, 1950, Papers of Stephen J. Spingarn.

18. Memorandum for the File on Internal Security and Individual Rights by Spingarn, August 21, 1950, Papers of HST, Files of Charles S. Murphy.

19. Papers of HST, Files of David D. Lloyd.

20. Memorandum of telephone conversation, August 18, 1950, Papers of James E. Webb. On the Acheson speech, see pp. 168–169 and n. 9.

21. Roger W. Jones, Bureau of the Budget, to William J. Hopkins, Executive Clerk, September 22, 1950, Papers of HST, Bill File.

22. Memorandum, September 1, 1950, Papers of HST, Files of David D. Lloyd.

23. The Supreme Court agreed in June, 1964.

24. The account of the veto of the McCarran bill and the fight to sustain the veto is taken from a memorandum for the Internal Security File, September 25, 1950, Papers of Stephen J. Spingarn (now at Harry S. Truman Library).

25. So designated in a memorandum for Charles S. Murphy from David E. Bell, March 12, 1951, Papers of Charles S. Murphy.

8

The Forces of Unreason

Failure of the Nimitz Commission

WHILE President Truman's attention was almost wholly engaged by the Korean War, the opposition pushed forward along the trail blazed by Senator McCarthy. Despite a "Declaration of Conscience" by seven Republican Senators, led by Margaret Chase Smith of Maine, denouncing the Wisconsinite for his use of smear tactics and for his general irresponsibility, the GOP leadership stood by him. Thus sustained, he charged that Senator Tydings, in the majority report of his subcommittee, had "tried to notify the Communists in the government that they were safe in their positions." They were not, however, because he, McCarthy, would persist in his mission, unafraid to confront the power of an administration "dedicated to the task of protecting the traitors, Communists, and fellow travellers in our government."[1]

Following an indication in McCarthy's earliest list of "cases," the Senate established a special subcommittee of its District of Columbia Committee to investigate homosexuality among federal employees. This subcommittee was to prove a vehicle of sorts for South Dakota's Karl Mundt, co-sponsor, during his House service, of the Mundt-Nixon bill. The White House quickly discovered that the subcommittee's counsel had prejudged the main issue under consideration. That is, he assumed that homosexuals were not only serious security risks, but perhaps the most serious of all; and that, because of their presumed special vulnerability to blackmail, they were automatic targets of Communist coercion. The subcommittee was depending on District police records of arrests for homosexual disorderly conduct and checking to see how many of those arrested were government employees. The counsel was of the opinion, however, that Senator Mundt would insist on seeing agency records, thus forcing the President to turn him down. Senator Hoey, chairman of the subcommittee, seemed anxious, by contrast, to do a thorough, unsensational job, giving full weight to medical evidence (as the counsel and, by implication, other members of the subcommittee were not prepared to do) .[2]

With antiadministration forces acting on the assumption that the Tydings subcommittee report would fail to discredit either Senator McCarthy or his methods of operation, members of the White House staff concerned with the problem—with the same doubts about the subcommittee's effectiveness—prepared a memorandum for the President on July 11, urging him to press for the commission proposed at the Blair House meeting of June 26.

> The argument has been made [they wrote] that the Korean situation has driven McCarthy off the front pages and we can therefore forget about this commission proposal.

It seems to us that the contrary is the case—the best time to set up such a commission is while McCarthy and company are not on the front pages since at such a time it does not so much create the appearance that such action has been forced by Senator McCarthy and his charges. We would indeed have been much better off if such a commission had been created last summer when there was a temporary lull in the hue and cry about loyalty and communism in the Government.

Furthermore, the creation of such a commission now might well be considered a statesmanlike response to the tensions and fears caused by the Korean aggression, rather than to McCarthy.

It seems to us pretty certain that in one form or another the same issue will be raised against the Administration again before the election (with a repeat performance in 1952) whether by Senator McCarthy or from some other source. For example, Senator Mundt, who is a member of the Hoey Subcommittee investigating sex perversion in the Government from the internal security standpoint, might very well step into McCarthy's shoes. Responsible people such as Bill Boyle [of the Democratic National Committee], [Secretary of the Navy] John L. Sullivan and Brien McMahon have told us that (although there is not so much public talk about it) the country is more concerned about the charges of homosexuals in the Government than about Communists. . . .

Attached is a memorandum of June 26 setting out the pros and cons on the commission proposal.[3]

The staff hoped that the President would include a plea for the commission in his forthcoming message to Congress on internal security legislation, and a draft was prepared along those lines. The commission proposal, however, was deleted from the message before it went to Congress, an omission that was particularly regretted by Averell Harriman, who had newly joined the White House staff as Special Assistant for

Mutual Security Affairs.[4] The most logical estimate is that the advice of the Big Four, or other congressional leaders, was responsible for the President's decision not to ask for the commission at that time.[5]

All the evidence indicates that Mr. Truman took bad advice on this question. It was already quite clear that his views of proper internal security legislation were not going to prevail in Congress. And press reaction to the months of attacks on the State Department and the Tydings subcommittee report showed that the administration was not getting its case across to the public. The so-called responsible newspapers, such as *The New York Times, Washington Post,* and St. Louis *Post Dispatch,* rejected both McCarthy's allegations and the means used to support them. This was not the whole of the fourth estate, however. The Hearst papers and McCormick-Patterson complex—Chicago *Tribune, New York Daily News,* and Washington *Times-Herald*—challenged the administration to disprove the charges and frequently behaved as if McCarthy had proved his point. Many prominent dailies across the country adopted the device of deploring McCarthy's methods while applauding his aims.

Further indication of the lengths to which the opposition would go was dramatically manifested when Secretary of Defense Johnson resigned on September 12, and Mr. Truman again called on George Marshall to come out of retirement to serve his country. Once the appointment of the distinguished general as Johnson's successor would have been universally welcomed; by now, however, the rancorous debate over China policy and subversion in the State Department had taken its toll. Senator William E. Jenner, an Indiana Republican, castigated Marshall as a "living lie" and "a front man for traitors," who, whether consciously or unwittingly, had shielded the Communists in the State Department who had handed China over to Mao.[6] Senator Leverett Saltonstall of Massachusetts, ranking Republican on the Armed Services Committee, sprang to Marshall's defense, but the die was cast. Senator Taft, while not joining in the vituperation, declared himself against the appointment, and GOP ranks closed behind him. Asked if his opposition was based on a dislike of military men in civil posts, Taft answered, "Oh, I suppose that's as good a reason as any."[7] His association of Marshall with what he regarded as the failure of the United States in the Far East was, of course, the motivating cause. When General Marshall was confirmed by the Senate, the vote ran painfully close to party lines. Bipartisanship was in mortal jeopardy.

After the first burst of approval for the administration's resistance to Communist aggression in Korea had died down, even that action began to seem flawed in the eyes of the President's opponents. In committing American forces to the defense of the Republic of Korea (South Korea) when the army of the Korean Democratic Republic (North Korea) invaded on June 25, 1950, Mr. Truman—according to Senator Taft—had "usurped" the power of Congress.[8] By taking action on executive authority alone, that is, he had bypassed the constitutional right of Congress to decide on war. In what was even a more effective appeal to popular opinion, Republicans accused the administration of having invited the attack.

Secretary Acheson, addressing the National Press Club the previous January 12, rather candidly delineated the American defense perimeter in the Pacific. Korea and Formosa were left outside the area to be defended by American arms, although they might depend upon economic and diplomatic assistance, and, under certain conditions, more direct aid through United Nations action.[9] The Secretary's critics assured the public that without this guarantee of immunity, the Soviet Union would never have sponsored North Korean aggression. It might seem that Stalin needed no more than the intelligence service available to an ordinary power to realize that American ground strength was very limited and that the Joint Chiefs of Staff, partly out of necessity, assumed that any future war would be a total war, with the fate of countries like Korea being decided by the victor after an awesome confrontation of the great powers. The United States government was not prepared materially, and the American people were not prepared psychologically, to fight a conventional war in a limited territory for limited objectives. Stalin would have felt safe in "unleashing" Kim Il Sung even if Mr. Acheson had never made his Press Club speech. But reason was not enough for Senator Wherry, who scourged the Secretary because "the blood of our boys in Korea is on his shoulders [*sic*]."[10] A whole Republican chorus rose in echo.

Faced with such an assault, David Lloyd believed that there were two major points to be made in the coming campaign:

1. That the main issue in the campaign is the revived isolationism which is now being expressed for the most part by the leaders of one wing of the Republican Party. This isolationism now takes the form of an attack on the policies of the Administration for failing to be aggressive enough. It comes from the same people who have done everything they could to hamper and impede our foreign policy before Korea. The political objective is to drive the isolationists out of Congress—an objective which for the most part, with only a few exceptions—would drive out the chief opponents of our domestic program as well.

2. To allay the Red scare by pointing out the political objectives of the ringleaders of the smear campaign, tying this in with the attack on our bi-partisan foreign policy.[11]

The White House staff was generally aware that, in taking this line, the administration would be making points for the future—just as they believed that although the veto of the McCarran Act might hurt in 1950, it would be an advantage in 1952. By then, the new law would have demonstrated its inability to control Communists and, quite probably, would have been declared unconstitutional.[12] The immediate outlook was bleak from any angle.

The congressional elections turned out quite as badly as many leading Democrats had feared. Millard Tydings, who, as a reward for his subcommittee report, had been selected as a special target by Senator McCarthy, was defeated for reelection in one of the most extravagantly vicious campaigns in American history. The contest featured, on the Republican side, the use of a faked photograph showing Tydings in apparently friendly conversation with Earl Browder, former leader of the American Communist party. Senator Lucas, for all his trimming, was unseated by Everett McKinley Dirksen, leaving Senate Democratic leadership in the still less certain hands of Ernest McFarland (who was to fall, in his turn, before Barry Goldwater in 1952). And, in the most closely watched race, in California, Representative Douglas was trounced by Representative Nixon. Mrs. Douglas, who had been attacked for leftist sympathies in the Democratic primary, was tailor-made for her opponent, whose great role in the Hiss case had won him a considerable reputation.[13] In his campaign against the "Pink Lady," Mr. Nixon was able to make good use of the arguments used by her conservative opponent in the primary. He documented her "soft attitude toward Communism" by citing her voting record in the House, accusing her of being "a member of a small clique which joins the notorious party-liner, Vito Marcantonio of New York, in voting time after time against measures that are for the security of the country." Mrs. Douglas retaliated by charging that her opponent had voted with Marcantonio against foreign aid (including aid to Korea), thus making him, as a Republican isolationist, the real dupe of Communism. The Nixon campaign had an answer for that: a flood of leaflets labeled "Douglas-Marcantonio Voting Record" (later to be known as the "pink sheets" and to number 500,000) showing that Mrs. Douglas had voted with the fellow-traveling New Yorker 354 times, but not listing many of the bills involved. The Nixon allegations stuck; the Douglas countercharges did not. The result was an impressive Republican victory.

Beyond the well-publicized Senate races, the overturn in the House was nearly great enough to restore the Republicans to the control of that body they had enjoyed in the Eightieth Congress. There was general agreement among members of the press corps that Senator McCarthy had played a large part in the outcome. On the morrow of the election, Arthur Krock, a widely read pundit, asserted that the real loser had been the State Department.[14] There was truth in the claim, although other issues besides Communist subversion and its alleged relation to foreign policy influenced the results: dislike of the Korean War as a war, dislike of it for its novel character, the fear of renewed wartime restrictions, rising inflation, and the growing distaste in many quarters for the power of labor unions, the institution of welfare measures, and sundry other (to them) exotic features of the domestic economy—all of these grievances being charged to the Democrats' account. Communism, of course, *had* been a major factor in many races (certainly decisive in Maryland and California), the State Department had been McCarthy's most profitable target, and the off-year victory was almost sure to encourage further Republican efforts to hobble the administration's foreign policy.[15]

Columnist Krock's views were supported by James H. Rowe, Jr., a former administrative assistant to FDR and a Washington attorney with important political connections:

> It is clear to me and I state it as a fact, not as an opinion, that no Democratic politican in the Senate or the House will undertake to defend the Department of State in the next session of the Congress. This is so clear to me after my own conversations with certain legislators that I regard it as self-evident. . . .
>
> Therefore, unless something is done the foreign policy of the United States is in deadly peril. I have no doubt that Taft and his group will, through reaction or compromise or out-and-out knifing, paralyze the Administration's foreign policy. I am convinced that they will do it and that in the process of doing it they will so weaken the United States, both in terms of prestige and in terms of military preparedness, that we will be suckers for the Russians.[16]

The elections did in fact increase the White House's sense of urgency about doing something to protect the State Department against indiscriminate attack. Throughout the summer, despite preoccupation with problems arising out of the Korean War and the struggle over internal security legislation, members of the President's staff had remained interested in a prestigious commission that would investigate and report on the loyalty program. Such an investigation, they were sure, would confirm the effectiveness of the program, and so promote public confidence in it—and by exposing the excessive zeal of some arbiters of loyalty, it might help recover public sympathy for traditional libertarian values.

In the aftermath of the elections, the staff returned to the question. Charles Murphy drafted a memorandum for Mr. Truman on November 15, observing that "[f]or various reasons it did not seem desirable to appoint such a Commission at earlier times this year when it was considered. However, the present seems to be an excellent time to appoint such a Commission."[17] Mr. Murphy, in support of his argument, pointed to the possibility of exploiting already apparent deficiencies in the McCarran Act, the desirability of heading off new investigations of the State Department, not to mention other departments and agencies, the chance to stimulate any public uneasiness on the score of McCarthy's extreme methods of operation, and, above all, the need to defend fundamental liberties.

Now, too, there was outside interest in, and support for, the plan. On November 20, Max M. Kampelman, Senator Humphrey's legislative counsel, wrote the Special Counsel to the President:

> I wanted you to know that the more we think about the proposal for a Commission the better do we like it. I have discussed it with Senator Humphrey, who asked me to say that he hopes you and the President will look favorably upon the idea. The election results seem all the more to point to the advisability of appointing such a Commission. Recent events seem to indicate that the Republicans will continue their McCarthyism tactics. There is reason

to believe that to appear a Commission now would take the sails
from their attack.[18]

The President himself, however, may have become less sure
of the merits of the idea. At least, George Elsey stated in a
memorandum of November 22 to Mr. Murphy:

> I talked with Clark Clifford this afternoon and, unless he hears
> from you to the contrary, he will plan to speak informally to the
> President on Friday or Saturday about the desirability of appoint-
> ing an Internal Security Commission in the very near future.
> Clark will make this an incidental matter and not the main pur-
> pose of his visit with the President.[19]

Whether a major job of persuasion was required, or
whether the staff simply wanted reinforcement against the
counterarguments of cautious legislative leaders, is not entirely clear. In any case, Mr. Truman wrote on November 25
offering ex-President Herbert Hoover the chairmanship of a
presidentially appointed bipartisan commission to report on
the question of "infiltration of Communists in the Government."[20] Hoover declined the next day, suggesting that the
problem came, not from Communists, but from "men in Government (not Communists) whose attitudes are such that
they have disastrously advised on policies in relation to Communist Russia."[21] He went on to urge rigorous investigation
of the past and present of these men, perhaps by Congress. An
informal commission would be inadequate. The President ac-
quiesced in Hoover's declination in a letter of December 7,
but asked for support.[22] A congressional investigation, he
stated, would lead to a partisan debate. The proposed commission would not only study "infiltration," but review the Gov-

ernment Employee Loyalty Program and similar programs, and review and evaluate all existing internal security laws, procedures, and practices, and recommend what changes, if any, should be made.

This proffered chairmanship poses a problem for the interpreter. Despite the bond of mutual respect between the President and the ex-President, Mr. Truman could hardly have been unaware that Hoover subscribed to the Republican "party line" in loyalty and security matters, even if he might put his arguments in somewhat more sophisticated terms. Was the offer serious? Or was it made in anticipation of a refusal, a gesture designed to placate a suspicious public opinion and startle an intransigent opposition leadership? We are left to speculate. It is hard to to be sure how much utility was left in making concessions to an opposition that would not be appeased—or how much value the President still placed in it. He had appointed Seth Richardson as chairman of the Subversives Activities Control Board created by the Internal Security (McCarran) Act, unquestionably as an indication that he would not deliberately undermine an Act of Congress. But, on the recommendation of Senator Humphrey, Senator Paul H. Douglas of Illinois, former Attorney General Francis Biddle, and Representative Andrew Jacobs, he appointed liberal ex-Representative Charles La Follette of Indiana to be a member of the same board.[23] He was not going to repeat the mistake of loading such a body with conservatives and bureaucratic types. It is true, of course, that Richardson's successor at the head of the Loyalty Review Board was the Old Guard ex-Senator Hiram Bingham of Connecticut, long an adherent and admirer of Herbert Hoover. That, however, appeared to be a replacement without a change.[24] The failure of the Senate, under McCarran's prodding, to confirm the La Follette appointment still did not render Mr. Truman's purpose in making the appointment wholly futile, nor did it demonstrate any merit in capitulating to the opposition temper.

After further reflection, the President offered the commission chairmanship, on January 4, 1951, to Admiral of the Fleet Chester W. Nimitz.[25] Nimitz accepted on January 9.[26] As a legitimate war hero and political neutral who could in no way be suspected of favorable sentiments toward communism, Nimitz was a good choice. His ignorance of any politics other than service politics, however, was a handicap and dictated the appointment to the commission of a member who could negotiate with congressional leaders certain essential matters, such as the exemption of the commissioners from conflict-of-interest statutes.

Mr. Truman established by executive order on January 23 the President's Commission on Internal Security and Individual Rights. Members of the commission, apart from Chairman Nimitz, were: Anna Lord Strauss, a prominent figure in the League of Women Voters; John A. Danaher, Washington attorney and former Republican Senator from Connecticut; Harvey S. Firestone, Jr., of the Firestone Tire and Rubber Company; Charles H. Silver, vice-president of the American Woolen Company and long active in New York Democratic politics; William E. Leahy, another prominent Washington attorney; Russell C. Leffingwell, partner in the Morgan Trust Company; the Right Reverend Karl Morgan Block, Protestant Episcopal Bishop of California; and the Most Reverend Emmet M. Walsh, Bishop Coadjutor of the Roman Catholic Diocese of Youngstown, Ohio.[27]

The commissioners were unquestionably of good repute, largely persons of means and property (with the usual bow to the clergy), an aggregation of the types of respectability—yet one has the inescapable feeling that they were second string. Although all were characterized by personal success, not one, except for the chairman, was popularly recognized as distinguished outside his home community. Yet a considerable number of "big names" had been considered by the White House staff in trying to form the commission.

Among the names apparently given the most consideration in preparing recommendations for the President were those of: Federal Judge Florence Allen; Archbishop Patrick A. O'Boyle of Wahington, D.C.; Edward Cardinal Mooney, Archbishop of Detroit; Henry Knox Sherrill, Presiding Bishop of the Protestant Episcopal Church; Herbert Hoover; former Supreme Court Justice Owen J. Roberts, who had headed the Pearl Harbor investigation; Fowler McCormick, chairman of the Board of Directors of International Harvester; Federal Judge Joseph C. Hutcheson; John J. Cavanaugh, president of Notre Dame; Learned Hand; Rabbi David de Sola Poole; Guy Stanton Ford, executive secretary of the American Historical Association; Samuel Cardinal Stritch, Archbishop of Chicago; Arthur Hays Sulzberger, publisher of *The New York Times;* Robert G. Sproul, president of the University of California; Milton Eisenhower, president of Kansas State College; James Bryant Conant, president of Harvard; Arthur H. Compton, president of Washington University; Harold W. Dodds, president of Princeton; Lawrence J. McGinley, president of Fordham University; Jaime Benítez, chancellor of the University of Puerto Rico; Governor James H. Duff of Pennsylvania; Marion B. Folsom, treasurer of the Eastman Kodak

Company; Walter Reuther; Arthur J. Goldberg, general counsel of the CIO; Admiral Nimitz; Major General William J.
(Wild Bill) Donovan, late head of the OSS; Thurgood Marshall; and Henry Ford II.[28]

On the recommended lists, the academic and clerical professions were heavily represented; on the commission as constituted, the former profession was not represented at all, and
the latter not at the level of reputation envisioned. The commission, furthermore, contained no member of the legal profession with judicial experience, although a number of jurists,
both active and retired, were suggested. A conscious effort was
made to recommend both important figures in the labor
movement and industrial and commercial executives; yet no
labor leaders served on the commission, while "business" was
proportionately better represented than on the suggested lists
—although, as in the case of the clergy, not on the level of national standing anticipated. No particular attempt seems to
have been made to secure any broad minority group representation, but several names on the lists of recommendations
were marked by the notation, "liberal Catholic," indicating
White House awareness of the religious and ethnic base of
one bloc of Senator McCarthy's supporters.[29] None of the
persons so labeled served on the commission.

Many of the persons on the suggested lists, to be sure, may
have been crossed off after consultation with the President or
after consideration of possible political complications. But
that would hardly account for the failure to secure a more
prominent commission—not in personal quality, but in public
repute—particularly since the anticipated standing of the commissioners was one of the strong arguments used for creating
the body. It is hard, then, to avoid the conclusion that a fair

number of designated commissioners declined to serve. Learned Hand, whose enlightened concept of jurisprudence and civil libertarian views had decorated the federal bench for many years, was approached and refused appointment as general counsel of the commission.[30] He pleaded not only his age but the unlikelihood that the commission could fulfill its stated aims, given the temper of the moment. At least four others on the suggested lists, apart from Nimitz and Hoover, were offered and declined appointment as commissioners.[31] It may be said that they, like Hand, saw little point in hazarding reputation on so poor a chance to perform a useful public service. Popular emotion, they felt, constituted an insuperable barrier to success.

Even if he had been obliged to take second best, as seems likely, President Truman greeted the Nimitz Commission with hopeful anticipation. At its first meeting, February 12, he addressed the commissioners, saying, "I have the utmost confidence in the manner in which the commission is set up. I have very great confidence in your chairman, and always have had. I am anxious that this job be done in the manner that will stop witch-hunting and give us the facts."[32] One scholar has expressed the opinion that the Nimitz Commission "was the most hopeful experiment in the complex, exacerbating, unending loyalty-security picture."[33] Its very creation must be considered a plus for the administration.

Not everyone, of course, looked upon the Nimitz Commission with pleasure. The congressional opposition, in particular, regarded it as a threat and was anxious to find ways to hamstring it. The opportunity to do so presented itself with the presumably routine request for special legislation to exempt commission personnel from the operation of certain con-

flict-of-interest statutes. This was standard procedure with
regard to members and employees of temporary, special
commissions.

John Danaher, who quickly became the commission's "man
of business," wrote to Admiral Nimitz that he had conferred
at length with Senator McCarran and Representative Francis
P. Walter of Pennsylvania, through whom the exemption bills
would be introduced, and that he expected early consideration in both branches of Congress.[34] Five days later, however,
Mr. Danaher was obliged to explain that McCarran had been
unable (he said) to get a quick report from the Judiciary
Committee and had had to appoint a subcommittee to look
into the matter. By March 2, the subcommittee had discovered some objections to the procedure, and Nimitz was informed that

> [t]hey said that the President had previously refused to permit the
> FBI files to be inspected by the Judiciary Committee, and that
> they are desirous of casting us into such a status that we will be
> amenable to a subpoena by the Senate either to submit the files
> which we procure or to testify concerning their contents after our
> examination of them. . . .
>
> It is perfectly clear that there are certain Senators on both sides
> of the aisle who for political or whatever reason resent the fact
> that the President raised our Commission just as both the House
> and Senate have reactivated their own inquiries into the field in-
> volving subversives.

Although the House committee approved the exemption
bill on March 13, the Senate body was in no particular hurry.
Mr. Danaher, rather under the spell of a former colleague,
wrote Chairman Nimitz on March 19 that while McCarran
was "outspokenly" for the bill, there was still hostility on the

full committee—perhaps a majority. Hope flared briefly that
the legislation might be unnecessary, after all, but Assistant
Attorney General Abraham J. Harris reported on March 21
that members and employees of the Nimitz Commission came
within the scope of the conflict-of-interest laws.

Senator McCarran obviously planned to stall as long as possible, and he had great resources to support so simple an aim.
The "hostility" on the Judiciary Committee was readily exploited for a negative vote. The MacArthur episode[35] made
antiadministration forces completely intransigent, and a personal appeal from the President to McCarran in May proved
futile. It was obvious then to the White House that there was
no point in pressing the issue for the time being. By October
11, it had been decided that the fight was completely hopeless,[36] and the Nimitz Commission was revoked by executive
order on November 14.

What would the Nimitz Commission have been like had it
survived? Would it have done the job Mr. Truman wanted it
to do? There are a few indications, and these are not hopeful.
Only once did the commission act in any way as a body. On
February 13, the Loyalty Review Board requested that the
basic loyalty standard be changed from "reasonable grounds"
to suspect disloyalty to "reasonable doubt" of an employee's
loyalty. Chairman Bingham was most anxious to secure the
change, to expedite the handling of cases, and it was decided
to circularize the members of the Nimitz Commission for
their opinions. The replies, which were received during late
February and early March, cannot be regarded as encouraging.[37] Only Anna Lord Strauss had any reservations about approving the change immediately, and she simply stated a
desire to hear arguments against the proposal. All the other

commissioners agreed that in the light of the prevailing national emergency, the change was justified. With such impressive support, the Loyalty Review Board was able to secure
the desired amendment.[38]

It is quite possible, of course, on a quick reading, that the
words "reasonable doubt" in the revised loyalty standard
could be confused with the classic protection afforded the accused in criminal proceedings. But in that case the reference
is to reasonable doubt of guilt, whereas the new loyalty standard referred, in effect, to reasonable doubt of innocence. The
amendment, in short, seriously impaired the protection
granted employees by reducing the degree of suspicion required for dismissal or denial of employment. Several members of the White House staff were aghast at the change.[39]

Were the commissioners aware of what they were recommending? Since it is unlikely that all of them read Bingham's
request carelessly, it must be assumed that they felt that
strengthening national security, as they conceived it, compen-
sated for a further infringement of employees' rights. And the
President was bound to take their views as representative of
an intelligent public opinion. The Nimitz Commission did
not act as a body in any other instance, but at least two of its
more prominent members regarded its task as primarily one of
toughening security measures. John Danaher, for example, reported to the chairman on March 9 that

> I feel confident that ways and means can be evolved through
> which a very substantial service can be rendered. In due course I
> will lay before the general counsel and, through him, the Commis-
> sion, a basis upon which we can expect collaboration of a high
> order [from the Un-American Activities Committee of the Ameri-
> canism Commission of the American Legion].[40]

Since the Legion was actively supporting McCarthy and calling monotonously for more stringent security measures, that was a remarkable proposal indeed. It recalled the working relationship between the Justice Department and the APL in World War I—with the difference, however, that the APL had not considered the Wilson administration to be a source of subversion and sabotage.

On March 20, another active member of the commission, Russell Leffingwell, wrote Nimitz:

> I get the impression that Congress has been too responsive to the views of the employees associations and the civil liberties associations, and has gradually made it even more difficult for the agencies to discharge undesirable employees for security reasons than to discharge them for other reasons of unfitness or unsuitability. . .
>
> I think employee tenure and civil rights generally have to be subordinated to the right of the nation to defend itself against Russia, which is the enemy of all civil rights and all the freedoms. . . .
>
> I am not going to change my mind about the primary right and duty of the nation to defend its security in the present emergency, even though that necessitates infringement of our cherished civil liberties.[41]

After Admiral Nimitz and Mr. Danaher conferred with the President on May 8, submitting the commissioners' resignations in consequence of the Senate Judiciary Committee fiasco, the former senator prepared a summary comment for Mr. Truman. Writing on July 17, he stated, in reference to the Nimitz Commission's goals:

[I]t can nowhere be denied that conditions now are vastly different

from those thought to exist in January. . . . Uncertainty existed
in the law. At least some confusion attended the administration of
the law. The Loyalty Review Board felt itself handicapped. However, [the Supreme Court has handed down decisions favorable to
the loyalty program and the security statutes]. By your amendment to Executive Order 9835 you granted to the Loyalty Review
Board a modified standard to be applied to cases under review,
pursuant to which opening and review of many cases can be
achieved. Clearly, these new weapons have been added to your ar-
senal in the fight to preserve the internal security of the United
States. . . .

Therefore, Mr. President, a very great deal has been accomplished in the last six months. . . . [S]everal months of study of
the over-all problem have led me to the conclusion that there is
no longer such need to turn to a commission so constituted as
was ours in January.[42]

Although Mr. Danaher complained of the administrative
tendency to confuse loyalty and security matters,[43] his overriding concern was with internal security, the enhancing of
which he saw as the commission's decisive purpose. One is led
irresistibly to the conclusion that if the Nimitz Commission
had been allowed to function, it would have conformed to the
popular emphasis on security at whatever cost, and that even
if it had increased public confidence in the loyalty program, it
could only have damaged the cause of personal freedom. Perhaps no such body could have done otherwise in a time of
such widespread popular hysteria; certainly this commission
did not seem up to more. Only a group of citizens so obviously distinguished, and dedicated to the nation, that their re-
putations were proof against slander could have afforded the
luxury of preaching truth and equity to the public. The Nim-

itz Commission lacked in the generality of its membership the individual stature that would have permitted it to court and survive criticism, and thus it could not have fulfilled the charge laid upon it by the President.

NOTES

1. Cabell Phillips, *The Truman Presidency: The History of a Triumphant Succession* (New York: The Macmillan Company, 1966), p. 389.

2. Memoranda for the Hoey . . . File, June 29 and July 10, 1950, Papers of HST, Files of Charles S. Murphy.

3. Memorandum from Charles S. Murphy, Stephen J. Spingarn, and George M. Elsey, Papers of Stephen J. Spingarn.

4. Memorandum for the File, August 15, 1950, Papers of Stephen J. Spingarn.

5. Interviews with George M. Elsey, March 29, 1967, and Stephen J. Spingarn, March 17, 1962.

6. *New York Times,* September 16, 1950.

7. Cited in William S. White, *The Taft Story* (New York: Harper & Bros., 1954), p. 90.

8. Ibid., p. 97.

9. John W. Spanier, *The Truman-MacArthur Controversy and the Korean War* (New York: W. W. Norton & Co., 1965), pp. 19–21, argues that the Acheson speech reflected military thinking that had left Korea out of the defense perimeter because of the American commitment to the idea of total war. The reliance on nuclear weaponry, and the consequent expectation of total war, was in good part imposed by budgetary considerations. It represented what a Republican Secretary of Defense with a particular flair for phrasing would call the "bigger bang for a buck." The Acheson speech, therefore, did not tell the Soviets anything they did not know. Trumbull Higgins, on the other hand, believes that the speech helped convince the Russians that the United States would not defend South Korea. Trumbull Higgins, *Korea and the Fall of MacArthur: A Précis in Limited War* (New York: Oxford University Press, 1960), pp. 13–15.

10. *New York Times,* August 17, 1950.

11. Memorandum, September 21, 1950, Papers of Charles S. Murphy.

12. Memorandum, September 20, 1950, Papers of HST, Files of David D. Lloyd.

13. The account of the California senatorial campaign is taken from

Earl Mazo, *Richard Nixon: A Political and Personal Portrait* (New York: Harper & Bros., 1959) , pp. 78–82.

14. *New York Times,* November 9, 1950.

15. Grenville and Young have put the basic problem exceptionally well: "The management of foreign policy in a democratic society poses a number of fundamental problems. Diplomacy can rarely be conducted successfully in the glare of public debate. At the same time, any responsible government has to win a broad measure of public support for its policies. To reconcile national interests and public feeling is frequently difficult. The task becomes complicated beyond measure–if not indeed impossible–if either party seeks to derive partisan political advantage from the handling of foreign policy. Unhappily, the division of powers and responsibilities embodied in the United States Constitution provides ample opportunity for members of Congress to undermine politically the diplomatic measures of an administration. By the same token (and it is sometimes overlooked) , the constitution also tempts the Executive to enhance its position by adopting a partisan posture in its dealings with the Legislature." John A. S. Grenville and George Berkeley Young, *Politics, Strategy, and American Diplomacy: Studies in Foreign Policy, 1873–1917* (New Haven: Yale University Press, 1966) , pp. vii–viii. In the years 1947–1953, Congress's opportunities were generally superior to the President's.

16. Letter to James E. Webb, November 22, 1950, Papers of James E. Webb.

17. Papers of HST, Files of Charles S. Murphy.

18. Papers of Charles S. Murphy.

19. Papers of HST, Files of Charles S. Murphy.

20. Papers of HST, Official File 2750–A.

21. Ibid.

22. Ibid.

23. Memorandum, Papers of HST, Official File, 2750–D.

24. Some conservatives, however, thought that Richardson was too deferential to the State Department and had failed to do all he might have to influence it to employ greater strictness in its loyalty and security procedures. William F. Buckley, Jr., and L. Brent Bozell, *McCarthy and His Enemies: The Record and Its Meaning* (Chicago: Henry Regnery Co., 1954) pp. 218–221.

25. Papers of HST, Official File 2750-A.

26. Ibid.

27. Ibid.

28. The names come from a memorandum dated June 1, 1950, another memorandum of apparently earlier date, and two more of obviously later date. Papers of Stephen J. Spingarn.

29. A view with strong support among scholars is that the new American Catholic middle class used its Church's longstanding anti-Commu-

nist position as proof of its own Americanism—often challenged in the past. This argument is clearly stated in Samuel Lubell, *Revolt of the Moderates* (New York: Harper & Bros., 1956), especially in the chapter on the "politicians of revenge."

30. Hand to Nimitz, March 11, 1951, Papers of HST, Records of the President's Commission on Internal Security and Individual Rights (hereafter cited as Nimitz Commission). Hand, it is true, had somewhat tarnished his reputation among civil libertarians by devising the interpretation of the "clear and present danger" test that enabled the Circuit Court of Appeals and, afterward, the Supreme Court, to uphold the conviction of the eleven Communist leaders tried under the Smith Act, and to determine that the act was not an unconstitutional invasion of rights guaranteed under the First and Fifth Amendments. See Wallace Mendelson, *The Constitution and the Supreme Court* (New York: Dodd, Mead & Co., 1959), p. 385. The administration, however, was hardly committed to any absolute interpretation of the First Amendment. The President's message covering his veto of the McCarran Act implies approval both of the Smith Act and the prosecutions conducted under it.

31. Private information.

32. Papers of HST, Records of the Nimitz Commission.

33. Harold M. Hyman, *To Try Men's Souls: Loyalty Tests in American History* (Berkeley and Los Angeles: University of California Press, 1959), p. 335.

34. This letter, and other correspondence concerning the exemption bills, is to be found in the Papers of HST, Records of the Nimitz Commission.

35. See below, chap. 9.

36. Charles S. Murphy to Professor E. M. Morgan of Vanderbilt University, Papers of HST, Official File 2750-A.

37. Papers of HST, Records of the Nimitz Commission.

38. Executive Order 10241, April 28, 1951, amending Paragraph 1 of Part V of Executive Order 9835 (March 21, 1947):
"1. The standard for the refusal of employment or the removal from employment in an executive department or agency on grounds relating to loyalty shall be that, on all the evidence, there is a reasonable doubt as to the loyalty of the person involved to the Government of the United States."
Papers of HST, Official File 252-K.

39. Interview with Donald A. Hansen, March 28, 1967.

40. Papers of HST, Records of the Nimitz Commission.

41. Ibid.

42. Papers of J. Howard McGrath, Correspondence of the Attorney General.

43. See p. 38 and n. 32.

9

Hail to the Chief

Korea and the Relief of MacArthur

PRESIDENT Truman's domestic problems were compounded by his relieving General of the Army Douglas MacArthur of United States and United Nations command in Korea, in April, 1951, for demonstrable impropriety of conduct.[1] To foes of the administration, however, the General had been dismissed not because he had violated the direct order of a superior—the unforgivable sin in any military book—nor because he had challenged civilian control over the making of national policy—one of the most persistent pieties in American political tables—but because he had wished, contrary to the desires of the President and Secretary of State, to fight Communism to a finish. On his return, the fallen hero was welcomed in city after city as a conqueror; even Democratic *caciques* dared not refuse him honor. Congress—or, rather, that large portion of it on whom the gods had laid their touch—voted him an invitation to expose his martyrdom before a joint session—an unprecedented reward for a man in official disgrace.

General MacArthur, who, even in the seventy-second year of his pilgrimage, could hope that his final destiny might be as yet unrealized, gladly displayed his concord with his hosts' most cherished beliefs. "Talk of imminent threat to our national security through the application of external force," he declared, "is pure nonsense." The real threat came not from the Chinese horde across the Yalu River in Manchuria, not from the Soviet spider counting coup in the center of his Kremlin web, but from "the insidious forces working from within which have already so drastically altered the character of our free institutions, . . . those institutions we proudly called the American way of life."[2] MacArthur thus spoke out for the view held by the Republican leadership. Let the President—to use Senator Wherry's considered language—"get rid of the alien-minded radicals and moral perverts in his administration"[3] and there would be no foreign challenge. Take the powder of drastic internal security measures and the national headache will go away.

It is even clearer now what the antiadministration leaders intended, and to whom they were appealing. McCarthy's role was to "demonstrate" that the difficulties the United States faced in the world were the result of policy made by traitorous elements in high places. "How can we account for our present situation," he asked, "unless we believe that men high in this government are concerting to deliver us to disaster? This must be the product of a great conspiracy on a scale so immense as to dwarf any previous venture in the history of man."[4]

This thesis appealed to a variety of people: to devotees of economy in government, who could foresee a reduction of defense budgets while national security was ensured by better police work at home; to those who had opposed American entry into World War II, and who regarded the postwar power of an aggressive Soviet Union and the consequent menace of Communist subversion as justification for their former position; to those so-called isolationists who upheld the American mission in Asia while entertaining the most deep-seated anti-European (and specifically anglophobe) sentiments, and who saw the Truman administration's cold war policies as a continuation of the betrayal of America's true interests that marked the Roosevelt administration's wartime priorities.[5] The controversy over General MacArthur's removal helped crystallize the feelings released by McCarthy's charges.

MacArthur was dismissed, quite simply, because he, a theater commander, publicly took issue with the policy of his Commander-in-Chief—a policy that had been made perfectly clear to him. To maintain not merely the policy, but the predominance of the civil authority—that is, the constitutional power of the President—MacArthur had to be stripped of his command. Some of President Truman's opponents at home affected to believe that nothing more was involved than a clash of opinion, and that the general had been petulantly dismissed for disagreeing with the administration. According to them, General MacArthur's plan for victory in Asia was the proper American program, while the President's insistence on maintaining self-imposed restraints on the use of our military resources was clearly contrary to the national interest. More than that, they implied, it probably had a sinister origin, the same pro-Communist elements in the State Department who had propelled the National government of China to destruction.

On June 25, 1950, as the North Korean attack developed,

the President agreed to a three-part American response after conferring with his principal military and diplomatic advisers. He ordered General MacArthur to evacuate Americans from South Korea, keeping the necessary airfields open to accomplish this task. Air Force units under MacArthur's command were to limit their operations to the area south of the 38th parallel, which divided the two Koreas, in carrying out this mission. The President also directed his Far Eastern commander to use air drops, or other expedient means, to get ammunition and other military supplies to the South Korean Army. Finally, the President ordered the United States Seventh Fleet into the Formosa Strait. This fleet movement—not to be announced until complete—had the twofold purpose of denying the Chinese Communists access to Formosa and preventing Chiang Kai-shek from attempting any adventure against the mainland. American policy was clearly to forestall the spread of hostilities to other parts of Asia.

The same evening, the United Nations Security Council unanimously passed a resolution calling upon the North Koreans to withdraw and agree to a cease-fire. The absence of the Soviet delegate, owing to his country's boycott of the Security Council over the issue of admitting Communist China to the UN, made the result possible.

The military situation in Korea had so deteriorated by June 27 that the President ordered the use of American naval and air forces of the Far Eastern command in support of South Korean defenders. These American units, however, were restricted to operations south of the 38th parallel. As Mr. Truman recalled later, "I wanted to take every step necessary to push the North Koreans back behind the 38th parallel. But I wanted to be sure that we would not become so deeply committed in Korea that we could not take care of other such situations as might develop."[6]

These steps were accompanied by a note to the Soviet government, asking for an end to the aggression: "In view of the universally known fact of the close relations between the Union of Soviet Socialist Republics and the North Korean regime, the United States government asks assurance that the Union of Soviet Socialist Republics disavows responsibility for this unprovoked and unwarranted attack, and that it will use its influence with the North Korean authorities to withdraw their invading forces immediately."[7] The position of the United States was strengthened by a second Security Council resolution directing UN members to assist South Korea in resisting aggression. It was hoped that this support for American action might induce the Soviets to call off their dogs.

There was some doubt in Washington that the Korean aggression represented a major thrust by the Communist world leadership. Many in the administration suspected that it was a diversionary attack designed as cover for some decisive Soviet assault, probably in Europe. For that reason, the greatest caution was shown in developing the American commitment to South Korea. For that reason, too, the President was at first inclined to accept Generalissimo Chiang's offer of up to 33,000 troops for use in Korea, since these might free one or two American divisions for possible employment elsewhere. Secretary Acheson opposed using the Nationalist soldiers because it would mean stripping Formosa of its natural defenders, an action that would have a peculiar look to other interested nations. He also pointed out, as did the military leaders, that the United States would have to transport these Chinese Nationalist troops to Korea and would probably face a serious problem in reequipping them. The Joint Chiefs of Staff, on the basis of information received from military observers in Formosa, further questioned the morale and general fighting quality of Chiang's forces. Convinced by this presentation, Mr. Truman decided to decline the Generalissimo's offer as gracefully as possible.

General MacArthur's trip to the front on June 29 convinced him that whatever chance there was of saving South Korea rested on the immediate intervention of American forces, and he requested permission to move two divisions of his command to Korea. The President was ready for the request, as the Army Chief of Staff, General J. Lawton Collins, had argued this view to him before receipt of MacArthur's report. On June 30, President Truman announced that General MacArthur had been authorized to commit any or all of the troops at his disposal to the defense of South Korea. In addition, naval units would establish a blockade of the whole Korean coast, and the Air Force was released to attack targets in North Korea. Targets close to the Soviet-Korean and Chinese-Korean borders, however, remained off limits.

The Soviet reply of June 29 to the American note of two days before blamed the South Koreans and their upholders for having provoked the war, but it also stressed the Kremlin's notion of the conflict as an internal affair of the Korean nation. Washington interpreted the Soviet reply as a signal that the USSR would not intervene directly, allowing its North Korean allies to carry the standard for the Communist cause. And since the Soviets showed no immediate signs of preparing an attack in Europe, the administration was doubly convinced that it had made the right decision in going to the aid of South Korea. The European allies of the United States

were also heartened by this indication that the far more precise American commitments to their own safety would be hon-
ored. Some of them indeed feared that the United States
might become entrapped in an Asian war, thus inviting a Soviet attempt against themselves, but they did not believe that
the limited goal set by the Truman administration—the resto-
ration of the status quo ante bellum in Korea—made that danger a pressing one.

Compelled to fight a coalition war as the agent of the
United Nations, and sensitive to the desires of its active allies,
most of whom were cosignatories of the North Atlantic
Treaty, the United States government moved cautiously in the
early days of the war.[8] But its commander on the scene—also,
perforce, the UN's commander—was not in real accord with
what he regarded as the administration's passive policy in the
Far East. At the end of July, he made a trip to Formosa, osten-
sibly to check on the capacity of Chiang's forces to defend the
island. On his return to headquarters in Tokyo, MacArthur
issued a statement praising the Generalissimo as a fellow fight-
er against Communism. Chiang, in Taipeh, talked of cooperation between the Unitd States and the Nationalist regime.
Suspicious of his commander's real feelings, President Truman sent Averell Harriman to Tokyo on August 3 to make
sure that the general properly understood the policy he was
supposed to execute. The talks went well enough on the surface, but Mr. Harriman reported his uneasiness to the President:

> For reasons which are difficult to explain, I did not feel that
> we came to a full agreement on the way we believed things
> should be handled on Formosa and with the Generalissimo. He

accepted the President's position and will act accordingly, but without full conviction. He has a strange idea that we should back *anybody* who will fight communism.[9]

In truth, General MacArthur was upset by Mr. Truman's policy toward Formosa; he believed that Chiang should be free to conduct raids against the mainland, to divert the attention of Chinese Communist forces, if nothing else. He apparently decided it would be necessary to make his views public. MacArthur sent a message to the annual encampment of the Veterans of Foreign Wars, to be read on August 28. Press associations and newspapers, unfortunately, had been sent copies of this letter correcting "the misconceptions currently being voiced concerning the relationship of Formosa to our strategic potential in the Pacific."[10] Formosa, he stated, was the key to American domination of the Pacific coast of Asia from Vladivostok to Singapore. When the White House learned of this message from the wire services, the President ordered MacArthur, through the agency of the Secretary of Defense, to withdraw it. This was quickly done—but it had already been publicly circulated.

The general's military success, nevertheless, had an important effect on his superiors. The spectacular victory at Inchon in September, guaranteeing that South Korea would be cleared of hostile forces and threatening the very existence of the invaders themselves, led the President to grant MacArthur the permission he had requested to cross the 38th parallel, to encompass the destruction of the North Korean Army. This was unquestionably a change of policy. The United States had intervened in June simply to restore the conditions existing prior to the invasion; its purpose had been to demonstrate that established arrangements could not be overthrown by force of arms. The new United Nations resolution secured by the American delegation—that the aim of the UN forces was to make possible free elections in a reunified Korea—cannot mask the essential purpose of the counterinvasion: the elimination of the North Korean Communist government. It must be speculated that the administration hoped, by inflicting a condign punishment on aggression, to accomplish several things at once. The danger of attacking a country supported by the United States would be clearly demonstrated. The shattering of the North Korean armed forces might dissipate any lingering Communist temptation to challenge the West in Asia, thus making any large-scale commitment of men and resources to that part of the world unnecessary. The victory at Inchon offered an unexpected opportunity to reunite the American people behind the administration's foreign policy, since even the most anti-Acheson Republican could only applaud the elimination of a Communist power.

However it read the new situation, the administration remained cautious even as it developed its departure in policy. MacArthur was warned to proceed only if he could reasonably discount the possibility of Soviet or Chinese intervention. He was instructed further to use only South Korean troops in any possible operations near the Chinese border. And the restrictions on naval and air operations already in force were continued. The government, in fact, had made a commitment to the British not to bomb beyond the Yalu without consulting them.

MacArthur, however, appeared to assume that directions received from Secretary of Defense Marshall on September 27 left him wholly free to use his judgment in deploying troops

north of the parallel. To make sure that there were no ambig-
uities in the general's understanding of American policy,
President Truman decided on a face-to-face meeting with the
theater commander who had not been home for more than a
decade. Because General MacArthur felt that he could not afford to come as far as Hawaii, the Commander-in-Chief
agreed to a meeting on Wake Island. According to a reliable
reporter, Anthony Leviero, who had his information from the
White House staff, "The basic principle of the policy that the
Administration would like General MacArthur to support is
that communism, especially in China, cannot be overcome by
force."[11] In other words, Mr. Truman was going to "sell" General MacArthur on the established policy of his government.

The general must have been a reluctant customer, since
such thinking had little in common with his own ideas on the
subject, but he seems not to have shown it. The President believed that he had made his position clear, and that MacArthur had accepted it. MacArthur, in his turn, reassured Mr.
Truman that there was no substantial danger of Chinese interference with operations above the 38th parallel. The
Chinese Communist regime, through its Foreign Minister,
Chou En-lai, had said publicly that a UN crossing of the parallel would be a direct threat to Chinese security. The Indian
Government had passed on reports from its admittedly pro-
Communist ambassador to China that Mao meant business,
and that a UN advance into North Korea would be countered
with force. As the American and allied troops proceeded effectively with the mop-up of the North Korean Army, however,
these indications were ignored. They were propaganda,
Chinese bluster, it was argued. The Secretary of State assumed
that the Chinese Communists could grasp the reasonableness

of our assurances that we had no designs beyond the Yalu. The Far Eastern commander assumed they had not the means to fulfill their threats.

Early in November, 1950, the so-called Chinese People's Volunteers—actually trained units of Communist China's regular army—swarmed across the border, overran forward UN elements, and drove back the main body of American and South Korean troops. Soon North Korea had been "liberated," and Communist forces—now Chinese rather than native—were once again advancing south of the 38th parallel. Once again, the problem for the United States and its UN allies was how to restore the conditions of June 24. Chinese intervention had reimposed on the administration its original policy. Both the State Department and General MacArthur had drastically miscalculated Peking's intentions, although both could claim plausible reasons for having done so; yet the real problem was dealing with brute fact.

General MacArthur would have forgotten Korea, in effect, and have dealt with the new enemy who now presented himself. That meant, for a beginning, removal of the inhibition on air strikes against military encampments, supply bases, and industrial facilities in Manchuria. It also meant blockading the Chinese coast and encouraging Chiang Kai-shek to harry the Communists' southern flank. The administration, being anxious to localize the conflict (and being under very considerable pressure from its European allies to do so), could not accept the General's plan for victory. What that plan was is best seen in the words of MacArthur's successor in the Far Eastern command, General Matthew B. Ridgway:

When MacArthur spoke of victory, he did not mean merely vic-

tory in Korea—the destruction of all hostile forces on the peninsula and the unification of the country under a democratic
government. What he envisaged was no less than the global defeat
of Communism, dealing Communism "a blow from which it
would never recover" and which would mark the historical turning
back of the Red Tide. His "program" included not merely driving to the Yalu, but destroying the air bases and industrial
complex in Manchuria, blocking Communist China's seacoast; de-
molishing its industrial centers; providing all necessary support
to Chiang's invasion of the mainland; and the transportation of
the Nationalist Chinese troops to Korea to beef up our ground
forces there. He sincerely believed that these moves would break
the Communist hold on the mainland. He was convinced that the
Chinese masses were ready to welcome Chiang back, and he had
persuaded himself that the Soviet Union would not intervene in
a conflict of the sort he had in mind. But if, in the course of
waging this preventive war on Red China, the threat of Soviet
intervention had jeopardized its success, it is not illogical to
assume that MacArthur would have urged the further step of an
attack upon the USSR (whose growing strength, he thought,
put time on its side). This would have been merely the logical
extension of his ultimate aim, the destruction of Communism
throughout the world by the use of armed force.[12]

MacArthur's official proposal for massive reinforcement of
UN ground forces in Korea, as a prelude to a major counterof-
fensive, coupled with the bombing of Chinese targets and the
naval blockade of the Chinese coast, was simply unacceptable
to the administration. While still committed to restoring
South Korea whole, on the basis of the status quo ante bellum,
it now seemed to the President and the State and Defense Departments that we could not afford an effort to win the war, in
the popular sense of the term.[13] The United States, in the

opinion of the Joint Chiefs of Staff, could not reinforce Korea
sufficiently to support a decisive offensive operation without
stripping the defenses of Europe and the nation itself. The renewed fear that Stalin had intended the Korean War as diversion to cover some European aggression ruled out such a
risk.[14] The UN allies of the United States, having agreed to
MacArthur's crossing of the 38th parallel with some trepida-
tion, now displayed positive reluctance to hazard further
large-scale undertakings; and the government, having actively
sought UN sanction, dared not now cast off the cloak of collective responsibility it provided.[15]

President Truman asked Congress to nearly quadruple the
defense appropriation and underscored his point on December
15 by declaring a state of emergency, to permit the rapid addition of about 1.2 million men to the armed forces. At the
same time, he was being subjected to pressures from two sides.
The UN General Assembly passed a resolution asking for a
cease-fire in Korea: allies and neutrals were ready to call quits.
From a distinctly different quarter, a majority of the Republicans in Congress, came a resolution asking the President to
dismiss Mr. Acheson because "he had lost the confidence of
the country." The clear implication of the resolution, against
a background of the politically successful McCarthy charges,
was that the State Department might betray the national interest in Korea, as it had supposedly done in China.[16]

General MacArthur did not hesitate to place his own views,
so contrary to those of his superiors, on public record. Early in
December he cabled the editors of *United States News &
World Report,* a magazine of conservative Republican orien-
tation, that he was hamstrung in Korea by "the extraordinary
inhibitions . . . without precedent in military history" that

denied him the opportunity to carry the war into the "privileged sanctuary" of the enemy. He also complained to the president of the United Press about the existing situation, which, as he saw it, "results largely from the acceptance of military odds without precedent in history—the odds of permitting offensive action without defensive retaliation."[17]

Ten days into the new year, MacArthur reported to the Joint Chiefs of Staff that if he were to be pinned down in Korea, under the present conditions and with the currently available forces, he could not answer for the safety of Japan. To establish a stable defensive position somewhere in South Korea, as recommended by the Joint Chiefs, might invite disaster in the rear. It would be better, under such circumstances, to withdraw from Korea. But MacArthur offered an alternative line of action: a naval blockade of China, unrestricted bombing of Chinese industries, communications, supply lines, and troop depots, acceptance of Nationalist Chinese reinforcements in Korea, and support of Nationalist diversionary actions against selected points on the China coast. The proposal was rejected at a National Security Council meeting on January 12, and the next day the President wrote MacArthur to emphasize the purposes to be attained by a successful resistance in Korea. Among the more important were: the demonstration that Communist aggression would not go unchallenged, the deflation of the now exaggerated prestige of Communist China, the granting of additional time to develop resistance to Communism in Asia, the honoring of our commitment to South Korea (which would, incidentally, give added value to our other international commitments), the improvement of prospects for a satisfactory settlement with

Japan, and the stiffening, by nations around the world threatened by Communist powers, of the resolve to resist.[18]

To lend further weight to his points, Mr. Truman sent the Army and Air Force Chiefs of Staff to Tokyo to spell out for the Far Eastern commander the international complications that went into the determining of American policy. MacArthur appeared to understand the situation as presented to him, and for the time being, at least, the theater commander seemed willing to follow the lead of the Commander-in-Chief.

Through the first three months of 1951, the fighting in Korea slowly diminished in intensity, and the UN allies slowly recovered their position. Seoul, the South Korean capital, was retaken in March, and it was clear that the area south of the 38th parallel would soon be again free of hostile forces. But it was equally clear that no decisive military victory could be won without the United States' investing more in men and resources than its other commitments—and perhaps the necessities of its own defense—made feasible. Taking into consideration both the broader interests of the country (as they saw them) and the anxieties of our allies in a coalition war, President Truman and his principal advisers concluded that if the government were to seek a cease-fire, the essential aims of the United States, South Korea, and the UN would be secured. South Korea would be restored, the North Korean aggression rendered futile, the collective responsibility of the UN vindicated—all thanks to the United States.

The State Department prepared a statement for the President's issuance, announcing that the United States was willing to discuss the termination of the war on the basis of the status quo ante bellum. It was considered quite possible that Peking was desirous of ending the conflict that it, too, could not win.

MacArthur was informed on March 20 that the President would soon make a public proposal for a cease-fire, and he was asked what he might need to maintain the current UN position in Korea. His reply was that his present forces were adequate for so limited a purpose, provided no additional restrictions were placed on his freedom of action.

The proposed statement, having been checked by the Defense Department and the Joint Chiefs of Staff, and apparently approved by MacArthur, was submitted to the governments of the allied nations on March 21. The statement emphasized that "the principal objective of repelling North Korean and Chinese Communist aggression against the South Korean Republic had been achieved," and suggested to the Chinese that "a prompt settlement of the Korean problem would greatly reduce international tension in the Far East and open the way for the consideration of other problems in that area by the processes of peaceful settlement envisaged in the Charter of the United Nations."[19]

Three days later, MacArthur offered publicly what he called a "military appraisal." Having commented on the deficiencies displayed by the Chinese forces, he went on to observe:

> These military weaknesses have been clearly and definitely revealed since Red China entered upon its undeclared war in Korea. Even under the inhibitions which now restrict the activity of the United Nations forces and the corresponding military advantages which accrue to Red China, it has shown its complete inability to accomplish by force of arms the conquest of Korea. The enemy, therefore, must by now be painfully aware that a decision of the United Nations to depart from its tolerant effort to contain the war to the area of Korea, through an expansion of

our military operations to his coastal areas and interior bases, would doom Red China to the risk of imminent military collapse. These basic facts being established, there should be no insuperable difficulty in arriving at decisions on the Korean problem if the issues are resolved on their own merits, without being burdened by extraneous matters such as Formosa or China's seat in the United Nations. . . .

Within the area of my authority as the military commander, however, it should be needless to say that I stand ready at any time to confer in the field with the Commander-in-Chief of the enemy forces in the earnest effort to find any military means whereby realization of the political objectives of the United Nations in Korea, to which no nation may justly take exception, might be accomplished without further bloodshed.[20]

Issuance of this communiqué, which was hardly a routine military appraisal as described, violated the injunction laid down by the Joint Chiefs of Staff the previous December 6 that all but the most routine statements by MacArthur had to be cleared with Washington. The wording and tone of this declaration, in effect, threatened Communist China with destruction if it did not agree to peace in Korea on pretty much the UN's terms. It certainly made it difficult for the enemy to believe that the United States government was seriously interested in a cease-fire. MacArthur later "confessed" that his intent had been to spike the administration's "secret plan" to buy peace in Korea by surrendering Formosa to the Communists and transferring Taipeh's seat in the United Nations to Peking.[21]

What the evidence for this "secret plan" may have been, it is hard to tell. The hope for a general settlement of Far Eastern questions had been expressed before, and the President now specifically called for a cease-fire prior to any general conference. Indeed, there was no guarantee that any such conference would ever take place. No one in the administration at this point believed in the innocence of the Chinese Communists. Although it was hoped that the historical and geopolitical sources of friction between China and Russia would sooner or later alienate Peking from its Soviet mentors, no one looked upon the Mao regime as friendly, or even normally trustworthy. What the administration wanted to do was to reduce the cost of containing Communist China.

News of the MacArthur communiqué reached Washington the night after its issuance and galvanized the administration's policy planners into action. Secretary Acheson met with a small number of concerned officials, including Under Secretary of Defense Lovett and Assistant Secretary of State Dean Rusk; they agreed, without dissent, that MacArthur had to be removed. Mr. Truman concurred, in principle, when they met with him the next morning. "By this act," he wrote later, "MacArthur left me no choice—I could no longer tolerate his insubordination."[22] Immediately, however, the President directed Mr. Lovett to have MacArthur sent a message from the Joint Chiefs reminding him of his duty under the "restraining order" of December 6. The message added, "The President has also directed that in the event Communist military leaders request an armistice in the field, you immediately report that fact to the JCS for instructions."[23]

The President had made up his mind to replace his overmighty general, but planning the details of the removal took some days. Not only was it politic as well as courteous to handle the matter delicately, but it was essential that allied and enemy governments, along with the American people, should understand just what MacArthur's relief meant, and what it did not mean. The delay, however, caused the removal to be carried out abruptly, under something like crisis conditions.

Joseph W. Martin, minority leader of the House of Representatives (and Speaker in the Eightieth Congress), wrote to MacArthur on March 8, observing that although the European aspects of foreign policy had been carefully examined, Congress had not had the benefit of the Far Eastern commander's views. Martin observed that he opposed weakening the American position in Asia out of overanxiety for Europe, reporting that in a recent speech he had urged using Generalissimo Chiang's troops to establish a second front in Asia. Since the general "always felt duty-bound to reply frankly to every Congressional inquiry into matters connected with [his] official responsibility," he answered Martin on March 20:

My views and recommendations, with respect to the situation created by Red Chinese entry into war against us in Korea, have been submitted to Washington in most complete detail. Generally these views . . . follow the conventional pattern of meeting force with maximum counterforce as we have never failed to do in the past. Your view with respect to the utilization of the Chinese forces on Formosa is in conflict with neither logic nor this tradition. It seems strangely difficult for some to realize that here in Asia is where the Communist conspirators have elected to make their play for global conquest, and that we have joined the issue thus raised on the battlefield; that here we fight Europe's war with arms while the diplomats there still fight it with words; that if we lose the war to Communism in Asia the fall of Europe is inevitable; win it and Europe most probably would avoid war and yet preserve freedom. As you point out, we must win. There is no substitute for victory.[24]

Representative Martin told some friends in the party and the press corps that he would drop a bombshell in the House on Thursday, April 5—and he was as good as his word. On that day he read MacArthur's letter of March 20 on the floor, presumably without the general's consent.[25] The President met next morning with Secretary Acheson, Secretary Marshall, Mr. Harriman, and General Omar N. Bradley, Chairman of the Joint Chiefs of Staff. Mr. Acheson recommended removal of MacArthur, but advised caution in the doing of it because of the political repercussions it was sure to provoke. He also suggested that the President have the unanimous advice of the Joint Chiefs before acting. General Marshall expressed concern about the difficulties that might overtake the military appropriation bill then before Congress if MacArthur were dismissed precipitately. Mr. Harriman was of the opinion that the General should have been fired two years before, when he showed a disposition to go his own way in the governance of Japan, without reference to United States policy. General Bradley regarded the question as primarily one of military discipline, and he believed that MacArthur had been obviously insubordinate. He did wish, however, to consult with his colleagues on the Joint Chiefs of Staff before offering a final recommendation.[26]

At a short meeting twenty-four hours later, Mr. Truman asked General Bradley to present the opinions of the Joint Chiefs on Monday morning. On April 9, accordingly, the Chairman reported the unanimous opinion of the service Chiefs of Staff that MacArthur be relieved. Secretaries Ache-

son and Marshall and Mr. Harriman concurred without further discussion, and the President commented that he had
made up his mind to take this step on March 24. It was firmly
decided that the recalcitrant General must be stripped of all
his commands, not merely that in Korea, as had been considered some days earlier. His replacement was to be General
Ridgway, then commanding the Eighth Army in Korea.

Secretary of the Army Frank Pace, who was presumed to be
at Eighth Army headquarters on an inspection, was designated to go to Tokyo and give the news to MacArthur in person. Some difficulty was encountered in locating Mr. Pace,
however, since he was in fact at the front. In the course of this
delay there was a leak of information, and the White House
learned on the evening of April 10 that the Chicago *Tribune*
would carry the story the next morning. The President decided at once that the administration could not afford the luxury of waiting for MacArthur to be notified personally, and,
at a press conference called at one o'clock on the morning of
April 11, Press Secretary Joseph Short released the news. General MacArthur thus learned of his dismissal from a radio
news broadcast—not quite the most graceful firing in history.
But, however the form, the mighty had fallen, perhaps to the
muffled strains of the *Magnificat.*

Congressional reaction to the news was instantaneous. Joe
Martin called a meeting of Republican leaders in his office
that morning at nine-thirty, and Senators Taft, Knowland,
and Bridges, and Representatives Charles E. Halleck of Indiana, Leonard Hall of New York, and Dewey Short of Missouri
gathered to confer with the House minority leader. A serious
discussion (initiated by Taft) of the possibility of impeach-
ing Mr. Truman occupied their attention for several minutes.

Martin, however, felt that the President had acted within his constitutional rights, even if the dismissal of MacArthur had been most unwise.

The Senators left for a time to meet with John Foster Dulles in Taft's office. Dulles, then Republican adviser to Secretary Acheson and the current symbol of bipartisanship, wanted to resign, but the Senators persuaded him he was of more use to the party where he was. When Taft and his colleagues returned to the larger meeting, it was agreed that Martin should approach Speaker Rayburn about inviting General MacArthur to address a joint session of Congress. The minority leader did so immediately after the party conference, and although the Speaker was not notably enthusiastic about the suggestion, he bowed to the precedent established by similar invitations to General Eisenhower and other returning heroes of World War II.[27] The Republican leaders were convinced that they had found a champion who would carry great weight with the public, and they were determined to make the most of him. Although Martin professed himself "appalled" by his own role in the general's relief, he nevertheless told himself that this deposed hero "might truly be the answer to our prayers."[28]

The GOP moved at once to the attack. The ebullient Senator Jenner expounded the "party line" interpretation of the controversy: "I charge that this country today is in the hands of a secret inner coterie which is directed by agents of the Soviet Union."[29] Party leaders, together with a few Democratic allies, prepared the way for a joint investigation of the affair by the Senate Foreign Relations and Armed Services Committees. On MacArthur's return, he was assiduously attended by Republican notables seeking to enlist his support for the

1952 campaign. Some of these, unquestionably, pictured him not only as Harry Truman's nemesis, but successor as well. And he was surely not discouraged by several weeks of enthusiastic public welcomes in which he was subjected to continuous demonstrations of popular adulation, while he and his congressional supporters were swamped by letters and postcards wishing him well in the struggle against the "boneheads" or "traitors" in Washington.

The Senate hearings, however, had the effect of deflating the picture of an omniscient MacArthur. Many Americans, to be sure, found their faith in him confirmed, but perhaps as many others discovered that his views, once elaborated and carefully examined, were less convincing than they had seemed at first blush and began to see sense in the administration's position. A very large body of citizens, including some who yet leaned to the general's outlook, came to find in his clash with the President nothing more menacing than an honest difference as to how the interests of the nation might be best served. Above all, MacArthur's love of pomp and frequent displays of personal vanity became boring, if not irritating, to a large element of the public; he tended to justify, by negative example, the principle of civilian dominance even to those unenamored of the President.

Viewed in retrospect, MacArthur's strategic plan for victory in Asia was flimsy, both militarily and politically. The Defense Department experts and the Joint Chiefs of Staff did not believe we could bomb Communist China into submission; the industrial plant to be destroyed, for one thing, provided only a small part of Peking's military equipment. General Hoyt Vandenberg, Chief of Staff of the Air Force, thought that the cost in men and planes of the operation would prevent us from maintaining adequate defenses at home and in Western Europe for two years thereafter. Air attacks across the Yalu, moreover, would have meant an end of the unspoken agreement that sheltered American bases in southern Korea and Japan. The Communists were not alone in possessing a "privileged sanctuary."

As for a blockade of the China coast, such a maneuver would have been accepted by the neutral nations only if made perfectly effective—and that could not have been done without closing the port of Hong Kong, a British Crown Colony, and the Soviet-held ports of Dairen and Port Arthur. The one step would have alienated an ally, the other invited World War III.

The opposition of President Syngman Rhee of South Korea was a major obstacle to the use of Chinese Nationalist troops in the defense of his country. "Freeing" Chiang to raid the mainland would have required a heavy investment of American equipment in the enterprise and a major commitment of American naval and air units. And, like MacArthur himself, the Joint Chiefs had little faith in the combat value of Chiang's army. There was no reason to believe that renewed contact with the Communist enemy would not lead to additional mass defections, and perhaps some grounds for suspecting that it would.

MacArthur's program, too, rested on the implicit thesis that Western Europe was of secondary importance to East Asia. The advanced technology and developed industrial plant, the trained manpower, the available air bases, the readily exploitable raw materials of Western Europe, not to mention our emotionally and politically potent bonds of culture and inheritance with that region, compelled the administration to reverse MacArthur's priorities.

> It was not therefore a "no-win" policy insinuated into our high councils by faceless subversives that guided the administration in its rejection of MacArthur's recommended program. It was essentially adherence to a basically different policy: a different interpretation of the word "victory"; a different view of the facts based on a better knowledge of the world situation.[30]

The opposition, however, preferred to believe with MacArthur that only subversives, faceless or not, could have deflected us from victory in Asia, victory to be won on the cheap with Chinese cannon-fodder from Formosa and sealed by daring fly-boys larking in the Manchurian skies, victory unchallenged by any sort of Soviet intervention.

NOTES

1. The JCS were convinced that MacArthur had to be relieved for three reasons. First, because he was not in sympathy with national policy in Korea, he would find it increasingly difficult to carry out the Chiefs' directives; second, he had failed to comply with a presidential directive to clear statements on policy with his superiors before making them public; third, his actions tended to jeopardize civilian control over the military authorities. Memorandum for W. Averell Harriman from Theodore Tannenwald, Jr., May 29, 1951, Papers of Theodore Tannenwald, Jr.

2. Norman A. Graebner, *The New Isolationism: A Study in Politics and Foreign Policy Since 1950* (New York: The Ronald Press Company, 1956), p. 28.

3. *New York Times,* August 15, 1950.

4. Cited in Graebner, *The New Isolationism,* p. 28.

5. This is one of the basic themes found in Graebner, *The New*

Isolationism. See also Samuel Lubell, *Revolt of the Moderates* (New York: Harper & Bros., 1951) , *passim.*

6. Harry S. Truman, *Memoirs* (Garden City, N.Y.: Doubleday & Co., 1956) , vol. 2, *Years of Trial and Hope,* p. 341.

7. John W. Spanier, *The Truman-MacArthur Controversy and the Korean War* (New York: W. W. Norton & Co., 1965) , p. 32.

8. George F. Kennan felt that UN involvement in the war was in no way necessary or called for. The United States had accepted the responsibilities of military occupation in South Korea, and these responsibilities could not be legally terminated in the absence of a Japanese peace treaty. The American right, even duty, to act unilaterally was therefore fully established. George F. Kennan, *Memoirs, 1925–1950* (Boston: Little, Brown and Co., 1967) , p. 490.

9. Cited in Truman, vol. 2, *Memoirs,* p. 351. Emphasis supplied.

10. Cited in Spanier, *The Truman-MacArthur Controversy,* p. 73.

11. *New York Times,* October 12, 1950.

12. Cited in Matthew B. Ridgway, *The Korean War* (Garden City, N.Y.: Doubleday & Co., 1967) , p. 145.

13. An excellent case could be made for the argument that the war had been won when the North Korean Army was driven in rout back across the thirty-eighth parallel. That victory was thrown away by the desire of the administration, the opposition leaders, and certain heads of allied governments for a more spectacular result. By the end of September, 1950, the original aims of the intervention had been completely achieved.

14. Although the initial fears of the State Department on this score seem to have been unfounded, it is reasonable to suppose that Stalin would have been tempted to move if the United States had made a full commitment of available forces to Korea.

15. Allied capitals were seriously alarmed when the President implied, during his November 30 press conference, that the atom bomb might be used in Korea, with the decision on its use left to the theater commander. A quick "clarification" of his remarks did not immediately allay apprehension. Cabell Phillips, *The Truman Presidency: The History of a Triumphant Succession* (New York: The Macmillan Company, 1966) , p. 329.

16. *Ibid.,* pp. 330–331.

17. Cited in ibid., pp. 329–330.

18. Truman, vol. 2, *Memoirs,* pp. 435–436.

19. *Ibid.,* pp. 439–440.

20. Douglas MacArthur, *Reminiscences* (New York: McGraw-Hill Book Co., 1964) , pp. 387–388.

21. *New York Times,* October 18, 1951.

22. Truman, vol. 2, *Memoirs,* p. 442.

23. *Ibid.,* p. 443.

24. MacArthur, *Reminiscences,* p. 386.

25. MacArthur took the position that since he had not given specific permission for the release of the letter, he should have been able to assume that Martin would not make it public. Ibid., p. 389. Martin, for his part, waited ten days to see if MacArthur would specifically request that the letter be withheld. Trumbull Higgins, *Korea and the Fall of MacArthur: A Précis in Limited War* (New York: Oxford University Press, 1960), pp. 114–115. One has the feeling that neither man was being wholly candid.

26. Truman, vol. 2, *Memoirs,* p. 447.

27. Joseph W. Martin, Jr., *My First Fifty Years in Politics,* as told to Robert J. Donovan (New York: McGraw-Hill Book Co., 1960), pp. 208–209.

28. Ibid., pp. 208, 209–210.

29. Cited in Phillips, *The Truman Presidency,* p. 345.

30. Matthew B. Ridgway, *The Korean War* (Garden City, N.Y.: Doubleday & Co., 1967, p. 149. The analysis of administration policy is taken from ibid., pp. 146–148. General Ridgway has been the only person to date given access to Mr. Truman's private papers.

10

Exit Fighting

DURING the last year and a half of its life, the Truman administration was continuously subjected to harassment on the score of its alleged "softness" toward Communism. The MacArthur controversy, by keeping public attention fastened on the administration's foreign and military policies, allowed the most vociferous of opposition spokesmen to keep questioning whether the President had been merely given "bad advice" or whether he had been duped into playing the Kremlin's game.

The most sensational attack, and the most bizarre, was made by Senator McCarthy on General Marshall on June 14, 1951. Or, rather, McCarthy delivered perhaps a third of a sixty-thousand-word speech on the Senate floor that day, causing the whole to be published in the *Congressional Record*.

The speech, as published, is largely a review of Marshall's career as Army Chief of Staff, presidential emissary to China, and Secretary of State. In his direction of allied strategy in World War II, in carrying out his mission to China in 1946,

McCarthy insisted, he consciously did Stalin's work. It was Marshall who, as Secretary of State, headed the most immense conspiracy in the history of man. He had blood on his hands. "[U]nless we understand the record of Marshall," the Senator asserted, "it will be impossible . . . to foretell the next move on the timetable of the great conspiracy."[1]

This attack was no more savage than that made on Marshall by Senator Jenner the previous September; in its language, in fact, it was no more violent and far less vulgar. But Jenner's charges, while they must have found some believers, did not damage the general's position, and they found no second until McCarthy decided to try a bolt. It is likely, of course, that the issue of Communists-in-government was so identified in the popular mind with McCarthy's name that allegations coming from him had a special authenticity to the susceptible. In this case, moreover, he presented what he called documentation, although it was for the most part a simple recital of Marshall's career. And even though McCarthy's interpretations were imposed upon the events and opinions cited, rather than drawn from them, some people were impressed by the apparent thoroughness. McCarthy's attack on Marshall stuck to some degree, and while the General's reputation was not *seriously* harmed, even in the summer of 1951, Marshall's position as a noncontroversial figure was ruined.[2]

The most reasonable explanation for the attack, and for the scatter-gun charges against persons close to the President that followed over the succeeding year, is that McCarthy was anxious to regain some control over what he must have regarded as *his* issue. It was particularly important to him since it was his only issue; his entire public reputation rested on it. The onset of the Korean conflict had driven him from the headlines, and the publication of the Tydings subcommittee report had briefly silenced his most powerful supporters, who waited to see if he would be damaged. Although his intervention in the congressional campaign had been well publicized, he was no longer carrying the ball in the Senate. The Republican leadership led the assault against the administration's foreign policy, while, on a lower level, Senator Mundt had managed to stake out the investigation of "perverts" as his own preserve. Now the so-called MacArthur hearings, in which he had no important part, held public attention. Since he had learned that neither the wildest implausibility nor even the total lack of evidence could inhibit acceptance of his charges at face value by a substantial number of people, the audacious derogation of highly placed persons must have recommended itself to him as a means of sustaining his place in the limelight.

While McCarthy was thus occupied with keeping his name before the public, more serious investigations in "his" field remained in other hands. The Internal Security Subcommittee of the Senate Judiciary Committee undertook, beginning in July, 1951, an investigation of the Institute of Pacific Relations, an international association of national research councils in ten countries with marked interest with Far Eastern affairs. The subcommittee argued, from the material it gathered, that by establishing "close organic relations with the State Department," a "group of persons operating within and about the Institute of Pacific Relations exerted a substantial influence on United States far eastern policy."[3] And because it was able to discover evidence of a Communist cell within the Institute, and to show that fellow travelers played an important role in making Institute policy,[4] it insinuated that it had proved a subversive origin for the policies that led to the "loss of China." It did find respectable academic former members of the Institute who considered Owen Lattimore to be a fellow traveler and it was able to produce some old correspondence that indicated Dr. Lattimore's sympathy for the Chinese Communists. It did not, however, demonstrate that his attitude sprang from an ideological bias.

Cases made out against certain State Department officials and Foreign Service officers are even more clearly suppositional. The Foreign Service men of whom General Hurley complained had misjudged the Chinese Communists precisely as Hurley had, although it led them to different conclusions. Error is not identifiable with treason, and there was no evidence offered that the men impugned had any affinity for Communist doctrine. Their tolerance of the Yenan group, indeed, grew out of the mistaken assumption that these were not real Communists. John Carter Vincent was supposed to have influenced Vice-President Wallace on his mission to China in favor of the Communists, but Vincent also recommended the recall of General Stilwell and his replacement by General Wedemeyer. Vincent's membership in the Institute of Pacific Relations proved nothing in itself, and the subcommittee's apparent shock that "Vincent of the IPR" influenced American policy was disingenuous in light of the man's position as director of the Far Eastern Division of the State Department. In still more tenuous fashion, the subcommittee regarded as suspicious Philip Jessup's calling of a conference at the State Department in October, 1949, during which the possibility of recognizing Red China was discussed.[5] As if the job of State Department officers were not to consider alternative possibilities on such questions!

The subcommittee, working at its job as McCarthy never did, established a serious question about Dr. Lattimore, but it was otherwise unable to add flesh to any of McCarthy's cases. It did manage, however, to thicken the prevailing atmosphere of doubt. McCarthy's talent was to raise questions, unsupported by data, which, in a time of suspicion, were taken by many people as answers. The repetition of names he had thrown out by a subcommittee under Democratic control had for some the impact of proof.[6] Certainly, fear of such a response induced extreme caution in Congress. It was not a great surprise, then, when it was reported on October 13, 1951, that the chances for confirmation of Ambassador Jessup as a member of the United States delegation to the General Assembly of the United Nations were very dim. Majority Leader McFarland had been informed that a number of southern Senators were committed against the appointment. Richard B. Russell of Georgia, a power in the Senate, appeared to be in full retreat from his decision to support confirmation; possibly the best to hope from him was that, out of a friendly feeling for McFarland, he would be absent when the vote was taken. As matters stood,

> Senator Sparkman as head of the subcommittee [would] issue some kind of a wishy-washy statement to the effect that his subcommittee has a vast amount of material to be examined, and recommending that the nomination be studied further (bottled up in the subcommittee). Although the vigorous supporters of Jessup were horrified at first at this surrender, they have come to the conclusion that this would be preferable to risking almost certain defeat on the floor.[7]

The White House could now be sure that the attacks on the

State Department would continue. On October 17, Matt Connelly was replying to Senator McCarran, who had inquired about a report filed through the District Intelligence Office of the Third Naval District to the effect that John Carter Vincent was a Communist. The informant filing the report had not revealed his source of information or provided any other evidence in support of it. On investigation, Connelly stated, the informant was determined to be a reserve officer, Lieutenant-Commander Robert Morris, at the time of writing special counsel to the Republican members of the Senate's Internal Security Subcommittee.[8] There was a suspicion in the White House that Mr. Morris, while not manufacturing evidence, was planting an allegation, so that he might provide the smoke if he could not establish the fire.

Several months later—on July 1, 1952—the President felt compelled to warn Attorney General James P. McGranery:

> I have heard a report to the effect that Senator McCarran may seek to have John Davies, of the State Department, indicted for perjury on the basis of testimony before his committee. I think this is just another example of witch-hunting, and if anything of the kind is tried, I would like for you to consult me before the Department of Justice takes any action.[9]

John Paton Davies had been cleared of suspicion by the Loyalty Board of the State Department on October 17, 1951, and the Loyalty Review Board reluctantly concurred on the following December 12. The Board's reluctance was occasioned by its taking upon itself to question Mr. Davies's political judgment (an exercise for which it was hardly qualified) rather than by doubt of his loyalty.[10] At the same time, it ruled against John Stewart Service, despite the no bill returned by the grand jury in the *Amerasia* case and several clearances by the departmental board.[11] He was dismissed by Secretary Acheson the next day.[12]

Charles Murphy, writing for the President, was obliged to direct the Archivist of the United States, on July 5, 1952, to deny the Internal Security Subcommittee any information concerning Owen Lattimore from the Roosevelt files.[13] The information, some of which was still classified, was available to the FBI and appropriate officials of the Justice Department, and since Lattimore had been indicted on seven counts of perjury by a federal grand jury after his testimony before the subcommittee the previous winter, the matter was now one for the courts to resolve.[14] The subcommittee had completed its useful work.

Senator McCarthy, in pressing his new attack, struck directly at the White House. Attacking the President's staff, he must have thought, might pay the highest dividends. An assault on David D. Lloyd, an administrative assistant since 1948, for his former membership in the National Lawyers' Guild, fizzled out.[15] McCarthy also publicly announced that the FBI had uncovered "derogatory information" concerning Philleo Nash, who had taken over David Niles's duties (although he was not appointed administrative assistant in his own right until December, 1952). "Tail-Gunner Joe" telegraphed the President on February 3, 1952, demanding that Mr. Truman make public the loyalty files.[16] At the insistence of the Loyalty Review Board and its parent body, the Civil Service Commission, which obviously felt intimidated, the White House created a special loyalty board to hear and judge Mr. Nash's record.[17] The hearing resulted in a complete clearance and, once again, McCarthy abandoned the "case."

McCarthy's career of slander, as we have seen, reached its peak in his denunciation of General Marshall. Many Senators were shocked by this attack and began, if they had not previously done so, to entertain the most profound misgivings about McCarthy's behavior. But the Senate was unable to muster sufficient courage, collectively or individually, to curb its Frankenstein monster; while no excess of his appeared to disconcert his hard-core supporters. President Truman greatly admired Marshall, perhaps above any other living man, but— because McCarthy did not go beyond assertion, and that under cloak of immunity on the Senate floor—he was unable to do more than denounce this incredible (and wholly unsubstantiated) charge. So long as McCarthy made his charges on the floor of the Senate, he was safe from the slander and libel laws; so long as he stuck to voicing suspicions without permitting them to be examined in serious investigations, he could convince a fair number of people that there *must* be something fishy about the persons accused. And as long as he was thus shielded from massive public doubt, his colleagues feared to challenge him, even to defend the office of the Chief Magistrate.

Meantime, the President and his staff found that they had to go on trying to supervise, as best they could, the administration of the loyalty program and the security laws. Boards continued their facile discoveries of subversive associations.[18] After the collapse of the Nimitz Commission, Mr. Truman sent the following memorandum to his Special Counsel:

I have been very much disturbed with the action of some of these

[Loyalty] Boards and I want to find some way to put a stop to their un-American activities. I wish you would have one of our staff boys look into this situation very carefully and make a recommendation to me.

Of course, it was the intention to have the Nimitz Commission go into these matters but it looks now as if we are not going to get any Nimitz Commission.[19]

Some little while later, the President followed up his request to Charles Murphy with a letter to the Executive Secretary of the National Security Council, asking that the NSC, utilizing the Interdepartmental Committee on Internal Security, and with the participation of the Civil Service Commission, investigate the administration of the Government Employee Security Program.[20] The ICIS report was transmitted to the NSC on April 29, 1952, and even in summary form it could hardly have been comforting reading for Mr. Truman:

The ICIS made no findings as to whether employees have been wronged by agency decisions in individual security cases. However, it did find certain defects in existing employee security programs: (1) some positions designated "sensitive" do not actually relate to national security; (2) some cases should have been handled on suitability rather than security grounds; (3) some suspensions of employees have been too hasty and not necessary in the interest of national security; (4) charges in some cases have been too vague to permit intelligent defense; (5) cases have not been adjudicated expeditiously; (6) some agencies have no procedural rules for handling security cases; (7) there is lack of uniformity in standards and procedures; (8) employees sometimes are coerced into resigning; (9) demotions to non-sensitive positions are not reviewed; (10) transfers are subjected to repeated investigations and clearances; (11) a person found a "security risk" can't get another job even in a non-sensitive agency; and (12) there is no central review of agency removal actions.[21]

Here, as in the loyalty program, is found something more than occasional unintelligent administration. There was clearly political bias in the application of regulations and, even more commonly, no doubt, fear on the part of subordinate administrators to take any but the harshest line under the prevailing circumstances. The reforms incident upon this report had not, unfortunately, been completed before the Truman administration left office, to be replaced by a regime far more prone to pursue the phantom of absolute security.

And the Truman administration went out of office, so far as loyalty and security matters were concerned, still bedeviled, as it had been for six years, by those who believed it possible to close every possible door to subversion by legislating against it, no matter what the cost to civil liberties. Nearly to the end, the President had to fight a largely unsuccessful rearguard action against drastic security measures raised up in Congress. The last major battle in this area was fought over the McCarran-Walter bill to revise the immigration laws. The White House staff advised against the measure because of its draconian and inequitable features.[22] And on June 21, 1952, Averell Harriman, who had become Director for Mutual Security the previous fall, wrote Mr. Truman:

Although the McCarran-Walter bill (H.R. 5678) will not materially affect our various mutual security programs, I personally feel very strongly that it does such violence to the traditions and heritage of this nation that I am compelled to urge you to veto it.

The bill represents the first major revision of our immigration

laws since 1924. As such I think it should make a contribution to
the solution of some of the problems we face in the world; it
should be in harmony with the spirit which animates our foreign
policy and our relations with other countries; and it should
strengthen our claim to leadership of the free world. Measured by
these standards, it is a thoroughly bad bill.

Except for two liberalizing provisions—the naturalization of
Japanese and other Asiatics and the establishment of quotas for
certain Asiatic countries hitherto barred—and some minor improvements, the bill retains most of the bad or outmoded features
of our present laws, and then goes on to add a whole series of
new provisions which in many ways will give us an even worse
statute than what we now have. I particularly wish to point out
that it reenacts provisions of the Internal Security Act of 1950,
which you so vigorously denounced at the time you vetoed it.

The legislation looks upon immigrants and aliens with suspicion and hostility. It establishes unjustifiably restrictive principles
of selection. It erects new and even more arbitrary barriers to
entry. It transforms naturalized citizens into an inferior class and
makes them subject to denaturalization on new grounds of uncertain effect. The bill retroactively subjects aliens to deportation for
acts which were not grounds for deportation when committed. It
curtails and, in some cases, removes the right of appeal and abol-
ishes the statute of limitations. References in the bill to persons
whose ancestry is one-half Asiatic is more in keeping with the Nuremberg laws than with American conceptions. It establishes
grounds for exclusion, denaturalization and deportation which are
unreasonable and unwarranted. It provides a basis for unreasonable search and interrogation of American citizens lawfully returning to this country. It does nothing to give us a fairer and more
up-to-date quota system that takes into account our new responsibilities in the world and the new relationship we are trying to
develop with other countries.

> This bill is another manifestation of that ugly trend among certain elements in our national life, which I can only characterize as mean, shortsighted, fearful and bigoted. I fervently hope that you can see your way to reject it in the most vigorous terms.[23]

State Department experts, the General Counsel of the Immigration Service, and other authorities were called in to advise the Senate Judiciary Committee in preparing this legislation. The Justice Department recommended its approval to the President. But Mr. Truman, under concerted pressure from a unanimous staff and other persons close to him, such as Mr. Harriman, decided in the end to veto the bill.[24]

The veto message was couched in the strongest terms:

> I am asked to approve the reenactment of highly objectionable provisions contained in the Internal Security Act of 1950 —a measure passed over my veto shortly after the invasion of South Korea. Some of these provisions would empower the Attorney General to deport any alien who has engaged or who has a purpose to engage in activities "prejudicial to the public interest" or "subversive to the national security." No standards or definitions are provided to guide discretion in the exercise of powers so sweeping. To punish undefined "activities" departs from traditional American insistence on established standards of guilt. To punish an undefined "purpose" is thought control.[25]

This crisp rejection of what so many believed to be an iniquitous measure was in vain. The McCarran-Walter Act, like the Internal Security Act before it, was passed over the President's veto. It was perhaps too much to expect Congress to do otherwise in an election year, particularly since the administration was without effective leadership in the Senate.

The issue of domestic Communism was agitated and exploited by the Republican opposition in 1952 as it had not been four years earlier. Moderates in both parties had hoped that the issue might be minimized when the GOP nominated General of the Army Dwight D. Eisenhower as its presidential candidate. General Eisenhower, a genuine popular hero of World War II, was a man of such obvious decency and common sense that it could be hoped that he might keep his party's campaign within bounds. Mr. Truman has recalled that even he felt, as the Eisenhower candidacy first took shape, that the right man might have emerged.[26] Since the President was a convinced and honest partisan, this feeling passed quickly, but a reasonable hope that the general would campaign on a high level persisted.[27] The Republicans' selection of Richard M. Nixon for second place on their ticket, however, was not comforting. Senator Nixon was as exclusively identified in the public mind with the Communist issue—albeit on a different level—as Senator McCarthy. His relative youth—he was thirty-nine years old, to the general's sixty-one —might be cited as a reason for the choice, but the fact remained that his exposure of Alger Hiss was at that time his sole claim to national prominence. There was evidence, moreover, that the Republican leadership in Congress still supported McCarthy. General Eisenhower's still-powerful defeated rival for the presidential nomination, Robert Taft, said of McCarthy's smashing primary victory in Wisconsin: "I didn't endorse him, you know, because I never interfere in other state primaries. But I did and do approve of his accomplishments in rooting out Communists and subversives in Government."[28] Who, precisely, had been rooted out Taft did not say.

The Democrats were themselves acutely conscious of the possibilities, whatever they might have hoped of Eisenhower. After the President had concluded that Governor Adlai E. Stevenson of Illinois would be his party's strongest candidate, the White House staff undertook to estimate if Stevenson's having given a deposition in support of Alger Hiss would injure him politically—without being able to reach a positive decision.[29] When Stevenson had become the Democratic presidential candidate, after long months of hesitation, the question was in some sense answered. The Republicans thought, at least, that he was vulnerable on the matter of his relations with Hiss. McCarthy, for example, was widely active in the campaign, but his efforts were best remembered afterward for his disingenuous reference to "Alger" Stevenson.[30]

It was, however, Senator Nixon, who, politically speaking, "owned" Hiss, who made the most of this point. Speaking on October 13 on a nationally televised program, he gave a long and detailed review of the Hiss case. His conclusion tied the case to the present campaign:

> Mr. Stevenson was a character witness, or should I say a witness for the reputation, and the good reputation, of Alger Hiss. He testified that the reputation of Alger Hiss for veracity, for integrity, and for loyalty was good. . . . This testimony . . . was given after all these facts, this confrontation in which Hiss had to look into Chambers' mouth to identify him, after these papers came out of the pumpkin, after all of those facts were known . . . it was voluntary on Mr. Stevenson's part . . . it was given at a time when he was Governor of Illinois and the prestige of a great state and the Governor of the state were thrown in behalf of the defendant in this case. . . . It is significant that Mr. Stevenson has never ex-

pressed any indignation over what Mr. Hiss has done and the treachery that he engaged in against his country.

Let me emphasize that there is no question in my mind as to the loyalty of Mr. Stevenson, but the question is one as to his judgment, and it is a very grave question. . . . In my opinion, his actions, his statements, his record disqualifies [*sic*] him from leading the United States and the free nations in the fight against Communism at home and abroad; because, you see, the election of Mr. Stevenson would mean four more years of the same policy which has been so disastrous at home and disastrous abroad for America.[31]

So far as issues went, none contributed more to Republican victory than the supposed threat of Communist subversion at home, neatly packaged with frustration over the course of the war in Korea. General Eisenhower's popularity, reputation, and extrapartisan aura enabled many normally Democratic and "independent" voters to register their negative emotions with a sense of affirmation.

NOTES

1. Richard H. Rovere, *Senator Joe McCarthy* (New York: Harcourt, Brace & Co., 1959) , pp. 172–177.
2. Rovere makes this point convincingly. Ibid., pp. 178–179.
3. Earl Latham, *The Communist Controversy in Washington: From the New Deal to McCarthy* (Cambridge, Mass.: Harvard University Press, 1966) , pp. 298–299.
4. Ibid., p. 302. The review of the IPR investigation is taken from ibid., pp. 296–316.
5. Ibid., p. 278
6. Since Pat McCarran was chairman of the Senate Judiciary Committee and its Internal Security Subcommittee and James O. Eastland of Mississippi was chairman of the special subcommittee of the latter body

investigating the Institute of Pacific Relations, the "proof" is a little unconvincing. Both Senators were inveterate opponents of the administration.

7. Memorandum for Charles S. Murphy from Kenneth W. Hechler, October 13, 1951, Papers of Charles S. Murphy.

8. Papers of HST, Official File 1279.

9. Papers of Charles S. Murphy.

10. Senator Taft himself learned what "derogatory information" could amount to on occasion while defending President Eisenhower's nomination of Charles E. Bohlen to be Ambassador to the Soviet Union. The appointment was under attack by a number of orthodox Republican conservatives as well as by McCarthy. Taft agreed to go with Senator Sparkman to read the FBI summary of its file on Mr. Bohlen. In reporting to the Senate on March 25, 1953, "Mr. Republican" referred to "sixteen pages of derogatory information" supposed to be in the files, saying, "The greater part of it consists of statements of persons who disagree with Mr. Bohlen's principles with respect to foreign policy. . . . In other words, they were statements of political differences with Mr. Bohlen." Cited in William S. White, *The Taft Story* (New York: Harper & Bros., 1954), p. 237.

11. The Review Board's attention was drawn to these facts by the White House. Interview with Donald A. Hansen, June 9, 1967.

12. The Review Board decision opened a door for Service's dismissal that had previously been closed. The behavior exposed in the *Amerasia* case suggested that he might be a de facto security risk, although he did not fall within the legal definition of such. Ironically, Service's dismissal was invalidated later by the Supreme Court on the grounds that the department had violated its own relevant regulations. Wallace Mendelson, *The Constitution and the Supreme Court* (New York: Dodd, Mead & Co., 1959) pp. 312–313.

13. Papers of Charles S. Murphy.

14. On May 2, 1953, Federal Judge Luther W. Youngdahl dismissed the first four counts of the indictment, and said that there were "serious doubts" about the validity of the other three. On August 24, 1953, the Justice Department asked the Court of Appeals to restore the four counts. On July 8, 1954, the Court of Appeals restored two of the counts but on June 28, 1955, the Attorney General ordered all charges dismissed. Latham, *The Communist Controversy*, p. 305 n.

15. Interviews with Stephen J. Spingarn, March 17, 1962, and Donald A. Hansen, March 28, 1967.

16. Papers of HST, Official File 3327.

17. Interview with Donald A. Hansen, June 9, 1967.

18. See pp. 48–50.

19. May 24, 1951, Papers of HST, Official File 2750-A.

20. July 14, 1951, Papers of HST, Official File 2750.

21. Memorandum, Papers of HST, Files of Martin L. Friedman.

22. Memorandum for the President from David D. Lloyd, May 3, 1952, Papers of HST, Files of David D. Lloyd.

23. Ibid.

24. Oral History Interview No. 8 (Donald A. Hansen, April 5, 1963), pp. 10–12. Harry S. Truman Library.

25. Papers of HST, Files of David D. Lloyd.

26. Interview with former President Truman, July 21, 1961.

27. Harry S. Truman, *Memoirs* (Garden City, N.Y.: Doubleday & Co., 1956), vol. 2, *Years of Trial and Hope*, p. 501.

28. Cited in White, *The Taft Story*, p. 87.

29. Charles S. Murphy to Samuel I. Rosenman, February 27, 1952, Papers of Charles S. Murphy.

30. Rovere, *Senator Joe McCarthy*, p. 182.

31. Cited in Earl Mazo, *Richard Nixon: A Political and Personal Portrait* (New York: Harper & Bros., 1959), pp. 67–68. At his news conference on February 6, 1969, President Nixon was queried about the fact that his nominee to be Ambassador to the United Nations, Charles Yost, had once testified to the good character of Alger Hiss. The President replied that that was in the past, that what mattered was what a man could do for his country now and in the future. The point, obviously, is not the eminently sensible answer, but that the question was asked at all. It seems likely that it was designed to evoke memories of what Senator Nixon had said so long ago, on this same score, about Governor Stevenson. Survivors of the Communist controversy—on both sides—have long memories.

11

The White House and
the Communist Issue

An Estimate

THE Truman administration cannot be held entirely blame-
less for its own predicament. The institution of the loyalty
program was accompanied by rather too much stress on protection against subversion and rather too little on protection
of traditional rights. Probably not enough time was allowed
to devise the program; certainly it was done under pressure.
Despite the President's genuine concern with how the program was administered, concerted efforts at reform were not
launched before second-line (or third-line) administrators
within the executive departments had yielded their judgment
to what must have seemed the greater power outside. The appointment of persons sympathetic—in some cases, far too sympathetic—to the opposition to key positions of administration
in the loyalty and security programs was surely a mistake. It
was too great a concession, even in the search for broad public
support, and the event proved it largely futile.

There can be no question, however, of the President's own

devotion to the principles of civil liberty. His commitment to traditional values of personal freedom was complete. But, although not truly a simple man, he shared some of the small-town simplicities of outlook characteristic of so much of his opposition; the complexities, both philosophical and practical, of the loyalty issue at least partly eluded him. To him, loyalty could not be defined: "You're either loyal to the United States, or you're not!"[1] The change in the loyalty standard, for example, apparently struck him as a useful administrative adjustment—the strong legal and philosophical objections of several members of his staff not convincing him otherwise—while the dangers inherent in confounding the requirements of security with the demand for loyalty never seemed evident to him. Mr. Truman, of course, was more than sincere in attempting to correct abuses by loyalty boards, although he was surprised as well as indignant at the frequency of their occurrence. Because of the strength and clarity of his own convictions, the President must have found it difficult to believe that others would deliberately trifle with individual liberties either out of prejudice or partisan purpose.

Some of the difficulties faced by the administration, along with some of the errors it made in dealing with them, were inherent in the President's institutional situation. An examination of certain aspects of that situation might repay us.

The President faced problems, to begin with, in imposing his will on the federal bureaucracy. That bureaucracy had expanded fairly rapidly with the New Deal's creation of many new executive and independent agencies, but it blossomed mightily during the Second World War. With the postwar economic boom and the advent of the cold war, it continued to grow at a regular, impressive pace. Its annual growth rate, indeed, was quite as imposing as that of the Gross National Product in the postwar period. Since the process has continued, the present structure dwarfs that of twenty years ago, but the youthful outlines of the exuberant monstrosity were fully apparent during the Truman years.

It is, of course, extremely difficult, if not impossible, for the President—any President—to keep tabs on how all his programs and directives are being carried out by this sprawling bureaucracy. Mr. Truman and his immediate aides, for instance, learned of peculiarities in the administration of the loyalty program through complaints by persons who had to be considered reliable. In most cases, subsequent checks confirmed the complaints.

The interests of federal employees are just not those of their ultimate superior. Nearly all want security, which means retention of employment. Most hope for promotion. Some aim at advancement to the highest ranks of the civil service. A few dream of achieving political place. All, from the most restlessly ambitious to the most stolidly content, are in some sense dependent upon being able to ride the shifting tides of opinion. The higher echelons of the permanent civil service, at least, not only follow the election returns, as the Supreme Court is reputed to do, but try to anticipate them. In serving today's master, it is advisable to avoid giving serious offense to tomorrow's.

The anxiety is greatest—and, frequently, the vulnerability, as well—at the level of the Assistant Secretaries and division heads in the Cabinet departments and the assistants to the director, and whatnot, in the agencies. These men, either higher-ranking civil servants or lesser political appointees, play a constant guessing game trying to determine where the actual power to reward lies—or, what is often more important, may lie in the near future. The civil servants in this class are better off than the others, since any political appointee, no matter how unobtrusive he has tried to make himself, is apt to disappear with the administration that has placed him—unless he has the rare luck, and lack of conviction, properly to stage-manage a judicious biting of the hand that has fed him. The climbing civil servant with an eye to the future, however, must be slow to identify himself with the brisk forwarding of any program that is clearly novel or controversial. Observing the administration and party in power, he knows, with King Solomon, that this, too, shall pass away. His problem is to make sure that its passing does nothing to interfere with his ascent to the next higher rung of the bureaucratic ladder. His tools are numerous. The order whose execution is delayed to the brink of oblivion by the difficulty of preparing to execute it, the division and subdivision of a program into sections, in the process of making assignments for execution, until the parts become hopelessly separated from one another and the whole is swallowed up in confusion, the interpretation of a policy in a rather different way from that intended by its framers (since the prose of government directives and instruction sheets is in no way outstanding for forthrightness and clarity) —all these will recommend themselves to the hopeful placeman.

The task of the lower-ranking civil servant, possessed of no more than routine ambition, so to speak, is less intricate but quite as exacting in its way. His job is to work hard, in terms of time and even of effort, without accomplishing anything his superiors seem not to want accomplished.

The nature of the bureaucracy could not fail to influence

the administration of the loyalty and security programs. Testimony before the Civil Rights Committee made it clear that common practice was for the chief executive officer of a department or agency to delegate supervision of the programs to a subordinate, who would, in turn, delegate them to a subordinate, or subordinates, of *his*. The poor devil who had the actual management of the business might feel (and with some justification) that his career depended upon his success in this job, or at least the avoidance of error. The loyalty and security programs were designed to keep the government free of subversives. A reading of the headlines—certainly after Joe McCarthy burst upon the scene—would make it obvious that the strictest vigilance against Communism was the strait path to advancement. In bringing charges or—what was safer, much safer—forcing a resignation, it was better to chance wronging an innocent man (certainly if the case was unclear) than to risk letting a subversive escape the net. The responsible officer, himself normally junior, would of course give the benefit of any doubt to the government—and himself.

No wonder the President looked at the government apparatus with wry humor, and a tinge of bitterness.

In the early summer of 1952, before the heat of the campaign, President Truman used to contemplate the problems of the General-become-President should Eisenhower win the forthcoming election. "He'll sit here," Truman would remark (tapping his desk for emphasis), "and he'll say 'Do this! Do that!' *And nothing will happen.* Poor Ike—it won't be a bit like the Army. He'll find it very frustrating."[2]

It needs to be said that all the obstacles to achievement erected by a bureaucracy are not the consequence of self-serving intrigue. Many, probably most, are raised up by honest misunderstanding, inertia, and incompetence. Timely stupidity has assisted more than one career. And McCarthy's heyday introduced simple fear as a widespread motive for inaction—or unjust action.

Conflicts among various departments and agencies, and within them, complicated the President's task of establishing coherent policies. Some of these conflicts arose from empire-building or jurisdictional disputes—both of which were encouraged by the proliferation of the bureaucracy and Roosevelt's custom of dividing responsibility for his new programs.[3] For some time, every government venture into a new field of activity meant the creation of a new agency. Often enough, the mandates given new agencies overlapped the functions of existing departments and agencies. Struggles between older departments and agencies to defend what were regarded as special privileges were common, as were open or covert contests for the control of some area of policy.

The Justice Department's resentment of the presence of the State and Treasury Departments' representatives on the President's Temporary Commission on Employee Loyalty is a case in point. If Justice had had to deal only with the War and Navy Departments, it might have encountered less philosophical and political resistance to its conception of a proper loyalty program—although the positions taken by Under Secretary of War Royall did not often sustain Chairman Vanech's expectations. The attitudes of several of the War and Navy alternates on the agenda subcommittee (particularly the chiefs of the counterintelligence services), where much of the real work of the commission was done, were in line with Justice's. L. V. Meloy, the Civil Service Commission alternate, generally sided with the Justice Department. Although Attorney General Clark was much less rigid than his deputy, the departmental outlook on this issue was broadly that of the law enforcement agencies; it regarded the question of potential subversion as largely a police problem. It was therefore principally concerned to close the loopholes through which suspects might escape.[4]

State and Treasury, joined from time to time by the War Department, fought to maintain the employee's right to an effective defense and to prevent the loyalty program from being turned into an agency for imposing political conformity. Their resistance was not wholly in vain, but it proved in the long run to be of limited practical effect.

One has the impression that Chairman Vanech's clumsy efforts to "blitz" the commission with his first draft report, and his prolonged, haggling efforts to secure acceptance of the FBI's definition of the scope and seriousness of the loyalty problem, distracted his opponents from giving adequate attention to matters of procedure. Their philosophical victories did not make up for the absence of any caveat on the use of the unsupported testimony of informers or for the failure to set out guidelines for the evaluation of derogatory information.

The President was quite probably in error when he gave the commission its head. If he had indicated in advance, at least in broad terms, what sort of program he wanted, the commission would have produced a more acceptable result. It is unlikely, to be sure, that Mr. Truman, personally, knew what a proper program might be—almost no one did, the problem being unprecedented—but he could have asked his staff to prepare an outline, or at worst a catalogue of limits, for the commission's use. He did not do this, and the White House staff of the time took no independent interest in the problem.

The worst features of the program, of course, were the consequence of the way in which it was administered, rather than with the way it was drawn up; but the administrators were left too much leeway by the drafters. In effect, many departmental and regional loyalty boards adopted the viewpoint of antiadministration elements in Congress as the norm for patriotism, and translated suspicion into reasonable doubt. The quality of the appointments to these boards was responsible for this result, but in this respect the departments and agencies simply followed the example set by presidential appointments to the Loyalty Review Board.[5] It was a bad example; appeasement once again produced the historically predictable consequence. It seems certain, too, that the hasty institution of a fairly drastic loyalty program, run by identifiable non-liberals, excited rather than reassured public opinion.

None of the weaknesses of the loyalty program, administrative, structural, or psychological, were beyond correction. Procedures could have been revised, administrative personnel replaced or brought under better discipline, and an administrative court of review established outside the Civil Service Commission (however it might have objected) , with a membership sufficiently prominent and an operation sufficiently public to promote popular confidence. These, or other reforms similar in effect, would have been adequate for all purposes at any time prior to the eruption of the debate over China, the climax of the Hiss case, and Senator McCarthy's serendipitous discovery of Communism. No reform was attempted, however, until it was, at least politically, too late.

That this was the case derived from Mr. Truman's rather traditional approach to his office. He believed that a President should govern through his Cabinet; like many of his southern and border-state colleagues in the Senate, he had been suspicious of Roosevelt's reliance on unofficial advisers and the nascent White House staff. "I propose to get Cabinet officers I can depend on and have them run their affairs, and when I can't depend on them I'll keep on firing Cabinet Members until I can get that kind."[6] The President, at least in the beginning, was thus committed to reliance on the Justice Department in loyalty and security matters. But, as one first-hand observer noted, "in the Truman Administration, the Justice Department tended to be evasive, sometimes downright unresponsive, in providing the Executive Office with forthright legal guidance on legislative or operational issues."[7]

Tom Clark, prior to his appointment as the government's chief law officer, had been a departmental career man who had risen through the Criminal Division to become Assistant Attorney General. A competent lawyer, his experience had stamped him with the enforcement viewpoint. He tended to subordinate considerations of civil liberty to the exigencies of crime control. A personal friend of the President, and completely loyal to him, Mr. Clark, who was given a relatively free hand, tried to run the Justice Department, administratively and politically, to what he felt was his chief's advantage. On the loyalty issue, that meant coming down on the side of severity. It also meant that the Attorney General had to go round and about the President's spontaneous bias in favor of maximal personal freedom.

Mr. Truman's second Attorney General, after Tom Clark's appointment to the Supreme Court, was Senator J. Howard McGrath, Chairman of the Democratic National Committee and formerly a popular Governor of Rhode Island. McGrath had a good legal mind, but he was a lazy administrator who generally left the running of the department to his subordinates. In the loyalty and security field, he consistently sought the line of least political resistance. In August, 1950, as we have seen, he tried independently to improve on the President's recommendations for internal security legislation by proposing a severe amendment of the Foreign Agents Registration Act that he hoped might buy off supporters of the McCarran bill. This maneuver not only ran counter to the President's wishes, but represented a serious miscalculation of the character and motives of the opposition.

When McGrath was hastily dismissed in the midst of a bizarre internal crisis over the investigation of corruption in government, James P. McGranery was named to replace him on the basis of an off-the-cuff recommendation by Matt Connelly.[8] Judge McGranery, who had been a Congressman, left little impress on the department in eleven months of service. He provided a fairly good imitation of the three wise monkeys of Nikko.

Despite the preeminence of the Justice Department in the loyalty-security area, numerous matters relevant to it came to the Special Counsel's office in the White House. This was particularly true from 1950 on, when Charles S. Murphy held the post. Complaints about the operation of the loyalty program, questions about presidential appointments, proposals for reviewing and revising procedures, and suggestions for legislation all wound up on his desk. Yet he had no real control over these matters. Rather, he

simply struggled with the backwash, the miscellany, the consequences, that the White House could neither evade [n]or ignore. In theory, the Attorney General might have provided coherent, consistent leadership in grasping the whole bundle of problems and getting a government-wide focus on them; conceivably the Nimitz Commission might have done so, or possibly even the National Security Council. But in practice, that kind of leadership was never obtained from these quarters or any other. And with nothing of that kind to tie to on the outside, the White House in general—and Murphy in particular—never saw a shred of a mandate—or any chance—for going it alone.[9]

Although President Truman was the founding father of the White House staff as we know it, he never used it, as Presidents Kennedy and Johnson did later, to watch over, prod, and, if need be, bypass the bureaucracy. The staff that Mr. Truman had put together by 1948 was energetic, very competent, and knowledgeable in the ways of the bureaucracy. Almost all of its members had come from other parts of the government, a full third of the civilian staff from the Bureau of the Budget. The staff men were therefore able to deal with the executive departments and agencies at both the top and second-line levels of administration. From time to time, they managed unobtrusively to adjust a dispute or spur an action somewhere in the bureaucracy. But they did not normally do so at the President's direction, and had to proceed with caution.

In the preparation of formal speeches, major statements, messages to Congress, and executive orders, in helping to draw up the administration's legislative proposals, in the review of enrolled bills, the staff, headed by the Special Counsel, found in the duty of stating policy a real opportunity to influence its making. Outside the area of stated assignments, however, it

had to be careful in intruding its advice. Any sort of intervention in foreign policy (apart from the Palestine question) had
to be carried out under the cover of a recognized function, as
the State Department was quick to resent poaching on its preserve.[10]

Clark Clifford, as Special Counsel, aspired to the role of
general policy adviser, but there were limits to his influence.
Charles Murphy tended to diffidence, and was not so inclined
to reach out beyond the point he was covered by assigned duties. In either case, however, it was always a question of influence rather than authority. This was true of all staff members.
John R. Steelman, despite the title of *The* Assistant to the
President, concentrated on labor-management relations, sedu-
lously avoiding any involvement in policy making in any
other field. He also served to shield the President from a myr-
iad of bureaucratic time-wasters. He protected himself by a
steady refusal to offer opinions outside his chosen domain.

The President regarded his staff as designed to give him
personal service, that is, to help do the things he had to, by
preparing speeches, messages, programs, etc. As he saw it, there
was no one else to help him with these things. The staff of the
National Security Council was politically neutral, and had
not been created, in any event, for general-purpose duties.
The Budget was useful (indispensable during the directorship
of James E. Webb) for preparing, screening, revising, and analyzing legislation, acting as a clearinghouse for bills offered by
the White House and the executive departments, and occasionally mediating interdepartmental disputes. But it could
not do for the President what his Special Counsel and administrative assistants could do. Given Mr. Truman's persistent
notion that the Cabinet should exercise its traditional func-

tions, it was little wonder that the staff was restricted as much as possible to purely White House services. Consequently, there can be no great surprise that although the staff was extremely well equipped to develop legislative programs, it was far less able to follow them up, promoting them and providing supporting material for congressional floor leaders. The next speech, the next message, the next proclamation, however comparatively trivial, would necessarily command their attention and compel them to leave the last job to other hands. Under these conditions, the "Truman White House rarely failed to state a better policy than it could implement in action by the governmental agencies."[11]

Very occasionally, as in the disastrous steel strike of 1952 or in loyalty-security matters generally from the advent of McCarthy, the President would direct the staff to act, on his behalf, to seek solutions for problems that could not be avoided by the White House. The prime task in such cases was to pick up the pieces left by departmental and agency failures. In a sense, such ventures by the staff were a form of personal service to the President, for it was a matter of his taking hold when his regular agents had proved insufficient or had defaulted.[12]

The White House staff, as such, could not undertake any positive action in the loyalty field because it was too closely identified with the President. It could discreetly investigate complaints against loyalty boards; it could bring under-the-table pressure to bear on erring agencies; it could propose, and plan for, what became the Nimitz Commission. It could not, so to speak, show its face. To do so would have invited a flood of abusive, irrational criticism of the President for meddling with the loyalty program to save "Reds."

It is at least possible that things would have been different if the President had assigned some member of the staff to special oversight of the loyalty program. It could not have hurt to have had the departments and their loyalty boards regularly reminded of the intent of the program, as understood at the White House. It might have helped to have had permanent staff liaison with the Justice Department, to make sure that it executed the President's desires; yet at the same time to reassure the FBI and the Internal Security Division of all necessary cooperation. It would have made sense to designate staff members to help prepare and direct the Tydings Subcommittee investigation of the McCarthy charges. And so on. But Mr. Truman simply did not use his staff that way. Neither Clark Clifford nor Charles Murphy, despite real executive ability and political "feel," ever had the extensive control over legislative planning or the broad right to speak authoritatively for the President, within the government, that characterized Theodore Sorenson's tenure as Kennedy's Special Counsel. Neither man possessed anything approaching the real power over domestic policy that Bill Moyers and Joseph Califano had during the Johnson administration. There was nothing in the Truman White House that remotely resembled the elaborate congressional liaison operations that General Wilton B. (Slick) Persons created for the Eisenhower administration or that Lawrence F. O'Brien maintained for Presidents Kennedy and Johnson.[13]

It is nevertheless unfair to criticize Mr. Truman for not having used his staff in a more audacious manner. The retrospective consideration of his experience was in good part responsible for the recent elaboration of the White House office and the delegation to it of substantial authority once delegated only to Cabinet Secretaries. It took a little time to see what was happening to the federal bureaucracy and to invent remedies for the inhibitions it laid upon a President. It was indeed a credit to President Truman that he organized and utilized the staff as well as he did, and that, in time, he put together so good a one. It has not had a good press, for, being made up largely of government career men, it was short on what is now meretriciously called style; and lacking real power, it had no political glamor. What influence it could exert depended wholly on the President's power (as is still true), and in the political (as opposed to the institutional, executive, or personal) sense, Mr. Truman has been our most embattled President since Hoover.

Any advertence to Mr. Truman's political weakness must refer to his position in Congress. At almost no time in his tenure of the White House—despite the miracle of 1948—could he have been regarded as a good bet politically. This fact made a strong impression on the leaders of both parties in both houses of Congress, as it certainly influenced some Cabinet members and top-level civil servants. His weakness on the Hill was made up of roughly equal parts of his own lack of prior political distinction, the incredible flabbiness and ineptitude of the Democratic leadership in the Senate, and the peculiar character of the congressional opposition.

Mr. Truman, to begin with, was an "accidental" President to a degree that has been true of no other Chief Executive since Chester A. Arthur.[14] Although he had a good reputation in the Senate, he had no personal following in it, and he was not a member of the fabled "club." His record and his personal qualifications, as understood in 1944, added up to availability, not authority. Senator Truman owed his nomination as Vice-President more to the party leaders' distaste for Mr. Wallace and their doubts about Mr. Byrnes's vote-getting abilities than to any recognized merits of his own. His succession to the presidency caused as much shock in Congress as elsewhere in the country, and it required a long time for the panjandrums of the powerful congressional committees to take him seriously. Some, indeed, never learned. Without strong leadership in Congress, the President had little hope of securing passage of most of his programs.

In the Senate, Mr. Truman never had any leadership that could be relied upon. While Senator Lucas's defection in the fight over the McCarran Act was an extreme example of the collapse of leadership, the floor leader could not deliver the votes unless superior powers, such as the leaders of the southern bloc, permitted it. Since, as we have observed, no real power inheres in the floor leadership, everything must depend upon the personal strength, parliamentary skill, and political understanding of the man who holds the post. It might be said that Mr. Truman was unfortunate in coming to the White House too late for Joe Robinson and too soon for Lyndon Johnson.

The Communist issue, it must be admitted, was a solvent for party discipline; particularly, it further weakened the bonds of allegiance tying numerous southerners to the administration. George Smathers overthrew Claude Pepper in the Florida Democratic primary of 1950 by arguing that Senator Pepper's support for the administration's civil rights program was a consequence of his pro-Communist sympathies. Vocal elements in the southern electorate, heartened by the idea that only Communists would agitate for racial equality, pressed their Senators and Representatives to line up behind

McCarthy, since the administration that had proposed the omnibus civil rights bill must needs be infested with Communists.

All the same, it is far from the impossible that the tactics used by Lyndon B. Johnson, as minority leader in what amounted to an equally divided Senate, to encompass the undoing of McCarthy in that body in 1954, would have worked in the immediate aftermath of the Tydings subcommittee hearings—or a year later, after the attack on General Marshall.[15] Unfortunately, the tactician was yet in the wings, and the President had only Scott Lucas and Ernest McFarland.

The situation in the House of Representatives, from the standpoint of leadership, was much better. This was certainly true at the top, although there were diminishing returns for the President down the line. Effective leadership, however, can accomplish less in the House than in the Senate. The House, because of its relatively small and often homogeneous constituencies, and the frequency with which the Representatives must renew their mandate, commonly registers public emotion, to use Manlio Brosio's expression. An issue so provocative all around of irrational reactions, as was the controversy over domestic Communism, could threaten the best party discipline. This was particularly true when important committee chairmen were swept up by an emotional tide back home.

Speaker Rayburn (minority leader in the Eightieth Congress) was an experienced and skillful legislator, a good partisan and loyalist, a friend of the President, and a personal supporter of most Fair Deal programs. He hated McCarthy, and those who imitated him or stood by him, and he was the only member of the "Big Four" whose agreement with the President's *attitude* toward the loyalty problem was sure. Rayburn nevertheless gave the President very cautious advice in this area. He was skeptical of the proposal for an investigative commission and he urged Mr. Truman to sign the McCarran bill. Very much a man of the House, and wise in its ways, "Mr. Sam" disliked having his principal invest too much prestige in hopeless causes. He felt it imprudent for the President to ask too often for support that he, the Speaker, could not deliver.

The Democratic floor leader of the House was John W. McCormack of Massachusetts, who had learned his trade in the hard and essentially unsentimental school of South Boston. He was (and is) a party man and knew the rules. Neither his origins nor his constituency inspired him to fight the "hard-liners" on security legislation, so that he did his duty in this field without great enthusiasm. He seemed to wish much of the time that the President would be sensible and join what he could not beat.

It is clear enough that the weakening of party discipline in both houses of Congress and the incompetence or cowardice of the Senate Democratic leadership undermined the President's efforts to control the bureaucratic leadership of the executive departments and agencies. The bureaucrats were naturally anxious to keep in the good graces of an opposition that showed every sign of coming to power in the near future.

Nothing more damaged the administration's efforts to offer coherent guidance in the loyalty and security fields than to be faced with a Republican opposition that refused to play the game. The game simply requires taking the patriotism and good faith in matters involving national security of one's op-

ponent for granted, while belittling his intelligence and judgment, or even questioning his common honesty in ordinary
domestic matters. Senator Goldwater, who was frequently accused of running an extreme campaign in 1964, never violated
this rule of minimal civility.

One can only speculate why the congressional leadership of
a whole party—and much of its state and local leadership as
well—gave itself over to a demagogy that might, if unchecked,
have subverted the structure of the state. Agitation of the idea
that the President and the Secretary of State would deliberately nourish Communism within the government of the
United States produced a degree of popular excitement that
came close, in some places, to ending ordinary political discourse. By support of McCarthy, the Republican leaders of
Congress foreclosed any possibility of a bipartisan examination of the genuine problems raised by the need for adequate
security within the government. They raised a barrier against
any rationalization of foreign policy. Where they would have
ended, had not General Eisenhower been elected President in
1952, is not at all sure. McCarthy's supporters set out to prove
that they held a monopoly of patriotism, and in the long run
demonstrated only that fanaticism is inimical to the democratic process and consistently threatens the constriction, if
not the paralysis, of democratic government.

Senator Taft, like the President, was an intense partisan.
His partisanship, however, unlike the President's, frequently
seemed irrelevant to the real world of politics and government. Taft apparently never understood the mediating function of the party system and its consequent crucial role in
giving life to the constitutional structure he professed to revere.
In using McCarthy, he adopted an argument that would have

been entirely discredited (and the party with it) by any appearance of compromise, or even cooperation, with the administration. The Republican position was, in more recent jargon, "non-negotiable." Mr. Truman may have been impolitic, but he was not inaccurate, in pinning the "red herring" label on his opponents' investigative activities. For many Republicans, the possibility of Communist infiltration of the government was not a problem, but an opportunity.[16] A terrible sense of frustration, born of an unusually prolonged period of electoral defeat, seems to have liberated a very substantial number of them from the restraints imposed by the historic consensus of the American party system. After the trauma of 1948, several of their most important leaders broke loose, too. They were able to go so far, in 1952, as to force upon General Eisenhower the public appearance of acquiescing in their fanciful attacks on his friend and mentor, General Marshall.[17]

The Truman administration, nevertheless, was never overwhelmed. Because, as his staff aides were inclined to believe, the President "could think better with his guts than [they] could with [their] heads,"[18] he was successful in fighting off the most dangerous efforts to ravage the Executive Branch. Where he was able to act without Congress, he could take decisive steps. Under the cover of his constitutional role as Commander-in-Chief, for example, he could order American troops into Korea in defense of an existing national commitment, and he could direct the racial integration of the armed services by executive order. The most important innovations in foreign policy, particularly with regard to Europe, had been put through before the winter of 1949–1950, but even afterward, the administration was able to secure legislation, more or less to its satisfaction, defining American responsibilities under the North Atlantic Treaty and keeping the foreign aid program afloat. This was largely the consequence of strong support from southern Democrats, who were committed on these issues.

The Communist controversy, on the other hand, did stultify the development of a new Asian policy.[19] And the price of victory elsewhere in the foreign policy field was the surrender of almost all the Truman domestic program. The crisis of confidence that we call McCarthyism played its part in the abandonment of so much of the Fair Deal through the timidity of executive agencies in pushing plans that might be damned as "socialistic."

The crisis was ended by time. The termination of the misunderstood Korean War, the passive resistance of a largely invulnerable Republican administration, and a revived public conscience (freed by relief to be pricked by shame) eventually checked most of the excesses symbolized by Senator McCarthy. When his censure finally came, it was in some part a belated vindication of the Truman administration, above all of the former President himself.

NOTES

1. Interview with former President Truman, July 21, 1961.
2. Cited in Richard E. Neustadt, *Presidential Power: The Politics of Leadership* (New York: John Wiley & Sons, 1960), p. 9. Neustadt's emphasis.
3. Administration of the programs initiated by the National Industrial Recovery Act, for instance, was divided. Title I, the industrial codes program, was given to the care of a new agency, the National Recovery

Administration. Title II, the public works program, was handed over to the Department of the Interior.

4. There is, of course, a strong tendency among liberals to discount the real problems of the police. To use an example that is not fanciful, consider the stickiness of the situation of a group of FBI men, Secret Service men, or city detectives, staked out at night in a driving rain, and being compelled to decide in a few seconds on a search and seizure which the Supreme Court may rule illegal, in a five-to-four decision, three years hence.

5. It is conceivable that because the Loyalty Review Board had only an advisory capacity, the President did not anticipate the influence it would attain.

6. Cited in Patrick Anderson, *The Presidents' Men: White House Assistants of Franklin D. Roosevelt, Harry S. Truman, Dwight D. Eisenhower, John F. Kennedy, and Lyndon B. Johnson* (Garden City, N.Y.: Doubleday & Co., 1968) , p. 91.

7. Richard E. Neustadt, "Notes on the White House Staff under President Truman," p. 25, Papers of Richard E. Neustadt.

9. Interview with Donald A. Hansen, June 9, 1967.

10. This was particularly true while General Marshall was Secretary of State. Anderson, *The Presidents' Men*, pp. 118–119.

11. Neustadt, "Notes . . .," p. 22.

12. This consideration of the role of the White House staff is largely based on ibid., pp. 14–25 et passim.

13. That there was no foreign-policy, or so-called national-security, expert in the White House to do for Mr. Truman what McGeorge Bundy, Walt W. Rostow, and Henry A. Kissinger have done for more recent Presidents was the result of President Truman's relations of trust with George Marshall and Dean Acheson.

14. Theodore Roosevelt, in 1900, had a national reputation as the commander of the "Rough Riders" and as reform Governor of New York. He was already the hero, if not quite yet the leader, of a major faction of the Republican party. Calvin Coolidge was at least as well known, and apparently as well qualified (to say the least) , as the head of his ticket, whose own nomination was something of an accident. Lyndon B. Johnson was master of the Senate in 1960 and, in his own right, a power in the Democratic party.

15. There is an excellent account of this "campaign" in Rowland Evans and Robert Novak, *Lyndon B. Johnson: The Exercise of Power* (New York: Signet Books, 1968) , pp. 92–97.

16. HCUA, for example, would have been quite willing to abandon the Hiss investigation after making its sensation. Until Mr. Nixon went to work, the committee did not have the evidence on which to proceed. Most of the members probably did not mind; they had made the headlines.

17. William S. White, *The Taft Story* (New York: Harper & Bros., 1954) , p. 193, finds this decision "Taftian to the core." General Eisenhower's account makes it clear that his staff made an exceptional effort to convince him that his silence on the charges against Marshall, for the duration of a campaign swing through Wisconsin, could not be construed as it came, in fact, to be construed. Having taken what purported to be good political advice, he discovered, as he related it, that "it gave the opposition and some segments of the press an opportunity to charge that I had 'capitulated' to the McCarthyites. This was, of course, completely untrue. Indeed, if I could have foreseen this distortion of facts, a distortion that even led some to question my loyalty to General Marshall, I would never have acceded to the staff's arguments, logical as they sounded at the time." Dwight D. Eisenhower, *The White House Years* (Garden City, N.Y.: Doubleday & Co., 1963) , vol. 1, *Mandate for Change, 1953–1956,* 318.

18. Interview with Stephen J. Spingarn, March 17, 1962.

19. Culpable as the Roosevelt and Truman administrations may have been in not consulting Republican leaders on the goals of Far Eastern policy, it must be understood that they were put off by their awareness of the rigidity and archaic quality of the Republican leadership's views of East Asia, particularly China. There probably never was much of a hope for an intelligent bipartisan policy in this area, one that would have come closer to the realities of the region than either party was able to get on its own.

APPENDIX 1

Executive Order 9835

Code of Federal Regulations. Title 3—The President. 1943–1948 Compilation, pp. 627–631. Washington: Government Printing Office, 1957.

The loyalty program hammered out by the President's Temporary Commission on Employee Loyalty was put into effect by Executive Order 9835 issued March 12, 1947.

EXECUTIVE ORDER 9835

PRESCRIBING PROCEDURES FOR THE ADMINISTRATION OF AN EMPLOYEES LOYALTY PROGRAM IN THE EXECUTIVE BRANCH OF THE GOVERNMENT

WHEREAS each employee of the Government of the United States is endowed with a measure of trusteeship over the democratic processes which are the heart and sinew of the United States; and

WHEREAS it is of vital importance that persons employed in the Federal service be of complete and unswerving loyalty to the United States; and

WHEREAS, although the loyalty of by far the overwhelming majority of all Government employees is beyond question, the presence within the Government service of any disloyal or subversive person constitutes a threat to our democratic processes; and

WHEREAS maximum protection must be afforded the United States against infiltration of disloyal persons into the ranks of its employees, and equal protection from unfounded accusations of disloyalty must be afforded the loyal employees of the Government:

NOW, THEREFORE, by virtue of the authority vested in me by the Constitution and statutes of the United States, including the Civil Service Act of 1883 (22 Stat. 403), as amended, and section 9-A of the act approved August 2, 1939 (18 U.S.C. 61 i), and as President and Chief Executive of the United States, it is hereby, in the interest of the internal management of the Government, ordered as follows:

PART I—INVESTIGATION OF APPLICANTS

1. There shall be a loyalty investigation of every person entering the civilian employment of any department or agency of the executive branch of the Federal Government.

a. Investigations of persons entering the competitive service shall be conducted by the Civil Service Commission, except in such cases as are covered by a special agreement between the Commission and any given department or agency.

b. Investigations of persons other than those entering the competitive service shall be conducted by the employing department or agency. Departments and agencies without investigative organizations shall utilize the investigative facilities of the Civil Service Commission.

2. The investigations of persons entering the employ of the executive branch may be conducted after any such person enters upon actual employment therein, but in any such case the appointment of such person shall be conditioned upon a favorable determination with respect to his loyalty.

a. Investigations of persons entering the competitive service shall be conducted as expeditiously as possible; provided, however, that if any such investigation is not completed within 18 months from the date on which a person enters actual employment, the condition that his employment is subject to investigation shall expire, except in a case in which the Civil Service Commission has made an initial adjudication of disloyalty and the case continues to be active by reason of an appeal, and it shall then be the responsibility of the employing department or agency to conclude such investigation and make a final determination concerning the loyalty of such person.

3. An investigation shall be made of all applicants at all available pertinent sources of information and shall include reference to:

a. Federal Bureau of Investigation files.

b. Civil Service Commission files.

c. Military and naval intelligence files.

d. The files of any other appropriate government investigative or intelligence agency.

e. House Committee on un-American Activities files.

f. Local law-enforcement files at the place of residence and employment of the applicant, including municipal, county, and State law-enforcement files.

g. Schools and colleges attended by applicant.

h. Former employers of applicant.

i. References given by applicant.

j. Any other appropriate source.

4. Whenever derogatory information with respect to loyalty of an applicant is revealed a full field investigation shall be conducted. A full field investigation shall also be conducted of those applicants, or of applicants for particular positions, as may be designated by the head of the employing department or agency, such designations to be based on the determination by any such head of the best interests of national security.

PART II—INVESTIGATION OF EMPLOYEES

1. The head of each department and agency in the executive branch of the Government shall be personally responsible for an effective program to assure that disloyal civilian officers or employees are not retained in employment in his department or agency.

a. He shall be responsible for prescribing and supervising the loyalty determination procedures of his department or agency, in accordance with the provisions of this order, which shall be considered as providing minimum requirements.

b. The head of a department or agency which does not have an investigative organization shall utilize the investigative facilities of the Civil Service Commission.

2. The head of each department and agency shall appoint one or more loyalty boards, each composed of not less than three representatives of the department or agency concerned, for the purpose of hearing loyalty cases arising within such department or agency and making recommendations with respect to the removal of any officer or employee of such department or agency on grounds relating to loyalty, and he shall prescribe regulations for the conduct of the proceedings before such boards.

a. An officer or employee who is charged with being disloyal shall have a right to an administrative hearing before a loyalty board in the employing department or agency. He may appear before such board personally, accompanied by counsel or representative of his own choosing, and present evidence on his own behalf, through witnesses or by affidavit.

b. The officer or employee shall be served with a written notice of such hearing in sufficient time, and shall be informed therein of the nature of the charges against him in sufficient detail, so that he will be enabled to prepare his defense. The charges shall be stated as specifically and completely as, in the discretion of the employing department or agency, security considerations permit, and the officer or employee shall be informed in the notice (1) of his right to reply to such charges in writing within a specified reasonable period of time, (2) of his right to an administrative hearing on such charges before a loyalty board, and (3) of his right to appear before such board personally, to be accompanied by counsel or representative of his own choosing, and to present evidence on his behalf, through witness or by affidavit.

3. A recommendation of removal by a loyalty board shall be subject to appeal by the officer or employee affected, prior to his removal, to the head of the employing department or agency or to such person or persons as may be designated by such head, under such regulations as may be prescribed by him, and the decision of the department or agency concerned shall be subject to appeal to the Civil Service Commission's Loyalty Review Board, hereinafter provided for, for an advisory recommendation.

4. The rights of hearing, notice thereof, and appeal therefrom shall be accorded to every officer or employee prior to his removal on grounds of disloyalty, irrespective of tenure, or of manner, method, or nature of appointment, but the head of the employing department or agency may suspend any officer or employee at any time pending a determination with respect to loyalty.

5. The loyalty boards of the various departments and agencies shall furnish to the Loyalty Review Board, hereinafter provided for, such reports as may be requested concerning the operation of the loyalty program in any such department or agency.

PART III—RESPONSIBILITIES OF CIVIL SERVICE COMMISSION

1. There shall be established in the Civil Service Commission a Loyalty Review Board of not less than three impartial persons, the members of which shall be officers or employees of the Commission.

a. The board shall have authority to review cases involving persons recommended for dismissal on grounds relating to loyalty by the loyalty board of any department or agency and to make advisory recommendations thereon to the head of the employing department or agency. Such cases may be referred to the Board either by the employing department or agency, or by the officer or employee concerned.

b. The Board shall make rules and regulations, not inconsistent with the provisions of this order, deemed necessary to implement statutes and Executive orders relating to employee loyalty.

c. The Loyalty Review Board shall also:

(1) Advise all departments and agencies on all problems relating to employee loyalty.

(2) Disseminate information pertinent to employee loyalty programs.

(3) Coordinate the employee loyalty policies and procedures of the several departments and agencies.

(4) Make reports and submit recommendations to the Civil Service Commission for transmission to the President from time to time as may be necessary to the maintenance of the employee loyalty program.

2. There shall also be established and maintained in the Civil Service Commission a central master index covering all persons on whom loyalty investigations have been made by any department or agency since September 1, 1939. Such master index shall contain the name of each person investigated, adequate identifying information concerning each such person, and a reference to each department and agency which has conducted a loyalty investigation concerning the person involved.

a. All executive departments and agencies are directed to furnish to the Civil Service Commission all information appropriate for the establishment and maintenance of the central master index.

b. The reports and other investigative material and information developed by the investigating department or agency shall be retained by such department or agency in each case.

3. The Loyalty Review Board shall currently be furnished by the Department of Justice the name of each foreign or domestic organization, association, movement, group or combination of persons which the Attorney General, after appropriate investigation and determination, designates as totalitarian, fascist, communist or subversive, or as having adopted a policy of advocating or approving the commission of acts of force or violence to deny others their rights under the Constitution of the United States, or as seeking to alter the form of government of the United States by unconstitutional means.

a. The Loyalty Review Board shall disseminate such information to all departments and agencies.

PART IV—SECURITY MEASURES IN INVESTIGATIONS

1. At the request of the head of any department or agency of the executive branch an investigative agency shall make available to such head, personally, all investigative material and information collected by the investigative agency concerning any employee or prospective employee of the requesting department or agency, or shall make such material and information available to any officer or officers designated by such head and approved by the investigative agency.

2. Notwithstanding the foregoing requirement, however, the investigative agency may refuse to disclose the names of confidential informants, provided it furnishes sufficient information about such informants on the basis of which the requesting department or agency can make an adequate evaluation of the information furnished by them, and provided it advises the requesting department or agency in writing that it is essential to the protection of the informants or to the investigation of other cases that the identity of the informants not be revealed. Investigative agencies shall not use this discretion to decline to reveal sources of information where such action is not essential.

3. Each department and agency of the executive branch should develop and maintain, for the collection and analysis of information relating to loyalty of its employees and prospective employees, a staff specially trained in security techniques, and an effective security control system for protecting such information generally and for protecting confidential sources of such information practicularly.

PART V—STANDARDS

1. The standard for the refusal of employment or the removal from employment in an executive department or agency on grounds relating to loyalty shall be that, on all the evidence, reasonable grounds exist for belief that the person involved is disloyal to the Government of the United States.

2. Activities and associations of an applicant or employee which may be considered in connection with the determination of disloyalty may include one or more of the following;

a. Sabotage, espionage, or attempts or preparations therefor, or knowingly associating with spies or saboteurs;

b. Treason or sedition or advocacy thereof;

c. Advocacy of revolution or force or violence to alter the constitutional form of government of the United States;

d. Intentional, unauthorized disclosure to any person, under circumstances which may indicate disloyalty to the United States, of documents or information of a confidential or non-public character obtained by the person making the disclosure as a result of his employment by the Government of the United States;

e. Performing or attempting to perform his duties, or otherwise acting, so as to serve the interests of another government in preference to the interests of the United States.

f. Membership in, affiliation with or sympathetic association with any foreign or domestic organization, association, movement, group or combination of persons, designated by the Attorney General as totalitarian, fascist, communist, or subversive, or as having adopted a policy of advocating or approving the commission of acts of force or violence to deny other persons their rights under the Constitution of the United States, or as seeking to alter the form of government of the United States by unconstitutional means.

PART VI—MISCELLANEOUS

1. Each department and agency of the executive branch, to the extent that it has not already done so, shall submit, to the Federal Bureau of Investigation of the Department of Justice, either directly or through the Civil Service Commission, the names (and such other necessary identifying material as the Federal Bureau of Investigation may require) of all of its incumbent employees.

a. The Federal Bureau of Investigation shall check such names against its records of persons concerning whom there is substantial evidence of being within the purview of paragraph 2 of Part V hereof, and shall notify each department and agency of such information.

b. Upon receipt of the above-mentioned information from the Federal Bureau of Investigation, each department and agency shall make, or cause to be made by the Civil Service Commission, such investigation of those employees as the head of the department or agency shall deem advisable.

2. The Security Advisory Board of the State-War-Navy Coordinating Committee shall draft rules applicable to the handling and transmission of confidential documents and other documents and information which should not be publicly disclosed, and upon ap-

proval by the President such rules shall constitute the minimum standards for the handling and transmission of such documents and information, and shall be applicable to all departments and agencies of the executive branch.

3. The provisions of this order shall not be applicable to persons summarily removed under the provisions of section 3 of the act of December 17, 1942, 56 Stat. 1053, of the act of July 5, 1946, 60 Stat. or of any other statute conferring the power of summary removal.

4. The Secretary of War and the Secretary of the Navy, and the Secretary of the Treasury with respect to the Coast Guard, are hereby directed to continue to enforce and maintain the highest standards of loyalty within the armed services, pursuant to the applicable statutes, the Articles of War, and the Articles for the Government of the Navy.

5. This order shall be effective immediately, but compliance with such of its provisions as require the expenditure of funds shall be deferred pending the appropriation of such funds.

6. Executive Order No. 9300 of February 5, 1943, is hereby revoked.

HARRY S. TRUMAN

THE WHITE HOUSE,
March 21, 1947.

APPENDIX 2

Truman to Bridges, March 26, 1950

Papers of Harry S. Truman, OF 419–K, Harry S. Truman Library.
Courtesy of Harry S. Truman Library.

Truman to Vandenberg, March 27, 1950

Papers of Harry S. Truman, OF 386, Harry S. Truman Library.
Courtesy of Harry S. Truman Library.

Bridges to Truman, March 29, 1950

Papers of Harry S. Truman, OF 419–K, Harry S. Truman Library.
Courtesy of Styles Bridges Papers, James J. Kiepper, Editor.

Vandenberg to Truman, March 29, 1950

Papers of Harry S. Truman, OF 386, Harry S. Truman Library.
Courtesy of Barbara Vandenberg (Mrs. John W.) Bailey.

When President Truman tried a personal appeal to the opposition
in an attempt to thwart McCarthy's attacks on the State Department, he turned to Arthur H. Vandenberg, ranking Republican
member of the Senate Committee on Foreign Affairs, and Styles
Bridges, who held that title while Vandenberg was kept away by illness. The President's letter to Vandenberg was a rather formal reci-
tation of the achievements of the bipartisan foreign policy, with

some general reference to the damage that might be done by its interruption, whereas his approach to Bridges was far blunter and more to the immediate point, as well as more personal in tone. While both Senators' replies were cordial (Vandenberg's almost effusive), it should be noted that both were extremely cautious and (particularly in the case of Bridges) noncommittal.

At Key West, Florida
March 26, 1950

Dear Styles:

I noticed a statement in the press this morning that you are joining the "wolf-hounds" in the attack on Dean Acheson. I am really sorry to hear this, and I don't believe you would do it if you fully understood all the implications involved in this unwarranted attack on the bipartisan foreign policy.

The approach which has been made recently by several Senators has been a most satisfactory one to the Politburo in Moscow. The communists have never had as much help from all the so-called disloyal people as they have had from these indefensible attacks on Mr. Acheson.

You know as well as I do that there never was a more capable and loyal public servant than Dean Acheson. I don't think there has ever been a public servant who has done a more honest or more conscientious job than he has done as Under Secretary of the Treasury, as Assistant Secretary and Under Secretary of State, and as Secretary of State.

I have no objection to your attacking me and the policies of the Administration on any subject you choose, but political attacks should be confined to domestic affairs and should not under any circumstances, at this critical time, upset the solid front here at home for our approach to the world situation.

I fear that you are thoughtless in not remembering that we are in the midst of what is termed a cold war, a much more difficult situation to handle than one where actual shooting is going on.

Dean and I explained to you and Senator Wherry on one occasion the exact situation in China. If you and your colleagues who are so anxious to find an issue for the coming campaign would care to discuss the effect which the present unwarranted attacks on the Secretary of State are having on the effective conduct of this cold war, I believe we can convince you that what you are proposing to do is not only unpatriotic, but is a most dangerous procedure, likely to cause a situation in which young Americans may lose their lives by the thousands. History will no doubt place the blame for that situation right where it belongs.

I am appealing to you as your old-time personal friend and Senate colleague, to weigh this situation carefully, to discuss it objectively with your colleagues, and then if you desire a further discussion of it with me personally, I will be glad to go into every detail with you, and anyone else you want to bring with you.

Sincerely yours,
/s/ HARRY S. TRUMAN

Hon. Styles Bridges
United States Senate
Washington, D.C.

At Key West, Florida
March 27, 1950

Dear Arthur:

I appreciated most highly your letter to Mr. Hoffman, supporting continuation of the full appropriation for E.C.A. I have been very much disturbed about the situation as it has been developing in the Congress with regard to the whole bipartisan foreign policy.

As you know, that bipartisan foreign policy was inaugurated back in the time when Cordell Hull was Secretary of State, and when I was Chairman of the Committee to Investigate the National Defense Program. In fact, I was one of the Senators who worked diligently on the B_2H_2 resolution. The first great result of our bipartisan policy was the setting up of the United Nations, and all of us are grateful for your own great contributions at that time. As a continuation of that policy, the salvation of Greece and Turkey was first inaugurated at the suggestion of the then Secretary of State, Mr. Byrnes, and General Marshall.

As you remember, we had a conference on the matter in the White House, at which you were present with several other Senators and Representatives of the Foreign Affairs and Foreign Relations Committees of the Congress. The European Recovery Program was a follow-up of the approach to the salvation of Greece and Turkey.

You remember, Dean Acheson, then Under Secretary of State, made a speech on the subject at Cleveland, Mississippi, in May 1947, which was followed by General Marshall's commencement address at Harvard University in June 1947. After that, several conferences were held by the President and Members of the Foreign Affairs and Foreign Relations Committees of the House and Senate, and the European Recovery Program was inaugurated.

There isn't any question in my mind that it has been a very successful Program, and that it must be continued to its logical conclusion. Still later, the North Atlantic Pact and the Military Aid Program were worked out on a bipartisan basis.

The approach of several Senators to the foreign policy program, in an effort to find an issue for the coming campaign this fall, is unfortunate. I am sorry that they can't find a domestic issue on which to carry on the campaign. It seems to me that that could be done if an intelligent approach were made to the subject.

I sent a communication to Chairman Kee of the House Committee on Foreign Affairs at about the same time you were writing to Mr. Hoffman. I am glad the letters were publicly distributed at the same time. They should have a very salutary effect in the effort to save the foreign policy. I am enclosing a copy of a letter which I have just sent to Styles Bridges on this same subject. As I said to Senator Bridges, the breakup of the bipartisan foreign policy at this time would mean but one thing—victory for Russia in Europe, and in all probability a definite approach to a shooting war, which none of us wants.

The unfortunate situation in the Far East, which came about as a result of the corrupt Chinese Nationalist government, has caused us much difficulty, through no fault of ours that I have been able to discover. I believe that the Chinese and Far Eastern situation eventually will be rescued from the totalitarian regime at Moscow. One of the most awful situations, as a result of the overthrow of the Nationalist government, will be the starvation of millions of innocent people in China. I am now endeavoring to find a way to alleviate that condition. The Chinese, as you know, are fundamentally anti-foreign, and we must be exceedingly careful to see that this anti-foreign sentiment is not turned in our direction.

I am making every effort possible to negotiate a treaty with Japan, which would be very helpful if we could get the cooperation of the Russians. We have never had that cooperation since hostilities ceased, and those of us who are familiar with the movements and the historical procedures following the German surrender know that every agreement made between us and Russia seems to have been made only to be broken at the convenience of the Russian government. You of course know this bit of history as well as I do.

You will notice in my communication to Senator Bridges that I told him I would be glad to talk with any group at any time on any subject which affected the foreign relations of the United States. Irresponsible attacks on the Secretary of State, I think, are the greatest asset that the Kremlin has in this country.

I sincerely hope that the Lord will be good to the country and hurry along your physical recovery, so that you can come back and take your proper place as the Minority Leader of the Program.

Sincerely yours,
/s/ HARRY S. TRUMAN

Hon. Arthur H. Vandenberg
United States Senate
Washington, D.C.

UNITED STATES SENATE
Washington, D.C.

March 29, 1950

Dear Mr. President:

Your recent communication to me was delivered to my office about noontime on Monday, March twenty-seventh. However, due to the fact that I was not in my office during the morning and was on the Floor of the Senate until mid-evening, your communication did not come to my personal attention until that time. This was after I had delivered a speech on the Floor.

I read your letter with care and the following morning called Matt Connelly, requesting him to convey a message to you expressing my appreciation for your thoughtful letter regarding the so-called campaign against Dean Acheson to which you referred. I presume that message was delivered to you.

Informally, I have arranged to see and talk with Dean Acheson in the very early future and I shall be glad to talk with you further on this matter when the opportunity presents itself after your return from Key West.

I hope you enjoy your vacation and return to Washington feeling physically fit.

With regards and best personal wishes to you as always,

Sincerely yours,

/s/ STYLES BRIDGES

The President
The White House
Washington, D.C.

UNITED STATES SENATE
Washington, D.C.

March 29, 1950

Dear Mr. President:

I deeply appreciate your personal letter of March 27.

Certainly there is much to be said for the argument you present. Certainly we cannot fundamentally "divide at home" in respect to foreign policy and expect to have much effective authority abroad. I deeply regret that my good wife and I are both on the side lines for the time being; and that I cannot take full part in these recurrent Senate crises. I am afraid I may be "out of service" for the session. But perhaps I can help here and there.

Dean Acheson has telephoned me your additional message and I shall hope to see him within the week.

Your very sincere personal message means immensely much to

me and you have done far more for me than my Doctors have.

I hope you have a delightful recess and come back to Washington "full of whistle stop beezum."

My wife joins me in our appreciation.

Please present my compliments to Mrs. Truman and Margaret.

With warm personal regards and best wishes,

Cordially and faithfully,

/s/ A. H. VANDENBERG

The President
The White House
Washington, D.C.

APPENDIX 3

Memorandum for Messrs. Murphy, Dawson, and Elsey
From Stephen J. Spingarn, July 20, 1950

Papers of Harry S. Truman, Files of Charles S. Murphy. Courtesy of the Honorable Stephen J. Spingarn.

This consideration of possibilities in the field of internal security legislation provides an excellent understanding of contemporary White House views of both the threat of subversion and the "McCarthy problem."

THE WHITE HOUSE
Washington

July 20, 1950

Memorandum for: Messrs. Murphy, Dawson and Elsey
From: Stephen J. Spingarn
Subject: A possible legislative proposal as an answer to the Mundt-
  Johnston-Ferguson Bill (the current version of the 80th
  Congress Mundt-Nixon Bill) ; plus consideration of
  establishment now of Commission on Internal Security
  and Individual Rights.

  The current version of the Mundt-Nixon bill is fast gaining strength on the Hill. It was reported by the Senate Judiciary Committee several months ago by a 12 to 1 vote, and I think it pretty certain that, in the present climate of affairs, it would pass the Senate if it were brought up. The companion bill has not been reported in the House yet this Congress, but it passed the House by a very large majority in the 80th Congress and I have no doubt it could readily pass again at this time.

271

The Republican Policy Committee has put the bill on their "Must List" and has asked the Democrats to do the same. The Democratic leadership is now struggling with the problem. A matter to be considered in this situation is S. 595, the Justice-sponsored internal security bill, which has been reported by the Senate Judiciary Committee and its companion bill, H.R. 4073, which has passed the House. Recently the President asked me to analyze this latter legislation and make a recommendation to him as to whether he should ask Senator Lucas to try to put it through the Senate. I gave the President a memorandum analyzing the bill and recommending that he ask Senator Lucas to secure passage. It is my understanding that the President has done this.

However, I have been informed that the Senate Democratic leadership feels that the Mundt-Nixon legislation will be hung on S. 595 if it is brought up and that the proponents of that legislation have the votes to make it stick. The American Legion and the United States Chamber of Commerce, among other organizations, are strongly backing the Mundt-Nixon bill. The Chamber of Commerce, for example, has recently written every Senator urging its enactment. As a result of the Korean situation and the general tenseness, the Congress is in a mood to pass very drastic legislation indeed in the anti-subversive field. The House action on July 17 in passing by a 362 to 15 vote the very drastic Hobbs bill (H.R. 10), which the President is strongly opposed to, is a sample.

I understand that the proposal has been put to the Democratic leadership in the Senate, that they add to S. 595 those provisions of the Mundt-Nixon bill which they feel they can swallow. Peyton Ford has been asked to look into this proposition and make a recommendation.

I wish to suggest the following as an addition to S. 595 as an answer to the proponents of the Mundt-Nixon bill, instead of an attempt to find something good in that obnoxious legislation.

My proposal is that legislation be added to S. 595 (or possibly submitted as a separate bill) requiring registration with the Department of Justice of all "subversive organizations" (i.e., both the left-wing and the right-wing subversive groups), and the furnishing by them to the Department of Justice of pertinent information about themselves and specifically the details about the size and source of their revenues, and the size and recipients of their expenditures.

Taking the Communist Party as an example, it has been stated by at least one expert on the subject that that Party raised a million dollars for the defense of the Scottsboro boys and actually spent only sixty thousand dollars for the defense. Similarly and more recently, the same expert states that the Communist Party raised some two million dollars for the defense of the eleven Communist leaders recently convicted in New York and spent only one or at the most two hundred thousand dollars of that sum for the actual defense.

The interesting question naturally arises: Where did the money come from and, more important, where did it go? To any serious counter intelligence organization, legislation (such as I propose) which would furnish means for finding an answer to these questions would be of far more value than all the superpatriot provisions of the Mundt-Nixon bill, even overlooking the fact that that bill goes far beyond the concepts of individual rights in a democratic state and indeed adopts the totalitarian methods of the police states which have been and are our enemies.

The designation of the subversive organizations under the foregoing proposal might be made by the Attorney General but this should certainly be done only after a hearing—this on both constitutional and policy grounds. The designation here should not be tied up with the Attorney General's subversive list under Executive Order 9835 (the Government employee loyalty program) though of course many organizations would be on both lists, since there are major legal and other differences in the considerations involved.

I have suggested the foregoing proposal to Peyton Ford, whose initial reaction was most favorable. He said that he was going to check it around with his people and if he got a favorable indication from them would try it out for size on the Hill.

Incidentally, the proposal is a variation of one made by the President's Civil Rights Commission in 1947. Morris Ernst has been the principal proponent. However, the President did not recommend this proposal in his Civil Rights Message to Congress on February 2, 1948. I can state from memory, however, that this did not represent any policy decision on his part against the proposal. We felt there was enough in the package already and simply did not recommend it for inclusion.

The Civil Rights Commission-Ernst proposal would apply to all organizations whether subversive or legitimate which attempted to influence public opinion. Thus, it would apply alike to the Communist Party, the Ku Klux Klan, the United States Chamber of Commerce, and the A.D.A. Such a proposal would naturally be highly controversial. However, my variation of this should apply only to organizations designated as subversive and would not (I would guess) be very controversial.

I am passing this information on to you because I think we are going to hear a lot more about this general subject before we hear less.

As a separate but related matter, I would like again to mention a proposal for a Presidential (or Hoover-style) Commission on Internal Security and Individual Rights, which was the subject of the President's June 22 Blair House meeting.

It seems to me that with a temporary quietus put on Senator McCarthy and his charges by the strong report of the Tydings Subcommittee this week and the action of the Senate Foreign Relations Committee yesterday in voting 11 to 0 to end the investigation, and 9 to 2 to send the Tydings Subcommittee report, without recommendation, to the Senate (as well as the Senate action today in receiving the report), that this is the ideal time to set up such a commission. Preferably (in my judgment) there should be Presidential action rather than legislation, unless we heavily discount the views of the Congressional leaders at the June 22 meeting at Blair House. If the commission were set up now it could not be argued very successfully that it was pointed at McCarthy, who is in eclipse for the moment. However, as has been pointed out before in previous memoranda, this eclipse is a temporary situation. McCarthyism is going to arise again and probably very soon although the man hurling the charges may not be McCarthy and the target may not be the State Department. The time to set up a commission is during a lull in the storm. If we had set one up last summer we would have been in much better shape now, and the whole McCarthy business would not have had the impact it did on the public mind.

Incidentally, even though we know McCarthyism is in a temporary lull, the public tensions created by the Korean situation probably makes the whole problem more acute than it has ever been. Just as an example, there is the almost incredible action taken on July 18 by the Birmingham, Alabama City Council in the anti-subversive field as reported by the Washington Post of July 19, and Representative Shafer's statement yesterday that all Communists should be put at once in concentration camps.

There is one angle on the commission proposal that requires particular consideration. The President has frequently intimated to us that he would veto legislation like the Mundt-Nixon bill if it reached him. Such a veto would be politically most courageous since it would please liberals, but I am afraid that a great majority of the American people would strongly react against it in the current climate of opinion. Possibly the veto could be softened if the President, at the same time, established a Presidential Commission on Internal Security and Individual Rights.

However, my own opinion is that it would be better to try to keep the Mundt-Nixon legislation from reaching the President by working up an alternative, possibly along the lines suggested in the earlier part of this memorandum, and also by establishing now the Presidential commission along the lines which we have discussed.

I hate to be in the position of the boy who cried "wolf" too often but I cannot help feeling that a decision on this commission proposal is pretty pressing and should not be overlooked, even in the stress of the workload created by the Korean aggression. As a matter of fact the success of this problem is very definitely and closely connected with the ability of this Government to act with the necessary strength and effectiveness, that can only be based on public confidence, in the present trying times.

/s/S.J.S.
S.J.S.

Note

    I should add that the Tydings Subcommittee, as the first recommendation in its report issued earlier this week, recommended a Hoover-style commission to study the whole Federal loyalty program only. Our commission proposal, of course, is much broader (and should be), including particularly internal security legislation. Senator Lodge, in his individual views in the same report, recommends a bipartisan commission (to be created by simple Senate resolution) to study State Department loyalty matters only.

APPENDIX 4

Veto message, Internal Security (McCarran) Act of 1950
Congressional Record, 81st Cong., 2nd sess. (1950),
96:15629–15632.

Memorandum for the Internal Security File, September
25, 1950
Papers of Stephen J. Spingarn, Harry S. Truman Library. Courtesy
of the Honorable Stephen J. Spingarn.

President Truman's message covering his veto of the Internal Security (McCarran) Act of 1950, was a masterpiece of its kind, bringing
together almost all possible objections to the legislation. The memorandum of Stephen J. Spingarn, then an Administrative Assistant to
the President, gives us some of the "inside" background of the President's decision to veto the bill and his unsuccessful fight to have the
veto sustained.

INTERNAL SECURITY ACT, 1950—VETO MESSAGE FROM THE PRESIDENT
OF THE UNITED STATES

The SPEAKER laid before the House the following veto message
from the President of the United States:

To the House of Representatives:

I return herewith, without my approval, H.R. 9490, the proposed
"Internal Security Act of 1950."

I am taking this action only after the most serious study and re-

277

flection and after consultation with the security and intelligence agencies of the Government. The Department of Justice, the Department of Defense, the Central Intelligence Agency, and the Department of State have all advised me that the bill would seriously damage the security and intelligence operations for which they are responsible. They have strongly expressed the hope that the bill would not become law.

This is an omnibus bill containing many different legislative proposals with only one thing in common: they are all represented to be "anticommunist." But when the many complicated pieces of the bill are analyzed in detail, a startling result appears.

H. R. 9490 would not hurt the Communists. Instead, it would help them.

It has been claimed over and over again that this is an "anticommunist" bill—a "Communist control" bill. But in actual operation the bill would have results exactly the opposite of those intended.

It would actually weaken our existing internal security measures and would seriously hamper the Federal Bureau of Investigation and our other security agencies.

It would help the Communists in their efforts to create dissension and confusion within our borders.

It would help the Communist propagandists throughout the world who are trying to undermine freedom by discrediting as hypocrisy the efforts of the United States on behalf of freedom.

Specifically, some of the principal objections to the bill are as follows:

1. It would aid potential enemies by requiring the publication of a complete list of vital defense plants, laboratories, and other installations.

2. It would require the Department of Justice and its Federal Bureau of Investigation to waste immense amounts of time and energy attempting to carry out its unworkable registration provisions.

3. It would deprive us of the great assistance of many aliens in intelligence matters.

4. It would antagonize friendly governments.

5. It would put the Government of the United States in the thought-control business.

6. It would make it easier for subversive aliens to become naturalized as United States citizens.

7. It would give Government officials vast powers to harass all of
our citizens in the exercise of their right of free speech.

Legislation with these consequences is not necessary to meet the
real dangers which communism presents to our free society. Those
dangers are serious and must be met. But this bill would hinder us,
not help us, in meeting them. Fortunately, we already have on the
books strong laws which give us most of the protection we need
from the real dangers of treason, espionage, sabotage, and actions
looking to the overthrow of our Government by force and violence.
Most of the provisions of this bill have no relation to these real dangers.

One provision alone of this bill is enough to demonstrate how far
it misses the real target. Section 5 would require the Secretary of Defense to "proclaim" and "have published in the Federal Register" a
public catalogue of defense plants, laboratories, and all other facilities vital to our national defense—no matter how secret. I cannot
imagine any document a hostile foreign government would desire
more. Spies and saboteurs would willingly spend years of effort
seeking to find out the information that this bill would require the
Government to hand them on a silver platter. There are many provisions of this bill which impel me to return it without my approval,
but this one would be enough by itself. It is inconceivable to me
that a majority of the Congress could expect the Commander in
Chief of the Armed Forces of the United States to approve such a
flagrant violation of proper security safeguards.

This is only one example of many provisions in the bill which
would in actual practice work to the detriment of our national security.

I know that the Congress had no intention of achieving such results when it passed this bill. I know that the vast majority of the
Members of Congress who voted for the bill sincerely intended to
strike a blow at the Communists.

It is true that certain provisions of this bill would improve the
laws protecting us against espionage and sabotage. But these provisions are greatly outweighed by others which would actually impair

our security.

I repeat, the net results of this bill would be to help the Communists, not to hurt them.

I therefore most earnestly request the Congress to reconsider its action. I am confident that on more careful analysis most Members of Congress will recognize that this bill is contrary to the best interests of our country at this critical time.

H. R. 9490 is made up of a number of different parts. In summary, their purposes and probable effects may be described as follows:

Sections 1 through 17 are designed for two purposes. First, they are intended to force Communist organizations to register and to divulge certain information about themselves—information on their officers, their finances, and, in some cases, their membership. These provisions would in practice be ineffective, and would result in obtaining no information about Communists that the FBI and our other security agencies do not already have. But in trying to enforce these sections, we would have to spend a great deal of time, effort, and money—all to no good purpose.

Second, these provisions are intended to impose various penalties on Communists and others covered by the terms of the bill. So far as Communists are concerned, all these penalties which can be practicably enforced are already in effect under existing laws and procedures. But the language of the bill is so broad and vague that it might well result in penalizing the legitimate activities of people who are not Communists at all, but loyal citizens.

Thus, the net result of these sections of the bill would be: no serious damage to the Communists, most damage to the rest of us. Only the Communist movement would gain from such an outcome.

Sections 18 through 21 and section 23 of this bill constitute, in large measure, the improvements in our internal security laws which I recommended some time ago. Although the language of these sections is in some respects weaker than is desirable, I should be glad to approve these provisions if they were enacted separately, since they are improvements developed by the FBI and other Government security agencies to meet certain clear deficiencies of the present law. But even though these improvements are needed, other provisions of the bill would weaken our security far more than these would strengthen it. We have better protection for our internal security under existing law than we would have with the amendments and additions made by H. R. 9490.

Sections 22 and 25 of this bill would make sweeping changes in our laws governing the admission of aliens to the United States and their naturalization as citizens.

The ostensible purpose of these provisions is to prevent persons who would be dangerous to our national security from entering the country or becoming citizens. In fact, present law already achieves that objective.

What these provisions would actually do is to prevent us from admitting to our country, or to citizenship, many people who could make real contributions to our national strength. The bill would deprive our Government and our intelligence agencies of the valuable services of aliens in security operations. It would require us to exclude and to deport the citizens of some friendly non-Communist countries. Furthermore, it would actually make it easier for subversive aliens to become United States citizens. Only the Communist movement would gain from such actions.

Section 24 and sections 26 through 30 of this bill make a number of minor changes in the naturalization laws. None of them is of great significance—nor are they particularly relevant to the problem of internal security. These provisions, for the most part, have received little or no attention in the legislative process. I believe that several of them would not be approved by the Congress if they were considered on their merits, rather than as parts of an omnibus bill.

Section 31 of this bill makes it a crime to attempt to influence a judge or jury by public demonstration, such as picketing. While the courts already have considerable power to punish such actions under existing law, I have no objection to this section.

Sections 100 through 117 of this bill (title II) are intended to give the Government power, in the event of invasion, war, or insurrection in the United States in aid of a foreign enemy, to seize and hold persons who could be expected to attempt acts of espionage or sabotage; even though they had as yet committed no crime. It may be that legislation of this type should be on the statute books. But the provisions in H. R. 9490 would very probably prove ineffective to achieve the objective sought, since they would not suspend the writ of habeas corpus, and under our legal system to detain a man not charged with a crime would raise serious constitutional questions unless the writ of habeas corpus were suspended. Furthermore, it may well be that other persons than those covered by these provisions would be more important to detain in the event of emergency. This whole problem, therefore, should clearly be studied more thoroughly before further legislative action along these lines is considered.

In brief, when all the provisions of H. R. 9490 are considered together, it is evident that the great bulk of them are not directed toward the real and present dangers that exist from communism. Instead of striking blows at communism, they would strike blows at our own liberties and at our position in the forefront of those working for freedom in the world. At a time when our young men are fighting for freedom in Korea, it would be tragic to advance the objectives of communism in this country, as this bill would do.

Because I feel so strongly that this legislation would be a terrible mistake, I want to discuss more fully its worse features—sections 1 through 17, and sections 22 and 25.

Most of the first 17 sections of H. R. 9490 are concerned with requiring registration and annual reports, by what the bill calls Communist-action organizations and Communist-front organizations, of names of officers, sources and uses of funds, and, in the case of Communist-action organizations, names of members.

The idea of requiring Communist organizations to divulge information about themselves is a simple and attractive one. But it is about as practical as requiring thieves to register with the sheriff. Obviously, no such organization as the Communist Party is likely to register voluntarily.

Under the provisions of the bill, if an organization which the Attorney General believes should register does not do so, he must request a five-man Subversive Activities Control Board to order the organization to register. The Attorney General would have to produce proof that the organization in question was in fact a Communist-action or a Communist-front organization. To do this he would have to offer evidence relating to every aspect of the organization's activities. The organization could present opposing evidence. Prolonged hearings would be required to allow both sides to present proof and to cross-examine opposing witnesses.

To estimate the duration of such a proceeding involving the Communist Party, we need only recall that on much narrower issues the trial of the 11 Communist leaders under the Smith Act consumed 9 months. In a hearing under this bill, the difficulties of proof would be much greater and would take a much longer time.

The bill lists a number of criteria for the Board to consider in deciding whether or not an organization is a Communist-action or Communist-front organization. Many of these deal with the attitudes or states of mind of the organization's leaders. It is frequently difficult in legal proceedings to establish whether or not a man has committed an overt act, such as theft or perjury. But under this bill, the Attorney General would have to attempt the immensely more difficult task of producing concrete legal evidence that men have particular ideas or opinions. This would inevitably require the disclosure of many of the FBI's confidential sources of information and thus would damage our national security.

If, eventually, the Attorney General should overcome these difficulties and get a favorable decision from the Board, the Board's decision could be appealed to the courts. The courts would review any questions of law involved, and whether the Board's findings of fact were supported by the preponderance of the evidence.

All these proceedings would require great effort and much time. It is almost certain that from 2 to 4 years would elapse between the Attorney General's decision to go before the Board with a case, and the final disposition of the matter by the courts.

And when all this time and effort had been spent, it is still most likely that no organization would actually register.

The simple fact is that when the courts at long last found that a particular organization was required to register, all the leaders of the organization would have to do to frustrate the law would be to dissolve the organization and establish a new one with a different name and a new roster of nominal officers. The Communist Party has done this again and again in countries throughout the world. And nothing could be done about it except to begin all over again the long dreary process of investigative, administrative, and judicial proceedings to require registration.

Thus the net result of the registration provision of this bill would probably be an endless chasing of one organization after another, with the Communists always able to frustrate the law enforcement agencies and prevent any final result from being achieved. It could only result in wasting the energies of the Department of Justice and in destroying the sources of information of its FBI. To impose these fruitless burdens upon the FBI would divert it from its vital security duties and thus give aid and comfort to the very Communists whom the bill is supposed to control.

Unfortunately, these provisions are not merely ineffective and unworkable. They represent a clear and present danger to our institutions.

Insofar as the bill would require registration by the Communist Party itself, it does not endanger our traditional liberties. However, the application of the registration requirements to so-called Communist-front organizations can be the greatest danger to freedom of speech, press, and assembly, since the Alien and Sedition Laws of 1798. This danger arises out of the criteria or standards to be applied in determining whether an organization is a Communist-front organization.

There would be no serious problem if the bill required proof that an organization was controlled and financed by the Communist Party before it could be classified as a Communist-front organization. However, recognizing the difficulty of proving those matters, the bill would permit such a determination to be based solely upon the extent to which the positions taken or advanced by it from time to time on matters of policy do not deviate from those of the Communist movement.

This provision could easily be used to classify as a Communist-front organization any organization which is advocating a single policy or objective which is also being urged by the Communist Party or by a Communist foreign government. In fact, this may be the intended result, since the bill defines "organization" to include "a group of persons permanently or temporarily associated together for joint action on any subject or subjects." Thus, an organization which advocates low-cost housing for sincere humanitarian reasons might be classified as a Communist-front organization because the Communists regularly exploit slum conditions as one of their fifth-column techniques.

It is not enough to say that this probably would not be done. The mere fact that it could be done shows clearly how the bill would open a Pandora's box of opportunities for official condemnation of organizations and individuals for perfectly honest opinions which happen to be stated also by Communists.

The basic error of these sections is that they move in the direction of suppressing opinion and belief. This would be a very dangerous course to take, not because we have any sympathy for Communist opinions, but because any governmental stifling of the free expression of opinion is a long step toward totalitarianism.

There is no more fundamental axiom of American freedom than the familiar statement: In a free country, we punish men for the crimes they commit, but never for the opinions they have. And the reason this is so fundamental to freedom is not, as many suppose, that it protects the few unorthodox from suppression by the majority. To permit freedom of expression is primarily for the benefit of the majority because it protects criticism, and criticism leads to progress.

We can and we will prevent espionage, sabotage, or other actions endangering our national security. But we would betray our finest traditions if we attempted, as this bill would attempt, to curb the simple expression of opinion. This we should never do, no matter how distasteful the opinion may be to the vast majority of our people. The course proposed by this bill would delight the Communists, for it would make a mockery of the Bill of Rights and of our claims to stand for freedom in the world.

And what kind of effect would these provisions have on the normal expression of political views? Obviously, if this law were on the statute books, the part of prudence would be to avoid saying anything that might be construed by someone as not deviating sufficiently from the current Communist propaganda line. And since no one could be sure in advance what views were safe to express, the inevitable tendency would be to express no views on controversial subjects.

The result could only be to reduce the vigor and strength of our political life—an outcome that the Communists would happily welcome, but that free men should abhor.

We need not fear the expression of ideas—we do need to fear their suppression.

Our position in the vanguard of freedom rests largely on our demonstration that the free expression of opinion, coupled with government by popular consent, leads to national strength and human advancement. Let us not, in cowering and foolish fear, throw away the ideals which are the fundamental basis of our free society.

Not only are the registration provisions of this bill unworkable and dangerous, they are also grossly misleading in that all but one of the objectives which are claimed for them are already being accomplished by other and superior methods—and the one objective which is not now being accomplished would not in fact be accomplished under this bill either.

It is claimed that the bill would provide information about the Communist Party and its members. The fact is, the FBI already possesses very complete sources of information concerning the Communist movement in this country. If the FBI must disclose its sources of information in public hearings to require registration under this bill, its present sources of information, and its ability to acquire new information, will be largely destroyed.

It is claimed that this bill would deny income-tax exemption to Communist organizations. The fact is that the Bureau of Internal Revenue already denies income-tax exemption to such organizations.

It is claimed that this bill would deny passports to Communists. The fact is that the Government can and does deny passports to Communists under existing law.

It is claimed that this bill would prohibit the employment of Communists by the Federal Government. The fact is that the employment of Communists by the Federal Government is already prohibited and, at least in the executive branch, there is an effective program to see that they are not employed.

It is claimed that this bill would prohibit the employment of

Communists in defense plants. The fact is that it would be years before this bill would have any effect of this nature—if it ever would. Fortunately, this objective is already being substantially achieved under the present procedures of the Department of Defense, and if the Congress would enact one of the provisions I have recommended—which it did not include in this bill—the situation would be entirely taken care of, promptly and effectively.

It is also claimed—and this is the one new objective of the registration provisions of this bill—that it would require Communist organizations to label all their publications and radio and television broadcasts as emanating from a Communist source. The fact is that this requirement, even if constitutional, could be easily and permanently evaded, simply by the continuous creation of new organizations to distribute Communist information.

Section 4 (a) of the bill, like its registration provisions, would be ineffective, would be subject to dangerous abuse, and would seek to accomplish an objective which is already better accomplished under existing law.

This provision would make unlawful any agreement to perform any act which would substantially contribute to the establishment within the United States of a foreign-controlled dictatorship. Of course, this provision would be unconstitutional if it infringed upon the fundamental right of the American people to establish for themselves by constitutional methods any form of government they choose. To avoid this, it is provided that this section shall not apply to the proposal of a constitutional amendment. If this language limits the prohibition of the section to the use of unlawful methods, then it adds nothing to the Smith Act, under which 11 Communist leaders have been convicted, and would be more difficult to enforce. Thus, it would accomplish nothing. Moreover, the bill does not even purport to define the phrase, unique in a criminal statute, "substantially contribute." A phrase so vague raises a serious constitutional question.

Sections 22 and 25 of this bill are directed toward the specific questions of who should be admitted to our country, and who should be permitted to become a United States citizen. I believe there is general agreement that the answers to those questions should be: We should admit to our country, within the available quotas, anyone with a legitimate purpose who would not endanger our security, and we should admit to citizenship any immigrant who will be a loyal and constructive member of the community. Those are essentially the standards set by existing law. Under present law, we do not admit to our country known Communists, because we believe they work to overthrow our Government, and we do not admit Communists to citizenship, because we believe they are not loyal to the United States.

The changes which would be made in the present law by sections 22 and 25 would not reinforce those sensible standards. Instead, they would add a number of new standards, which, for no good and sufficient reason, would interfere with our relations with other countries and seriously damage our national security.

Section 22 would, for example, exclude from our country anyone who advocates any form of totalitarian or one-party government. We, of course, believe in the democratic system of competing political parties, offering a choice of candidates and policies. But a number of countries with which we maintain friendly relations have a different form of government.

Until now, no one has suggested that we should abandon cultural and commercial relations with a country merely because it has a form of government different from ours. Yet section 22 would require that. As one instance, it is clear that under the definitions of the bill the present Government of Spain, among others, would be classified as "totalitarian." As a result, the Attorney General would be required to exclude from the United States all Spanish businessmen, students, and other nonofficial travelers who support the present Government of their country. I cannot understand how the sponsors of this bill can think that such an action would contribute to our national security.

Moreover, the provisions of section 22 of this bill would strike a serious blow to our national security by taking away from the Government the power to grant asylum in this country to foreign diplomats who repudiate Communist imperialism and wish to escape its reprisals. It must be obvious to anyone that it is in our national interest to persuade people to renounce communism, and to encourage their defection from Communist forces. Many of these people are extremely valuable to our intelligence operations. Yet under this bill the Government would lose the limited authority it now has to offer asylum in our country as the great incentive for such defection.

In addition, the provisions of section 22 would sharply limit the authority of the Government to admit foreign diplomatic representatives and their families on official business. Under existing law, we already have the authority to send out of the country any person who abuses diplomatic privileges by working against the interests of the United States. But under this bill a whole series of unnecessary restrictions would be placed on the admission of diplomatic personnel. This is not only ungenerous, for a country which eagerly sought and proudly holds the honor of being the seat of the United Nations, it is also very unwise, because it makes our country appear to be fearful of foreigners, when in fact we are working as hard as we know how to build mutual confidence and friendly relations among the nations of the world.

Section 22 is so contrary to our national interests that it would actually put the Government into the business of thought control by requiring the deportation of any alien who distributes or publishes, or who is affiliated with an organization which distributes or publishes, any written or printed matter advocating (or merely expressing belief in) the economic and governmental doctrines of any form of totalitarianism.

This provision does not require an evil intent or purpose on the part of the alien, as does a similar provision in the Smith Act. Thus, the Attorney General would be required to deport any alien operating or connected with a well-stocked bookshop containing books on economics or politics written by supporters of the present government of Spain, of Yugoslavia or any one of a number of other countries. Section 25 would make the same aliens ineligible for citizenship. There should be no room in our laws for such hysterical provisions. The next logical step would be to "burn the books."

This illustrates the fundamental error of these immigration and naturalization provisions. It is easy to see that they are hasty and ill-considered. But far more significant—and far more dangerous—is their apparent underlying purpose. Instead of trying to encourage the free movement of people, subject only to the real requirements of national security, these provisions attempt to bar movement to anyone who is, or once was, associated with ideas we dislike, and in the process, they would succeed in barring many people whom it would be to our advantage to admit.

Such an action would be a serious blow to our work for world peace. We uphold—or have upheld till now, at any rate—the concept of freedom on an international scale. That is the root concept of our efforts to bring unity among the free nations and peace in the world.

The Communists, on the other hand, attempt to break down in every possible way the free interchange of persons and ideas. It will be to their advantage, and not ours, if we establish for ourselves an "iron curtain" against those who can help us in the fight for freedom.

Another provision of the bill which would greatly weaken our national security is section 25, which would make subversive aliens eligible for naturalization as soon as they withdraw from organizations required to register under this bill, whereas under existing law they must wait for a period of 10 years after such withdrawal before becoming eligible for citizenship. This proposal is clearly contrary to the national interest, and clearly gives to the Communists an advantage they do not have under existing law.

I have discussed the provisions of this bill at some length in order to explain why I am convinced that it would be harmful to our security and damaging to the individual rights of our people if it were enacted.

Earlier this month, we launched a great Crusade for Freedom designed, in the words of General Eisenhower, to fight the big lie with the big truth. I can think of no better way to make a mockery of that crusade and of the deep American belief in human freedom and dignity which underlie it than to put the provisions of H. R. 9490 on our statute books.

I do not undertake lightly the responsibility of differing with the majority in both Houses of Congress who have voted for this bill. We are all Americans; we all wish to safeguard and preserve our constitutional liberties against internal and external enemies. But I cannot approve this legislation, which instead of accomplishing its avowed purpose would actually interfere with our liberties and help the Communists against whom the bill was aimed.

This is a time when we must marshal all our resources and all the moral strength of our free system in self-defense against the threat of Communist aggression. We will fail in this, and we will destroy all that we seek to preserve, if we sacrifice the liberties of our citizens in a misguided attempt to achieve national security.

There is no reason why we should fail. Our country has been through dangerous times before, without losing our liberties to external attack or internal hysteria. Each of us, in Government and out, has a share in guarding our liberties. Each of us must search his own conscience to find whether he is doing all that can be done to preserve and strengthen them.

No considerations of expediency can justify the enactment of such a bill as this, a bill which would so greatly weaken our liberties and give aid and comfort to those who would destroy us. I have, therefore, no alternative but to return this bill without my approval, and I earnestly request the Congress to reconsider its action.

Harry S. Truman

The White House,
September 22, 1950.

September 25, 1950

MEMORANDUM FOR THE INTERNAL SECURITY FILE
Subject: Chronology of events on veto of Wood-McCarran anti-
      subversive bill, H. R. 9490

On September 13 at staff, the President told Mr. Murphy and me that he wanted this bill very carefully analyzed when it reached the White House as a basis for his decision as to whether or not to veto it. His thinking, of course, has been consistently against this type of legislation as he indicated at his press conference of September 7. The President told us that although the Big Four had urged him to sign the bill at their meeting with him earlier in the week, he had declined to give them any commitment. However, he had told them in response to their request that he would not hold up the bill the full ten days when it reached the White House but would act on it promptly so that in the event he vetoed it Congress would have an opportunity to act on his veto.

Mr. Murphy and I agreed that I should begin work immediately getting the necessary analysis of the bill (still in conference) ready and preliminary drafts of a veto message. We made arrangements with Peyton Ford to have Bob Ginnane, and others at Justice, begin work at once on an analysis of the bill and Justice's version of a veto message as well as a signing statement. I also alerted Roger Jones of Budget and Adrian Fisher of State. I had previously requested from Don Hansen of Treasury, a draft of a possible veto message and on September 13 he furnished me this. I similarly requested Ken Hechler and Dick Neustadt to prepare their version of veto messages, which I received a day or so later, and I prepared a draft myself on September 15 and 16. All of these drafts were prepared without knowledge as to what shape the final bill would emerge from conference in but on the assumption that it would largely follow the pattern of the bill as passed by the Senate. I also asked Philleo Nash to prepare a possible signing statement and he did so.

At his press conference on Thursday, September 14, with the bill still in conference, the President was asked whether he was going to veto it and replied that he could not tell what he was going to do until it reached him and he had analyzed it. This apparently seemed to some people on the Hill a softening of the position he had expressed at his press conference the previous week and I received several calls from the Hill, including one from Senator Humphrey, about the matter. The seven Senators and twenty Representatives who had voted against the bill were concerned that they would be out on a limb if the President did not veto the bill. I told Seantor Humphrey and the others who called me that I, of course, did not know what the President was going to do on the bill but that I did not understand that his September 14 statement should be construed as any weakening of his September 7 position. I pointed out that the Senate and House versions of the bill were completely different and that it was theoretically possible that a reasonably good bill could emerge from the conference. Consequently, the President could hardly commit himself until he saw what the conferees did.

On Monday, September 18, at which time we had a confidential committee print of the conference agreement although the report had not yet been signed, I arranged with Charlie Murphy to have Dave Bell spend the day studying the various veto message drafts and prepare the next-stage-draft using the best ideas from all of them. Dave Bell prepared a so-called second draft which was available Tuesday morning. This was a great improvement over the previous draft but in my opinion was still not punchy and quotable enough, particularly because it did not set out in crisp, sharp, lucid fashion a list of major defects in the bill. On Tuesday the conferees filed their report. Dave Bell worked out a third draft during the day which was only a minor refinement of the previous draft. Wednesday, I prepared a lengthy memorandum of comments and suggestions on the Bell draft which I supplemented with another memorandum on Thursday. A Justice draft of veto message came over about this time. Bob Ginnane was the principal draftsman of this. It contained some good material but we thought that the structure of the White House draft was much better and decided to continue to use that as the vehicle. Also, on Wednesday the President told us that he had talked to Vice President Barkley, who had been urging him to sign the bill, and that he told the Vice President that he did not think he was going to be able to sign the bill. It seemed evident at this point that the President's mind was made up to veto the bill.

Thursday, September 21 we worked almost all day in Mr. Murphy's office on the veto message. Present were Charlie Murphy, Dave Bell, Dick Neustadt, Peyton Ford, Bob Ginnane and myself.

Both Houses had approved the conference report on Wednesday and the bill actually reached the White House early Thursday afternoon. We worked until about midnight Thursday and got out a fourth draft. The President had read the previous draft and had made comments and suggestions which were incorporated in the fourth draft. By this time the draft was in pretty good shape. This was the fourth draft.

The next morning, Friday, we met again the first thing in Mr. Murphy's office and made some further substantial changes in the draft which was now the fifth draft. There was a Cabinet meeting that morning and the Attorney General personally brought over and gave the President his recommendation for a veto. Defense and CIA had orally advised Roger Jones that they were against the bill and State (Adrian Fisher) had written Jones a letter to that effect.

At 11:00 a.m. we met with the President to go over the fifth draft. In addition to the President, the following were present: Charlie Murphy, Charlie Ross, George Elsey, Dave Bell, Dick Neustadt, Peyton Ford and myself. These meetings lasted from 11:00 a.m. until 1:30 p.m. and quite a few changes were made in the draft as a result.

The President also decided to add a little cover sheet note to each mimeographed copy of the veto message going to Congress, urging each Member of Congress to carefully read and study the veto message before taking any further action on it, i.e., before voting to sustain or over-ride the veto. This was in the form of a direct appeal from him, with his facsimile signature on each copy. As far as I am aware, this action was without precedent, and it was an indication of the deep conviction of the President on this subject. Also, instead of the usual single-spaced veto message release on both sides of the page, this veto message was advisedly double-spaced and only on one side of the page, so as to make it easier to read and absorb.

Mr. Miller took the veto message to the House of Representatives about 4:00 p.m. Friday. Despite the President's request that the veto message be carefully studied before a vote was taken, the House promptly voted to over-ride the veto by a vote of 286 to 48.

The Senate then took up the matter with every indication that there might be a vote to over-ride the veto in the course of Friday evening. The House had already passed a Concurrent Resolution for an adjournment until November 27th at the end of its Saturday session, and the original Senate plan was to stay in session until a few minutes after midnight Friday night, and then pass the same resolution and leave without any further session on Saturday other than the few minutes after midnight. However, around 11:00 p.m. Friday evening, following a telephone conversation with Charlie Murphy, the President called a number of Senators who favored sustaining the veto, including Senators Humphrey and Kilgore, and encouraged them to continue the debate on the matter well into Saturday, so that there would be an opportunity for press, radio and public reaction to the Friday veto message.

As a result, the debate continued all night Friday.

About 5:00 a.m. Saturday morning, Senator Langer, the only Republican supporting the veto, after holding the floor for hours, fainted and had to be removed to Bethesda Naval Hospital. Senator Humphrey immediately took over the floor. About 9:30 Saturday morning, Mr. Sims, Senator Humphrey's Assistant, called me to say that the Senator wished advice as to the President's views as to the course of action to be followed from there on in connection with the fight to sustain the veto. The view of Senator Humphrey and the Senators associated with him, was to continue the debate until about 2:00 o'clock in the afternoon and then let the matter come to a vote. They felt that on the one hand the maximum amount of public reaction possible in a limited period would be obtained by that time, and on the other that there would be an adverse reaction if they attempted to carry the debate through midnight Saturday, since it would thus have the appearance of a filibuster, and they were carefully trying to avoid any suggestion that they were carrying on a filibuster.

I told Mr. Sims I would talk to the President and let him know. At the President's staff meeting a little later in the morning I sought his advice on Senator Humphrey's inquiry. The President said that it was a matter for the Senators to decide; that if by carrying the debate on until midnight they could completely avoid a vote to override the veto, he would favor that course of action; but if that action would only delay but not avoid the vote, he would favor a vote at whatever time Saturday afternoon Senator Humphrey and his associates thought they had gotten the maximum possible public reaction on the matter. I passed this information on to Senator Humphrey.

Saturday afternoon, after lunch, I was in Charlie Murphy's office when the President called him from Blair House to say that he had talked to Senators Chavez and McFarland. The President said that Chavez said that he would vote to sustain the veto (and he

later did so), and that McFarland indicated that if his vote was necessary to sustain the veto, he would vote that way. The President
was encouraged by his talks with Chavez and McFarland and asked
that Murphy and the rest of us talk to other Senators to see if we
could get any further support for the veto. (At the President's direction, Charlie Murphy had earlier called the Democratic National
Committee and asked them to make a maximum effort in the matter.) Charlie Murphy called one or two other members of the Staff,
notably Don Dawson, and passed on the President's message. Murphy
and I made several calls to the Hill. I talked to Senator McMahon, but he was obviously set to over-ride the veto, and he discouraged the possibility of any support for the veto in any quarter.
Charlie Murphy called Senator Hill, who was friendly, but committed to vote to over-ride the veto.

About 4:30 p.m. the Senate voted to over-ride the veto by 57 to
10.

The veto message has already attracted a good deal of praise,
even from quarters not normally friendly to the Administration.
Thus, for example, the Washington *Daily News* (a Scripps-Howard
newspaper) on Saturday, September 23rd, had a long editorial praising the message highly. Bob Ginnane, of Justice, told me Saturday
that Senator Graham had told him that he had overheard Senators
Hill, Russell and McFarland discussing the veto message and that
they had agreed it was a very powerful document. They said they
were still going to vote to over-ride, but they were definitely shaken
in their position by the veto message. They indicated (said Graham) that they had not expected it to contain so powerful and tell-
ing an argument against the bill.

S.J.S.

APPENDIX 5

Wallace to Truman, September 19, 1951

Papers of Harry S. Truman, OF 1170, Harry S. Truman Library. Courtesy of Robert B. Wallace.

Senator McCarran's investigation of the Institute of Pacific Relations during the summer and fall of 1951 (it continued into early 1952) brought back to public attention the possible influence exerted on America's Far Eastern policy by Owen Lattimore and John Carter Vincent. Senator McCarthy had accused them of pro-Soviet bias (at the very least) in the spring of 1950. Henry Wallace, who had by that time radically altered his outlook on foreign policy questions, wrote the President denying that Lattimore or Vincent had played any important role during his mission to China in 1944.

Sept. 19, 1951

Hon. Harry S. Truman,
President of the United States,
Washington, D.C.

Dear Mr. President,

During the last three weeks there has been considerable newspaper and radio controversy as to what part John Carter Vincent and Owen Lattimore played in my trip to the Far East in 1944. This controversy arose from certain testimony before the Senate Committee on Internal Security during August. Therefore I have decided to make available to you for what disposition you care to make of it the complete file of my reports to President Roosevelt on my Far Eastern trip in 1944. Parts of these reports were at one time looked on as secret but with the situation as it is today there is no reason why these reports should not be made available to the public. I shall, of course, take no steps to publish this letter myself but I wish you to feel completely free to handle it in any way which you deem will best minister to the welfare of the United States.

The following comments as well as the documents themselves should clear up any confusion as to what I was trying to do in China. The part of various individuals in my trip will also be made more clear. In March of 1944 I wrote Secretary Hull asking him to designate someone to accompany me on the projected trip and the State Department named John Carter Vincent, then Chief of the Division of Chinese Affairs. The OWI sent Owen Lattimore to handle publicity matters in China. I passed through Soviet Asia on my way to China but China where the situation was critical, formed the sole subject of my recommendations to President Roosevelt. These recommendations were contained in two related documents:—

First, a message drafted in Kunming, China on June 25, 1944 but which because of difficulties of communication from Kunming, was cabled to the President from New Delhi on June 28, 1944. This was divided into two parts, the first part being a quick resume of the political situation in China and of my talks in the days immediately preceding with Generalissimo Chiang Kai-shek; and the second part, a resume of the military situation, its implications and requirements.

Second, a formal report to President Roosevelt covering the whole trip, including also certain longer term proposals about American policy in China which I presented in person at the White House on July 10, 1944.

These were the only documents originated by me and contained all recommendations of mine resulting from the trip. Mr. Vincent, of course, transmitted to the State Department the detailed, reportorial account of my conversations with the Generalissimo which have already been published in the State Department White Paper.

There has been testimony before the Senate Internal Security Committee that Messrs. Vincent and Lattimore were members of the Communist Party at that time and were relied on by the party leadership to "guide" me along the party line. Hence it is important to specify the parts that these two men took in the recommendations that I presented to President Roosevelt. As to Mr. Lattimore, he had no part whatever. He did not contribute to and to the best of my knowledge knew nothing about either the cable from New Delhi or the formal report to the President delivered in Washington. He offered me no political advice at any time sufficiently significant to be recalled now, and when we were together, he talked chiefly about scholarly subjects of common interest such as the history of Chinese agriculture and the relationship of the nomadic tribes with the settled peasantry.

Mr. Vincent as the designated representative of the State Department was naturally consulted by me when we were travelling together. Aside from serving as reporter at the meetings with Chiang Kai-shek, his most important part was his assistance in the preparation of the two-part cable sent from New Delhi. In Kunming, the knowledge I had already gained in Chungking of the urgency of the Chinese situation, and of the grave dangers of the Japanese offensive then going on in East China was heavily underlined by General C. L. Chennault's presentation to me of the current military picture. In the light of this presentation and in response to Chiang Kai-shek's request made of me on June 24 I decided to cable Pres. Roosevelt on June 26. Mr. Vincent joined in the advance discussions of the projected cable, was present while it was drafted and concurred in the result. The finished cable was, of course, mine but I was disturbed by the fact that I was making far-reaching recommendations without having had an opportunity to consult the Theater Commander, General Joseph Stilwell. My recommendations were so drastic that Vincent would certainly have urged that I get in touch with Gen. Stilwell if he (Vincent) had had objections. Instead Vincent concurred in the cables of June 28.

On the other hand, as both Mr. Vincent and Secretary of State Dean Acheson have stated, Mr. Vincent took no part in the preparation of my formal report to President Roosevelt on July 10 and to the best of my knowledge was not aware of its contents. I wrote the July 10 report myself and went along to the White House to present it to the President. In doing the work of writing I made use of various memoranda which had accumulated during the journey, some no doubt from Vincent. However, the strongest influence on me in preparing this final report of July 10 was my recollection of the analyses offered me by our then Ambassador to China, Clarence E. Gauss, who later occupied one of the Republican places on the Export-Import Bank Board.

With regard to the two-part Kunming–New Delhi cable of June 28, it should be said that the military recommendations contained therein were the most important contribution I made while in China. These recommendations were that *China be separated* from the command of Gen. Stilwell, that *Gen. Wedemeyer should be considered* in the choice of a new military commander in China, and that the new commander should be given the additional assignment of *"Personal representative"* of the President at Chungking. The name and record of Gen. Wedemeyer are enough to indicate that the purport of these recommendations was the opposite of pro-communist.

Some months later the change of military command I proposed to the President was carried out at the most urgent plea of Chiang Kai-shek. History suggests that if my recommendations had been followed when made, the Generalissimo would have avoided the disasters resulting from the Japanese offensive in East China later that summer. And if Chiang's government had thus been spared the terrible enfeeblement resulting from these disasters, the chances are good the Generalissimo would have been ruling China today.

The political section of the Kunming–New Delhi cable of June 28 should be read with the atmosphere of that time in mind. Much emphasis had been placed from the very beginning of the war on the primary importance of "beating the Japs," and by the spring of 1944 even the most conservative American publications were urging that the Chinese communists could contribute substantially to this end. Roosevelt talked to me before I left, not about political coalition in China, but about "getting the two groups together to fight the war." Chiang Kai-shek for internal political reasons had, on his own initiative so I was informed, opened talks between the Nationalists and the Communists but, so he told me, with no prospect for success. When I cabled the President that "the attitude of Chiang Kai-shek towards the problem is so imbued with prejudice that I can see little prospect for satisfactory long term settlement" I was referring not to "political coalition" but to this "military problem" of "getting the two groups together to fight the war." On the other hand, when I said that the disintegration of the Chungking regime will leave in China a political vacuum which will be filled in ways which you will understand," I was, of course, warning against the possibility of a Communist political triumph in China.

The July 10 report does not recommend any political coalition between the government of Chiang Kai-shek and the Chinese communists. It was written, however, against a Chinese political background which is still quite unknown to most Americans. In brief, one of the worst of several ills from which the Chungking government was suffering at the time, was the absolute control of all positions of political, military and economic power by an extreme pro-Asian, anti-American group within the Kuomintang. This was much emphasized by Ambassador Gauss who plainly stated that this group in Chungking was doing the Chinese communists' work for them. The more Western-minded, more efficient and more pro-American Chinese Nationalist leaders had been so completely driven from power that Dr. T. V. Soong's appearance as interpreter at my talks with the Generalissimo was authoritatively reported to be his first emergence from a sort of informal house arrest, while the most highly praised of the Chinese Generals, General Chen Cheng, now Prime Minister in Formosa, had been dismissed from all command some months before. These facts are hinted at in my report to Roosevelt on July 10 in which it is noted as "significant" that "T. V. Soong took no part in the discussions (with the Generalissimo) except as interpreter," while General Chen Cheng is mentioned along with Generals Chang Fa-kwei and Pai Chung-hsi as the sort of men who might rally the Chinese armies to greater efforts.

In this concluding section of this final report to President Roosevelt on July 10, a coalition is in fact suggested but not with the Communists. Instead President Roosevelt is urged to use American political influence to "support" the "progressive banking and commercial leaders," the "large group of western trained men," and the "considerable group of generals and other officers who are neither subservient to the landlords nor afraid of the peasantry." In short I urged President Roosevelt to help the Generalissimo's government to help itself, by bringing back to power the better men in the Chinese Nationalist ranks. These better and more enlightened Nationalists, being more able to stand on their own feet, were somewhat more independent of the Generalissimo than the extreme pro-Asia groups. Hence, it was necessary to point out to President Roosevelt that if the desired changes were made in the Chinese Nationalist government, the Generalissimo's future would depend on his "political sensitivity," and his ability to make himself the real leader of the reconstituted administration. Internal reform at Chunking was, in short, my proposed means of avoiding the "revolution" and insuring the "evolution" that are referred to earlier in this report of July 10. It is worth noting that the Generalissimo must have been thinking along parallel lines, since the extremists began to lose their control and Dr. Soong and Gen. Chen Cheng were brought back to power by the Generalissimo himself during the same month that I rendered my report to President Roosevelt.

Such were the recommendations, such was the direction of the influence of my trip to the Far East in the spring of 1944. During the years immediately following the end of the war my thinking about Chinese problems underwent a sharp change. My views during this later period are known as are now my views in 1944. Recent events have led me to the conclusion that my judgment in 1944 was the sound judgment. I append herewith a copy of the two-part Kunming—New Delhi cable of June 28 in the War Department paraphrase given to me when I returned to Washington and of the final report to Pres. Roosevelt of July 10 as presented by me to him.

Wishing you health and strength in shouldering
the tremendous burdens ahead,
Mrs. Wallace joins me in asking you to
convey to Mrs. Truman and Margaret
our best regards,
Sincerely yours,
/s/ Henry A. Wallace

Selected Bibliography

Manuscript Collections Located at
Harry S. Truman Library
Papers of OSCAR L. CHAPMAN
Papers of CLARK M. CLIFFORD*
Papers of DAVID D. LLOYD
Papers of J. HOWARD MCGRATH
Papers of CHARLES S. MURPHY
Papers of RICHARD E. NEUSTADT
Papers of STEPHEN J. SPINGARN*
Papers of THEODORE TANNENWALD, JR.
Papers of HARRY S. TRUMAN
     Bill File
     Files of Clark M. Clifford
     Files of Martin L. Friedman
     Files of David D. Lloyd
     Files of Charles S. Murphy
     Files of Stephen J. Spingarn
     Files of the White House Official Reporter
     Official Files
     President's Personal Files

*Portions of the Papers of Clark M. Clifford and of Stephen J. Spingarn were seen by the author while they were in the possession of Messrs. Clifford and Spingarn, prior to their donation to the Truman Library.

Records of the President's Commission on Internal Security and Individual Rights [Nimitz Commission]
Records of the President's Committee on Civil Rights
Papers of JAMES E. WEBB

Personal Interviews

Honorable Thurman Arnold, *June 7, 1967*
Honorable George M. Elsey, *March 29, 1967*
Honorable Donald A. Hansen, *March 28 and June 9, 1967*
Honorable Charles S. Murphy, *March 29, 1967*
Honorable Stephen J. Spingarn, *March 17, 1962*
Honorable Harry S. Truman, *July 21, 1961*

Harry S. Truman Library Oral History Project

Oral History Interview No. 8 (Donald A. Hansen, April 5, 1963).

Public Documents

U.S. *Congressional Record.* Vols. 91–98.
U.S. Senate, Committee on Armed Services and Committee on Foreign Relations. *Hearings to Conduct an Inquiry into the Military Situation in the Far East and the Facts Surrounding the Relief of General of the Army Douglas MacArthur from his Assignments in that Area.* 82nd Cong., 1st sess., 1951.
U.S. Senate, Subcommittee of the Committee on Foreign Relations. Hearings Pursuant to S. Res. 231, *A Resolution to Investigate Whether There Are Employes in the State Department Disloyal to the United States.* 81st Cong., 2nd sess., 1950.

Newspapers Regularly Used

The New York Times
Washington Post

Biographies, Diaries, Memoirs

BYRNES, JAMES F. *Speaking Frankly.* New York: Harper & Bros., 1947.
CARR, ALBERT Z. *Truman, Stalin, and Peace.* Garden City, N.Y.: Doubleday & Co., 1950.

CLARK, MARK. *From the Danube to the Yalu.* New York: Harper & Bros., 1954.

DANIELS, JONATHAN. *The Man of Independence.* New York and Philadelphia: Lippincott, 1950.

DJILAS, MILOVAN. *Conversations with Stalin.* Translated by Michael B. Petrovich. New York: Harcourt, Brace & World, 1962.

EISENHOWER, DWIGHT D. *The White House Years.* Garden City, N.Y.: Doubleday & Co., 1963. Vol. 1, *Mandate for Change, 1953–1956.*

EVANS, ROWLAND, and NOVAK, ROBERT. *Lyndon B. Johnson: The Exercise of Power.* New York: Signet Books, 1968.

HILLMAN, WILLIAM. *Mr. President.* New York: Farrar, Straus and Young, 1952.

KENNAN, GEORGE F. *Memoirs, 1925–1950.* Boston: Little, Brown and Co., 1967.

LILIENTHAL, DAVID E. *The Journals of David E. Lilienthal.* New York: Harper & Row, 1964. Vol. 2, *The Atomic Energy Years, 1945–1950.*

MACARTHUR, DOUGLAS. *Reminiscences.* New York: McGraw-Hill Book Co., 1964.

MARTIN, JOSEPH W., JR. *My First Fifty Years in Politics.* As told to Robert J. Donovan. New York: McGraw-Hill Book Co., 1960.

MAZO, EARL. *Richard Nixon: A Political and Personal Portrait.* New York: Harper & Bros., 1959.

MILLIS, WALTER, ed. (with the collaboration of E. S. Duffield). *The Forrestal Diaries.* New York: Viking Press, 1951.

NIXON, RICHARD M. *Six Crises.* Garden City, N.Y.: Doubleday & Co., 1962.

RIDGWAY, MATTHEW B. *The Korean War.* Garden City, N.Y.: Doubleday & Co., 1967.

ROVERE, RICHARD H. *Senator Joe McCarthy.* New York: Harcourt, Brace & Co., 1959.

TRUMAN, HARRY S. *Memoirs.* 2 vols. Garden City, N.Y.: Doubleday & Co., 1956.

VANDENBURG, ARTHUR H., JR., ed. (with the collaboration of Joe Alex Morris). *The Private Papers of Senator Vandenberg.* Boston: Houghton Mifflin Co., 1952.

WEDEMEYER, ALBERT C. *Wedemeyer Reports!* New York: Henry Holt & Co., 1958.

WHITE, WILLIAM S. *The Taft Story.* New York: Harper & Bros., 1954.

WHITNEY, COURTNEY. *MacArthur: His Rendezvous with Destiny.* New York: Alfred A. Knopf, 1956.

WILLOUGHBY, CHARLES, and CHAMBERLAIN, JOHN. *MacArthur, 1941–1951.* New York: McGraw-Hill Book Co., 1954.

Secondary Works

ANDERSON, PATRICK. *The Presidents' Men: White House Assistants of Franklin D. Roosevelt, Harry S. Truman, Dwight D. Eisenhower, John F. Kennedy, and Lyndon B. Johnson.* Garden City, N.Y.: Doubleday & Co., 1968.

BELL, DANIEL, ed. *The Radical Right.* Garden City, N.Y.: Doubleday Anchor Books, 1964.

BONTECOU, ELEANOR. *The Federal Loyalty-Security Program.* Ithaca, N.Y.: Cornell University Press, 1953.

BUCKLEY, WILLIAM F., JR. and BOZELL, L. BRENT. *McCarthy and His Enemies: The Record and Its Meaning.* Chicago: Henry Regnery Co., 1954.

CARR, ROBERT K. *The House Committee on Un-American Activities, 1945–1950.* Ithaca, N.Y.: Cornell University Press, 1952.

CHASE, HAROLD W. *Security and Liberty: The Problem of Native Communists, 1947–1955.* Garden City, N.Y.: Doubleday & Co., 1955.

COOKE, ALISTAIR. *A Generation on Trial.* New York: Alfred A. Knopf, 1950.

CORWIN, EDWARD S. *The President: Office and Powers, 1787–1948.* 3rd rev. ed. New York: New York University Press, 1948.

DRAPER, THEODORE. *American Communism and Soviet Russia.* New York: Viking Press, 1960.

FAIRBANK, JOHN K. *The United States and China.* Cambridge, Mass.: Harvard University Press, 1958.

FEIS, HERBERT. *The China Tangle: The American Effort in China from Pearl Harbor to the Marshall Mission.* New York: Atheneum, 1965.

FILENE, PETER G. *Americans and the Soviet Experiment, 1917–1933.* Cambridge, Mass.: Harvard University Press, 1967.

GELLHORN, WALTER. *Security, Loyalty, and Science.* Ithaca, N.Y.: Cornell University Press, 1960.

GOLDMAN, ERIC. *The Crucial Decade: America, 1945–1955.* New York: Alfred A. Knopf, 1956.

GRAEBNER, NORMAN A. *The New Isolationism: A Study in Politics and Foreign Policy since 1950.* New York: Ronald Press Co., 1956.

GRENVILLE, JOHN A. S., and YOUNG, GEORGE BERKELEY. *Politics, Strategy, and American Diplomacy: Studies in Foreign Policy, 1873–1914.* New Haven: Yale University Press, 1966.

HIGGINS, TRUMBULL. *Korea and the Fall of MacArthur: A Précis in Limited War.* New York: Oxford University Press, 1960.

HIGHAM, JOHN. *Strangers in the Land: Patterns of American Nativism, 1860–1925.* New York: Atheneum, 1965.

HOWE, IRVING and COSER, LEWIS. *The American Communist Party: A Critical History, 1919–1957.* Boston: Beacon Press, 1957.

HUNTINGTON, SAMUEL B. *The Soldier and the State: The Theory and Politics of Civil-Military Relations.* Cambridge, Mass.: Harvard University Press, 1957.

HYMAN, HAROLD M. *To Try Men's Souls: Loyalty Tests in American History.* Berkeley and Los Angeles: University of California Press, 1959.

KENNAN, GEORGE F. *Russia and the West under Lenin and Stalin.* New York: Mentor Books, 1962.

KIRKENDALL, RICHARD S., ed. *The Truman Period as a Research Field.* Columbia, Mo.: University of Missouri Press, 1967.

LASCH, CHRISTOPHER. *The American Liberals and the Russian Revolution.* New York: Columbia University Press, 1962.

LATHAM, EARL. *The Communist Controversy in Washington: From the New Deal to McCarthy.* Cambridge, Mass.: Harvard University Press, 1966.

LONGAKER, RICHARD P. *The President and Individual Liberties.* Ithaca, N.Y.: Cornell University Press, 1961.

LUBELL, SAMUEL. *The Future of American Politics.* New York: Harper & Bros., 1951.

———. *Revolt of the Moderates.* New York: Harper & Bros., 1956.

MENDELSON, WALLACE. *The Constitution and the Supreme Court.* New York: Dodd, Mead & Co., 1959.

MOOREHEAD, ALAN. *The Traitors.* New York: Harper & Row, 1963.

NEUSTADT, RICHARD E. *Presidential Power: The Politics of Leadership.* New York & London: John Wiley & Sons, 1960.

OSGOOD, ROBERT E. *Limited War: The Challenge to American Strategy.* Chicago: University of Chicago Press, 1957.

PACKER, HERBERT L. *Ex-Communist Witnesses: Four Studies in Fact-Finding.* Stanford, Calif.: Stanford University Press, 1962.

PHILLIPS, CABELL. *The Truman Presidency: The History of a Triumphant Succession.* New York: The Macmillan Company, 1966.

PRITCHETT, C. HERMAN. *Civil Liberties and the Vinson Court.* Chicago: University of Chicago Press, 1954.

REES, DAVID. *Korea: The Limited War.* New York: St. Martin's Press, 1964.

ROSS, IRWIN. *The Loneliest Campaign: The Truman Victory of 1948.* New York: The New American Library, 1968.

SPANIER, JOHN W. *The Truman-MacArthur Controversy and the Korean War.* New York: W. W. Norton & Co., 1965.

WARREN, FRANK A., III. *Liberals and Communism: The "Red Decade" Revisited.* Bloomington, Ind.: Indiana University Press, 1966.

WEST, REBECCA. *The New Meaning of Treason.* New York: Viking Press, 1964.

WESTERFIELD, H. BRADFORD. *Foreign Policy and Party Politics: Pearl Harbor to Korea.* New Haven: Yale University Press, 1955.

Index